INTRODUCING

THEOLOGIES OF
RELIGIONS

INTRODUCING

THEOLOGIES OF RELIGIONS

Paul F. Knitter

ORBIS BOOKS

Maryknoll, New York 10545

Thirteenth Printing, March 2013

Founded in 1970, Orbis Books endeavors to publish works that enlighten the mind, nourish the spirit, and challenge the conscience. The publishing arm of the Maryknoll Fathers and Brothers, Orbis seeks to explore the global dimensions of the Christian faith and mission, to invite dialogue with diverse cultures and religious traditions, and to serve the cause of reconciliation and peace. The books published reflect the views of their authors and do not represent the official position of the Maryknoll Society. To learn more about Maryknoll and Orbis Books, please visit our website at www.maryknollsociety.org.

Manufactured in the United States of America

Library of Congress Cataloging-in-Publication Data
Knitter, Paul F.
    Introducing theologies of religions / Paul F. Knitter.
        p.   cm.
    Includes bibliographical references and index.
    ISBN 1-57075-419-5 (pbk.)
    1. Theology of religions (Christian theology)   I. Title.
BT83.85 .K63 2002
261.2 – dc21
                                            2002002843

For Rose and Paul,
My parents,
In loving memory
And gratitude

Contents

Part I
THE REPLACEMENT MODEL
"Only One True Religion"

Preface

I hope this book rings two bells: an alarm bell and an invitation bell. As an alarm, it seeks to alert Christians (but not only Christians) to the pressing need to take other religions more seriously, to get to know them, talk with them, work with them. As an invitation, the book intends to show the exciting, life-giving, world-benefiting, faith-deepening benefits that result from engaging and learning about persons who follow other religious ways. The urgent need is also a promising opportunity. It is said that in our present age, religious people have to be religious interreligiously. To walk one's own faith-path, one needs to be walking with others from different paths. This book will describe how Christians are trying to do that and the kind of problems and opportunities they are facing.

I've tried to do this before — back in 1985 with *No Other Name? A Critical Survey of Christian Attitudes toward World Religions.* The present book started out as a revision of that earlier study. But as I began to gather all the materials on what Christians have been experiencing in, and what theologians have been saying about, their encounter with other religions over the past two decades, I realized I couldn't just revise my survey of 1985. I'd have to write a new book. There were so many new voices and viewpoints. So much had changed.

But I realized that I had changed too. Thanks especially to the gentle prodding of my wife, Cathy, I came to understand that I didn't want to write another book aimed primarily at my fellow theologians in the academy. From my own pastoral experiences with students and fellow believers in congregations and parishes, I'd come to see more clearly what a pressing, often agonizing, question "the other religions" have become for Christians. I wanted to speak to these fellow travelers, who make up that "broader audience" of ordinary folk who are informed, intellectually alive, and interested in or struggling with religion and religious faith. To speak to them, I'd have to tune into their real questions, converse with them in a clear, engaging manner, but at the same time offer them some solid, reputable theology to think about.

As I was pondering whether and how to do this, Orbis Books just happened to launch its new "Introducing" series, aimed at informing a broader audience of interested readers about what is going on in contemporary theology. Click! My originally intended revision could be another entry in the impressive and growing line-up of this Introducing series. William Burrows, managing editor at Orbis and friend and colleague in editing the Faith Meets Faith series over the past years, thought it was a good idea. But there was one big hitch. In such a series, my task would be to describe and analyze, not take sides! As they say in the academy, no advocacy. In *No Other Name?* I did my critical review of theologies of religions basically as a framework, or launching pad, for proposing my own (at that time, I called it "theocentric") model. In this book, there could be only the review of the various models for a Christian theology of religions — critical, yes, but evenhanded.

This hitch turned out to be a blessing. Of course, the goal of objectivity, even-handedness, and nonadvocacy is impossible. But it's also worthwhile. I think the never-fully-successful effort I have made in this book to present the different Christian theologies of religions as accurately and attractively as possible has paid off. Those who have read the manuscript as it was taking shape have told me that my resolve to keep my mouth shut has better enabled them both to understand the different theologies more clearly and to assess them more independently. And, I must admit, the effort has paid off for me personally as well. Yes, I still have my own approach to other faiths. But in trying to portray all the perspectives as convincingly as possible, in both their strengths and weaknesses, I have become more aware of the limitations of my own model, and of the need for continued dialogue with the other models, than I have ever been during the forty years or so since I have been struggling with and writing about how Christians can understand other religions.

But because this twofold task of writing clearly for people who don't speak "theologese," and of writing accurately without taking sides, is so daunting, I knew I would need help. I got it. And I'm grateful. The biggest help came from a group of twelve fellow members of Robert Bellarmine Parish. As each chapter laboriously took shape on my computer screen, I would e-mail or fax it to each of them. After they read it, we would gather at one of our homes and they would tell me, kindly but candidly, how successful I had been in reaching the "informed and interested lay reader." Over the many months, we formed a kind of "base theological community" — a community of faith seeking understanding — in which we questioned and supported each other and shared hopes that what we were doing might make a difference in the broader church, and world. The gratitude I feel requires that I say thank you to each of them by name: Kristen Corcoran, Tom and Diane Flautt, Mike Harmon, Ruth Holtel, Karen Hurley, Sean and Mary O'Dwyer, Julie and Ken Rothe, Lou Vera, Sam Weller. I should add to that list two other persons with whom I have an even deeper community: my wife, Cathy, and my son, John. They too accompanied me, chapter by chapter, telling me with an honesty that only love permits what they liked and disliked, what excited them, or lost them.

I also received a hefty amount of advice from the twenty-five students in my graduate course titled "The Uniqueness of Christ" in the fall semester of 2000. We worked our way through a first draft of this book, and with a candor born of trust, they told me what they thought of both the theological content and the style. Often sobered, I was mainly encouraged — especially when at the end of the semester, the students asked me which of the theological models I preferred. My efforts to hold my own theological cards close to my chest must have worked.

But I needed help not only in reaching out to that "broader audience" but also in making sure that what I was offering was solid, and accurate, theology. For this I turned to my peers, especially to those whose ideas I was trying to describe accurately and fairly. So I owe a heartfelt and humbled thank you also to S. Mark Heim of Andover Newton Theological School, Jim Fredericks of Loyola Marymount University, Jack Healy of Fordham University, and especially Jacques Dupuis of the Gregorian University in Rome. All of them read the entire manuscript; all of them told where they thought my own perspectives were fogging over what they or others were really saying. I hope I made good use of their advice. I say the same of the peer-reviewer who is my closest friend and sharpest critic — Bill Burrows of Orbis Books. He was this book's good shepherd, keeping me from going astray but always keeping me going.

Finally, a few words on how the book might be used. While I tried to write for a diverse audience, the faces I continually had before me as I wrote these pages were those of my undergraduate students at Xavier University. I could feel their looks of confusion or boredom every time I slipped into too much theological shoptalk or speculation. I hope this book will speak especially to them. It can serve as a primary text for courses on Christian attitudes toward other religions" or on "dialogue among world religions." And I think it would be an appropriate introductory text for general "world religions" courses. A structure that has proven successful for me is to spend about three-quarters of the semester on the substance of this book, having two or three students do class reports on some of the readings listed at the end of each chapter; the final weeks of the course would then be a case study of dialogue with a particular religion using a text like Francis Clooney's *Hindu Wisdom for All God's Children* or Leo LeFebure's *The Buddha and the Christ*. For graduate courses, each chapter of the book can serve as an introduction to a deeper discussion of the various models based on further reading of some of the primary sources given at the end of each chapter. Finally, as I discovered in my own experience at Bellarmine Parish, the book can make for vigorous conversation for an adult education course or parish discussion group.

So I hope this book does work as a bell that will both alert and invite Christians to take other religions more seriously. In doing so — no matter what theological model they end up with — Christians will, I believe, both deepen their own faith and increase their ability to bring this world a little closer to what Jesus called the Reign of God.

If this book helps that happen, I can't think of a better way to begin my retirement from Xavier University.

PAUL F. KNITTER, Professor Emeritus
Xavier University, February 25, 2002

Abbreviations

AG   *Ad Gentes* (Decree on the Church's Missionary Activity; Vatican II)

DP   *Dialogue and Proclamation* (document issued jointly by the Commission on Interreligious Dialogue and the Congregation for the Evangelization of Peoples)

GS   *Gaudium et Spes* (Pastoral Constitution on the Church in the Modern World; Vatican II)

LG   *Lumen Gentium* (Dogmatic Constitution on the Church; Vatican II)

NA   *Nostra Aetate* (Declaration on the Relationship of the Church to Non-Christian Religions; Vatican II)

RM   *Redemptoris Missio* (The Mission of the Redeemer; encyclical on missionary work; John Paul II)

UR   *Unitatis Redintegratio* (Decree on Ecumenism; Vatican II)

Introduction

Christianity and Other Religions

Problem and Promise

The title of this chapter attempts to capture what this book is all about. Through-out these pages we will be examining and assessing why the reality of many other religions has become for Christians both a big problem and a big — maybe even bigger — promise. Bewildered, often befuddled, by the diversity and vital-ity of other religions, Christians are facing questions and challenges they never had to confront before (at least not in this intensity). That's the problem. But these unsettling questions are also prompting new discoveries and insights about humanity, divinity, and Christianity itself. And there's the promise. This book wants to take seriously and honestly both the problem and the promise.

In a sense, the problem is not new. From the clouded origins of the human species, as the spark of consciousness broadened and gave rise to the driving concern for the meaning of life, there have always been many religions, each with its own "ultimate" answers. But today, the presence, power, and richness of other religious traditions have vigorously entered Christian awareness. Our contemporary intercommunicating and interdependent planet has made us aware, more clearly but also more painfully than ever before, of the multiplicity of religions and of the many different ultimate answers.

At times the new approach becomes painful because the quantity of informa-tion and quality of our new awareness of other religions today set off a barrage of questions that religious persons of the past, secure in their own isolated religious camps, never had to face with such urgency:

- Why are there so many different religions?

- If God is one, should there not be one religion?

- Are all the religions valid in God's eyes — all equally effective in putting people in contact with the Divine?

- Are their differences more a matter of varied colors than of conflicting content? How should the religious traditions relate to each other?

- More specifically, how should my religion relate to the others?

- Might I learn more from them than what I have learned from my own? Why do I belong to one religion rather than another?

1

These questions constitute the agenda for Christians trying to understand themselves and their faith in relation to their religious neighbors and *their* faiths. The attempt of Christian pastors and theologians to answer questions such as those listed above constitutes the discipline called "theology of religions." In that discipline, pastors such as bishops and popes, as well as theologians, study the Christian Scriptures and tradition to ascertain the responses of their forebears in Christianity. They go on to study the insights of scholars known as "historians of religion" and "comparative religionists." They read the fundamental texts and enter into dialogue with the followers of other religious traditions in order to understand them better. And then pastors and theologians of religions return to their fellow Christians to explain what they have learned. Often they suggest ways in which Christian teachings on other religious traditions should be changed. Their proposals have excited intense debates among theologians and reactions from church teaching authorities.[1]

The title of this book is *Introducing Theologies of Religions.* In it I attempt to lay out the major theological positions on the relation of Christianity to other religious Ways and on the role of the many religions in the divine plan. The book is intended for persons who want to begin the systematic study of the theology of religions. It will quickly become clear that there have been and are *many* points of view. Consequently, this book is, in a sense, on "theologies" of religion. My task is to summarize and describe these theologies as accurately as I can. The pastors and theologians I am writing about often differ radically with one another about the adequacy of positions espoused by others. I cannot reconcile their differences. I hope, though, that the persons I discuss will each say, "You have stated my position fairly."

I gave a number of the authors discussed in this book the entire manuscript and asked for their opinions. One of them said I had done well enough summarizing his position but complained that laying things out as if they were objects of consumer choice seemed a betrayal of the goals of systematic theology — which, rather than simply presenting choices, tries to lay out the truth in a coherent fashion and then offers an argument that answers the major questions in the most adequate way possible. Doing theology the way this book does, he was saying in effect, does not do justice to the Christian theological task of understanding religious pluralism in a way that takes seriously both the core truths of Christianity and those of the "others."

I have a great deal of sympathy with that observation. Indeed, at an earlier stage in my career, I thought I had written a book that solved the key problems in a manner Christians would judge adequate.[2] The controversies that book stirred

---

1. Two documents of the Catholic Church are especially useful in illustrating this dynamic. See Pope John Paul II's encyclical *Redemptoris Missio* ("On the Permanent Validity of the Church's Missionary Mandate," December 7, 1990) and the declaration of the Congregation for the Doctrine of the Faith's *Dominus Iesus* ("Declaration on the Unicity and Salvific Universality of Jesus Christ and the Church," August 6, 2000).

2. See Paul F. Knitter, *No Other Name? A Critical Survey of Christian Attitudes toward the World Religions* (Maryknoll, N.Y.: Orbis Books, 1985).

up quickly disabused me of the notion that the task of articulating a universally acceptable Christian theology of religions would be easy. Yet it still seems to me that texts such as Acts 4:12 need to be interpreted today in ways that do justice to the increasingly common Christian experience of grace, power, and truth in other religious Ways. That Lukan text reads: "There is no salvation through anyone else, nor is there any other name under heaven given to the human race by which we are to be saved." In the Gospel of John, a whole series of texts is epitomized in the following verses:

> For God so loved the world that he gave his only Son, so that everyone who believes in him might not perish but might have eternal life. For God did not send his Son into the world to condemn the world, but that the world might be saved through him. Whoever believes in him will not be condemned, but whoever does not believe has already been condemned, because he has not believed in the name of the only Son of God. And this is the verdict, that the light came into the world, but people preferred darkness to light, because their works were evil. (John 3:16–19)

For many Christians trying to take their religious faith seriously, the questions rising from such biblical texts are pressing and often painful. They cannot run away from these questions if their own faith is to be honest. But because of such texts, traditional Christian teaching had it that theirs was the only true religion and that what was good in other religions was only there to prepare followers to receive the Gospel and enter the one true religion — Christianity.

The theology of religions, or, as it is put in a new formulation of that term, the "theology of religious pluralism,"[3] wrestles with such issues. For those who are not troubled by the fact that religious plurality does not seem destined to end, there is little need to go beyond the surface. Issues can be solved by simply citing Scripture. Most theologians of religion have not accepted such pat answers, and this book attempts to introduce the reader to what they have been saying.

Above all, there has been a growth in the sentiment that religious plurality needs to be taken account of in our changed historical circumstances. What the Muslim could say and think about the Christian and Jew in a former age no longer seems adequate. What Christians once said to dismiss summarily the claims of Islam needs similarly to be reexamined, above all in the light of experiences that reveal the grace and truth present in our Muslim neighbors. This same equation, I believe, fits in the case of what we learn when we study such traditions as Judaism, Buddhism, Hinduism, Confucianism, and African and Native American traditionalism. The rest of this chapter sets the stage for efforts to face and perhaps answer questions concerning whether the persistent diversity and plurality of the religions of humankind have a positive significance that each religious Way needs to consider. Before we can really search for answers,

---

3. See Jacques Dupuis, *Toward a Christian Theology of Religious Pluralism* (Maryknoll, N.Y.: Orbis Books, 1997), 7–13.

we must be well aware of the content, urgency, and complexity of the question. So in what follows in this introductory chapter, we will explore:

1. Why is the age-old fact of religious diversity being experienced differently in the world of today?

2. Why does this experience suggest to many people a "new age" and the need for a radically new way for religions to relate to one another?

3. Why does this view of a new age dawning and proposals for a new way of understanding and relating to the religious "other" cause questions and headaches for so many?

I do not come to this task without many opinions that have been forged on the anvil of personal study and prayer. The most important influence on me, however, has been the opportunity I have had to enter into dialogue with brothers and sisters in other religious traditions from across the globe. At another level, the plight of the world's wretched poor, the political use of religion that impedes dialogue, and the precarious situation of Mother Earth have affected me deeply. In recent years, I have devoted two books to discussing religious plurality and the world situation in the light of currents in recent history.[4] Events after September 11, 2001, have only made the issues I wrote about then seem more important and maintaining optimism that religion can be a force for peace more precarious. Study, prayer, interreligious dialogue, and action to promote justice, peace, liberation, and the integrity of creation have changed me. No one would believe me if I said I have written this book in a completely "objective" fashion. My life as a scholar and as a Christian interested in realizing the Gospel vision of the peaceful reign of God has led me to a bias in favor of practical cooperation and the dialogue of life as religious persons struggle to create a better world. I am aware today, more than ever in the past, that this practical cooperation does not trump the question of truth. Above all, perhaps, there lingers the fact that the way in which the reality of universal *relativity* is interpreted often pitches many people into the arms of the pernicious dogma of *relativism,* which holds that differences don't matter and that the debate, argument, study, and dialogue needed to gain *truth* are outdated in our postmodern world. About such "postmodern" ideas, more later. In this introduction it may suffice to say that — even if this book may subtly and perhaps sometimes blatantly apply a practical, pragmatic standard in judging proposals for understanding Christianity vis-à-vis other religious Ways — I know we, in the present context of pluralism, are many years away from an understanding of religious claims to possess truth that will command general acceptance globally.

---

4. See my two most recent books, Paul F. Knitter, *One Earth — Many Religions: Multifaith Dialogue and Global Responsibility* (Maryknoll, N.Y.: Orbis Books, 1995) and *Jesus and the Other Names: Christian Mission and Global Responsibility* (Maryknoll, N.Y.: Orbis Books, 1996).

The Many Religions:
A Newly Experienced Reality

Today the reality of other religions no longer exists only across the border, in distant lands. It has moved into neighborhoods throughout the world, but nowhere more unavoidably than North America and Europe. To know something about another tradition, one no longer has to be a scholar or world traveler. All one has to do is visit the local bookstore, turn on the television, or browse the Web. What was once esoteric material for the delight of the scholar is now the popularly written and beautifully illustrated religious paperbacks that fill the shelves of American and European bookstores. Translations of the Bhagavad Gita, the Tao-Te-Ching, and the Dhammapada are to be found alongside the Bible. Commentaries on the meaning and value of Hinduism, Buddhism, Taoism, and Islam by Huston Smith, Joseph Campbell, Thich Nhat Hanh, and the Dalai Lama are selling just as well — if not better — than the works of Christian writers. Series on public television enable viewers to explore the depths and beauty of other religious paths. This openness is especially the case on college campuses, where courses on Asian religions, Islam, and Native American traditions often fill up more quickly than courses in Christian theology. Further, it has been my experience that in studying other religions, students are generally not content simply to learn about their teachings or practices — about Nirvana or Karma or Brahman or the Tao. They raise questions about evaluating the traditions, about their "truth," and about comparisons with Christian teachings. Students increasingly feel that to be firm in their own religion they have to be acquainted with others.

But the kind of knowledge of other religions that really touches and ruffles Western Christians is not coming by way of books and courses. It also arrives in the dialogue of life with friends one meets in the neighborhood, at work, or in civic organizations. Not only are ideas migrating, so are people. In the 1960s, Wilfred Cantwell Smith described a state of religious affairs that has grown more prevalent and personal throughout the ensuing decades:

> The religious life of mankind from now on, if it is to be lived at all, will be lived in a context of religious pluralism.... This is true for all of us; not only for "mankind" in general on an abstract level, but for you and me as individual persons. No longer are people of other persuasions peripheral or distant, the idle curiosities of travelers' tales. The more alert we are, and the more involved in life, the more we are finding that they are our neighbors, our colleagues, our competitors, our fellows. Confucians and Hindus, Buddhists and Muslims, are with us not only in the United Nations, but down the street. Increasingly, not only is our civilization's destiny affected by their actions; but we drink coffee with them personally as well.[5]

5. Wilfred Cantwell Smith, *The Faith of Other Men* (New York: Harper & Row, 1962), 11.

Because Christians are sharing not only their classrooms and work sites but also their dinner tables and even their marriage beds with persons of other religions, they find that once-foreign faiths take on different dimensions and power in their own lives. To have a friend, a colleague, a family member, or a spouse who has found meaning through a religious path that is starkly different from Christianity not only impresses; it disturbs. A Zen Buddhist may find peace through a practice that does not even talk about the existence of God. A Hindu discovers "salvation" in the realization that there is no essential difference between herself and a tree. What do such claims on the lips of neighbors and friends mean for Christian life and belief? Such people are normal, happy human beings, getting their jobs done and raising their families as well as, perhaps better than, we are. They live lives of love, of service, of commitment.

Theology of religions is for persons who do not want to sit back and complacently conclude that all that is fine for others but means nothing for them. At a practical level, it is human to want to learn more about the religiously "other." That practical search has ramifications in questions about what their lives and beliefs mean for us as Christians. In raising such questions, Christianity — which long held that outside the church there was no salvation — is encountering other religions and seeking to understand them in their own right and in terms of what they mean for their own tradition.

For some Christians, the persistence of religious diversity after some nineteen centuries of Christian missionary activity is unsettling. Certainly the achievements of Christian mission are extensive and laudable. Thanks to the sweat and blood of generations of missioners, the Christian church is present on all continents and in almost every nation. After two thousand years of missionary labors, Christians at the turn of the millennium number 33.2 percent of the world population. The majority of these Christians, moreover, live in Africa, Asia, and Latin America. Christianity is a world religion today as never before in its history. Also, as Gandhi recognized, the vision and values of the Nazarene, as contained in the Sermon on the Mount, have notably influenced cultures that staunchly refuse to call themselves Christian. Still, if we consider global conversion to be the goal of Christian mission, the results are disheartening.

There have, of course, been vast numbers of converts to Christianity. But the bulk of these converts have not come from the so-called world religions — Hinduism, Buddhism, Judaism, and Confucianism. For the most part, people born in these religions, which were formed during what Karl Jaspers called the "Axial Period" (900 B.C.E. to 200 C.E.), and in Islam, which began in the seventh century, have never converted to Christianity. Nor does it seem likely that this will change in the foreseeable future. When conversions occur from one axial religion to another, they are, for the most part, offset by converts moving in the other direction. While Christians constitute the most populous of the religions (around 1.9 billion in 1998), Muslims occupy an impressive, and growing, second place with 1.2 billion.

Plurality: A Significant Fact
of Religious and Cosmic Life

Awareness of the continuing multiplicity and vitality of religions is pushing many to say, "There is no one-and-only way for all." To those led in this direction, a similar judgment is often applied also to cultures, philosophies, and economic systems. And when that occurs, many of our contemporaries come to believe that their structures of rationality, consciousness, nationhood, and religion are one among many. Edward Schillebeeckx puts it for his fellow Christians as follows: "The unshaken certainty that one continues to possess the truth oneself while others are mistaken is no longer a possibility." In that context, to say that one's own Way is the only possibility for grasping religious truth is to live in a "time warp."[6]

To those who would agree with Schillebeeckx, plurality is not a situation to be tolerated until Christians can devise a master plan that will herd all these "other" sheep into one corral. To those convinced by anthropological, historical, and sociological studies that there is no one, superior way, multiplicity is the stuff of reality, the way things are and function. Is this something Christians can and should accept? Or does it lead to a denial of fundamental religious truth? Such are the questions that lie behind the declarations of church pastors and theologians who are wrestling with such issues.

And it should be quickly noted that these are the same questions that Muslims, Hindus, and others are asking. Indeed, it is resistance to the so-called relativism of the Western academy that inspires many Muslim teachers today. We should not deceive ourselves by thinking that the answers to such questions are easy.

It is clear that many university-educated persons in the West and elsewhere are convinced that religious traditions are not reliable ways of stating the truth about the universe. Indeed, on the part of many, it is an axiom that religion leads to conflict, backwardness, superstition, and hatred. To what extent should Christians (or Jews, Muslims, or Buddhists for that matter) agree with such views? If one lets these legitimate criticisms of religion into one's tradition, does their point of view constitute an acid that not only scours away abuses and outdated thinking but also may corrode even the core attitudes one needs to enter into religion as mystery and spirituality? These are questions that, even when they are not on the surface in discussions that follow, make many theologians and religious teachers uneasy with modernity.

Still, multiplicity from atoms to molecules to plants to bugs to humans is what science today shows us is necessary for the existence and functioning of the world. Out of the chaos comes new and different ways for responding to developmental dead ends and crises. Reality is intrinsically complex, rich, intricate, mysterious. As Edward Schillebeeckx puts it, plurality is not just a "matter

---

6. Edward Schillebeeckx, *The Church: The Human Story of God* (New York: Crossroad, 1990), 50–51.

of fact" but a "matter of principle." If we boil the "many" down to "one," we would harm ourselves and maim the world. "Logically and practically," Schillebeeckx says, "multiplicity now takes priority over unity."[7]

And yet awareness of pluralism does not lead simply to a total celebration of diversity; nor is the pluralism without its problems. Many are troubled by the way relativity is easily equated with a relativism that has no room for discussing truth-claims and degrees of value. I believe a conviction is growing that the many religions cannot exist side-by-side as nonrelated, sovereign bodies. Do not, many ask, the crises of our age constitute a call to the religions to cooperate in their solutions? Can the many religions legitimately live in lazy tolerance, or, even worse, in a state of warfare? If they do so, can humanity's and earth's environmental problems be overcome? Schillebeeckx again helps us draw conclusions as to what this means for religious persons: "The multiplicity of religions is not an evil which needs to be removed, but rather a wealth which is to be welcomed and enjoyed by all.... There is more religious truth in all religions together than in one particular religion.... This also applies to Christianity."[8]

It would seem that the religions of the world have to come together, not to form a new, singular religion but to form *a dialogical community of communities*. The most appropriate image for the religious future of humankind is perhaps to be found not in pictures of thriving churches, synagogues, temples, and mosques but in what the world witnessed and thousands experienced at the World Parliament of Religions in Chicago in 1993 and Cape Town in 1999. Here representatives of the major religious communities of the world gathered to affirm and practice the need to talk to and listen to each other. They were a dialogical community on an international scale, imaging what can also take place on the local scene.

A Community of Communities?

A dialogical community of communities among the world's religions is still more a dream than a clear concept. To try to get some sense of what this dream contains, we can examine the reasons why many people hold that it is not only possible but necessary.

We turn first to philosophers since it is their culturally recognized job to describe, interpret, and direct how people, at a given stage of history, understand or should understand their world and themselves. Among the various schools of philosophy within contemporary Western culture, there is one that proposes a vision of reality that many ordinary persons sense to be true of their individual lives: that the world and everything in it are evolutionary or in process. We are, in other words, not in a state of being but in a process of becoming.

---

7. Ibid., 163.
8. Ibid., 166–67.

A number of philosophers articulate this view in different but fundamentally compatible ways. Alfred North Whitehead and Charles Hartshorne see a world involved in an adventure of creativity through process. Pierre Teilhard de Chardin's universe evolves painfully but steadily from the biosphere to the noosphere to the unity of the Omega Point, which he identifies with the cosmic Christ at the eschaton. Some contemporary Buddhists elaborate Gautama's discovery of a constantly changing world through a process of dependent co-origination. Aurobindo's Hinduism envisions a world in evolution toward divinization. Thomas Berry's and Brian Swimme's grandiose evolutionary "Universe Story" has found great resonance among persons concerned with the plight of the environment.[9]

The vision these thinkers present is pointedly different from the worldview that guided the mind and imagination of Western civilization for most of its existence. For the majority of Europeans throughout the Middle Ages and into the Renaissance, creation came forth from the hand of God as a finished product, stable, and hierarchically ordered. One was not to tamper with this order. Humans were to keep their place in relation to God. Within the divinely constituted order of things, social classes were also to keep their places; God willed serfs to be serfs and lords to be lords. Although change occurred, the medieval worldview considered change a corruption and a spur for Christians to desire the unchanging world of eternity with God.

A confluence of many events and discoveries changed this image of an unchangeable world. The profound disruptions of the French Revolution and the Industrial Revolution set persons thinking that the social order might not be as unalterable and divinely established as they had thought. Even more disruptive of the stability of things was Darwin's discovery of biological evolution. His *On the Origin of Species* demanded that creation, if it was to be believed in at all, be seen not as a one-time event but as a continuous process, still unfinished and undetermined.

Then came the insights and discoveries of the "new physics," pioneered by Albert Einstein, which over a period of twenty to thirty years thoroughly remodeled the Newtonian universe. Reality was no longer seen as a well-ordered machine, made up of discrete parts neatly linked to each other. Rather, it was a buzz of activity, of constant process, in which the parts could not even be neatly determined and located. At its deepest, subatomic level, the world did not seem to show any "basic building blocks" or "beings," but rather an intricate, ever-changing, and interrelating process of activity or becoming.

It was especially the new physics that prompted philosophers to suggest the

---

9. Alfred North Whitehead, *Process and Reality* (New York: Free Press, 1969); Charles Hartshorne, *The Divine Relativity* (New Haven: Yale University Press, 1948); Pierre Teilhard de Chardin, *The Phenomenon of Man* (New York: Harper & Row, 1961); Joanna Macy, *Mutual Causality in Buddhism and General Systems Theory: The Dharma of Natural Systems* (Albany: State University of New York Press, 1991); Thomas Berry and Brian Swimme, *The Universe Story* (San Francisco: HarperSanFrancisco, 1992).

following: if everything is a becoming rather than a being, the becoming takes place through interrelating. In that context, we can be only by becoming, and we can become only in relating. Nothing, whether an electron or a human being, can be "an island unto itself." "Every-thing" and "every-body" are profoundly and dynamically interrelated, to the point that what a "thing" or "body" is, is constituted by its relationships. "We are our relationships" has become almost a cliché. It is difficult to grasp this as literally true, for we still look upon things as substances rather than events; we deem ourselves primarily individuals rather than partners.

The very structure of our language prevents us from grasping that we are our relationships. We begin our thinking and speaking with nouns that are then followed by verbs; the subject generally must precede the predicate. If we could speak and feel the language of the Hopi Indians, which is made up primarily of verbs that serve as nouns, we might be closer to the way we and the world really are. We are not first of all individuals who later relate; rather it is our relating — how we do it and with whom or what — that makes us (or gives us the semblance of being) individuals. We are not "becomings" but "becomings with." Cut off the "with," and we cease to exist.

The philosophical perspective we're trying to explore views the multiplicity, or plurality, of creation as empowered with a potential for ever greater unity — even though it can't really say just where this potential will end. The many are called to be one. But it is a one that does not devour the many. The many become one precisely by remaining the many, and the one is brought about by each of the many making its distinct contribution to the others and thus to the whole. It is a process that aims at an ever more pervasive concentration of the many in each other and thus in a greater whole. Whereas individualization is weakened, personalization is intensified; the individual finds its true self as part of other selves. So there is a movement not toward absolute or monistic oneness but toward what might be called "unitive pluralism": plurality constituting unity. Or, in simpler, more engaging terms: the movement is toward a truly dialogical community, in which each member lives and is itself through dialogue with others.

Can this philosophical vision serve as a lens to interpret the new experience of religious pluralism described in the first section of this chapter? The world religions are confronting each other as never before, and they are experiencing a new sense of identity and purpose because they, like atoms and humans and cultures, are sensing the possibilities of a more pervasive unity through better relationships with each other. Just as philosophy and science are calling Western culture from a static, individualistic understanding of reality, so many religious persons are awaking to a more dynamic and dialogical way of understanding themselves. Believers within various religions are feeling more and more intensely the challenge of finding and developing their individual identities within the broader community of other religions. To be Christian or Hindu, one must be part of this wider religious community. Today, so it seems, one must be religious *interreligiously.*

A simple analogy might make all this clearer and reveal its relevance for our issue of dialogue: we might compare "truth" or "the way things are" to the starry universe around us. There is so much of it, and it is so far away, that with our naked eyes, we really can't see what's there. We have to use a telescope. But by enabling us to see something of the universe, our telescope also prevents us from seeing everything. A telescope, even the mighty ones used by astronomers, can take in only so much. This describes our human situation. We're always looking at the truth through some kind of cultural telescope, the one provided us by our parents, teachers, and broader society. The good news about this situation is that our telescope enables us to see; the bad news is that it prevents us from seeing everything.

So what can we do? How can we see more of the truth than what our limited cultural and religious telescope permits? The answer is simple — and it tunes us into our topic of a dialogical community of religions: by borrowing some-one else's telescope! If we can look through our neighbors' telescopes — even though these new telescopes might seem strange to us and difficult to adjust our eyes to — we can see things that we missed with our own. And the more differ-ently built and angled these telescopes are, the more new things we're going to be able to see. With other telescopes, really different from our own, we can see areas of the universe that our telescopes weren't able to reach or weren't able to bring into focus. And the more telescopes we manage to use, the more our vision and understanding of truth will expand. Thus, we come to the conclusion that felt right to us from the beginning: truth is known through conversation.

Scholars who speak out of what we are calling a postmodern awareness also offer us another reason for the necessity of conversation: the truth that we see through our own cultural-religious telescope is not only limited but dangerous. In not realizing that the truth we have is limited, we see it as the only truth, or the whole truth, or the superior truth — not only for ourselves but for all people. And here, according to these scholars, is where we need to be suspicious of our truth-claims, for at this point truth can become ideology. According to the so-called masters of suspicion (Nietzsche, Freud, Marx), as well as women and other oppressed groups, when one group holds up its truth as the absolute truth it will eventually use that truth to take advantage of others. Truth becomes ideology when a group or society or religion pursues, affirms, and proclaims something as true not only because they believe that it really is so but because — whether they realize this or not — it maintains their power over others.

Ideology is the use of one's own "truth" as a means to promote one's per-sonal, economic, or class welfare at the cost of others. One group's advantage becomes the criterion for determining what truth is. As Michel Foucault has pointed out, truth-claims easily become power-claims.[10] This can make belief that one has the truth very dangerous.

---

10. Michel Foucault, *Power/Knowledge: Selected Interviews and Other Writings, 1972–1977* (New York: Pantheon Books, 1980).

Examples of how truth is dangerously turned into ideology are rife in the history of all religions and cultures. Why have Christian preachers told the poor that their poverty will gain them a higher place in heaven? Was it to console the poor or to keep them from rebelling against the wealthy landowners who were often contributing financially to the church? Why do Brahmins (religious authorities in Hinduism) insist that the caste system is a requirement of the eternal, sacred law of Dharma? Because they have discovered this law through their study and meditation or because their own power and prestige are secured by the caste system?

How can we protect ourselves against the worm of ideology? Self-examination won't work. Ideology is like bad breath. You need someone else to tell you that you have it. We need to talk to people who use other telescopes to look at the universe of truth to hear from them not only how our truth looks to them but how our proclamation of truth affects them. Perhaps they will reveal how it excludes, demeans, or exploits them.

To put all this in the language of what is called hermeneutical theory (the exploration into how humans know or interpret the truth), we can take up the challenge of what Jürgen Habermas calls the task of "communicative praxis."[11] To know the truth we must be engaged in the practice of communication with others; that means really talking with and listening to people who are significantly different from us. If we're talking just with ourselves or with our own kind, or if there are some people whom we simply exclude from the conversation and can't imagine ourselves talking to, then we are possibly cutting ourselves off from the opportunity to learn something we haven't yet discovered.

To have our own mother tongue and yet be able to understand and converse in other cultural or religious languages is to feel the wonder and necessity of becoming what we might call "world citizens." The term can be misunderstood or misused — as if becoming part of the global village required us to totally leave our home village. Our root identities are always local; and to a great extent, they remain so. What we are talking about here is the need, and the exciting opportunity, for also becoming citizens of other villages. We take what we have inherited from our own village and in the light of what we learn as we visit other villages, we appreciate both the value and the limitations of what our own village has given us. In this sense, all of us today are being called toward some degree of world citizenship. Two of the greatest threats facing the community of nations and cultures are the nationalism and fanaticism that grow among those who have never left their village and who think that it is superior to all others.

This call is not heard by all religious persons and communities. It is often perceived as a threat by those whose theologies don't allow it. Because the face of the stranger is still too threatening, many religious communities respond to the new world situation with a kind of cultural isolationism that hijacks religious traditions and puts them in the service of ethnocentric nationalism.

---

11. Jürgen Habermas, *The Theory of Communicative Action,* vol. 1 (Boston: Beacon Press, 1984).

In the coming chapters we will be exploring and weighing the various ways in which Christians, over the past half-century especially, have been trying to come to grips with this new experience of religious pluralism and this newly felt need for a dialogical community of religions. In all the models for a Christian theology of religions we discuss, theologians and church authorities seek to preserve the values of the universal scope of the Christian claim and their knowledge of the particular, historical sources of those claims without falling into either relativism or absolutism.

Although the theologies of religion we shall examine are often bewilderingly complex, they all deal with the challenge that Wilfred Cantwell Smith posed in 1962:

> How does one account, theologically, for the fact of humanity's religious diversity? This is really as big an issue, almost, as the question of how one accounts theologically for evil — but Christian theologians have been much more conscious of the fact of evil than that of religious pluralism.... From now on any serious intellectual statement of the Christian faith must include, if it is to serve its purpose, ... some sort of doctrine of other religions. We explain the fact that the Milky Way is there by the doctrine of creation, but how do we explain the fact that the Bhagavad Gita is there?[12]

But in order to explain why the Bhagavad Gita is there, Christians will have to readdress the fundamental question, Why is Christianity here? A new way of understanding other religions implies a new way of understanding Christianity. Christians do indeed face both problems and promises when they honestly and lovingly face the reality of other religions.

Further Readings

Braybrooke, Marcus. *Faith and Interfaith in a Global Age*. Grand Rapids, Mich.: Co-Nexus Press, 1998, 9–16, 103–32.

Bryant, M. Darroll. "Do All Religions Teach the Same Thing? Exploring the Unity and Diversity of Religions." *Dialogue and Alliance* 11 (1997): 43–58.

Campbell, Joseph. *The Hero with a Thousand Faces*. Princeton, N.J.: Princeton University Press, 1968, 3–46.

Ching, Julia. "Living in Two Worlds: A Personal Appraisal." In *A Dome of Many Colors: Studies in Religious Pluralism, Identity, and Unity*. Ed. Arvind Sharma and Kathleen M. Dugan. Harrisburg, Pa.: Trinity Press International, 1999, 7–22.

Cousins, Ewert. "The Convergence of Cultures and Religions in Light of the Evolution of Consciousness." *Zygon* 34 (1999): 209–20.

Crawford, Cromwell S. "The Future of Religion at the Dawn of the 21st Century: Paradox of Pluralism." *Dialogue and Alliance* 13 (1999): 5–14.

De Mey, Peter. "Ernst Troeltsch: A Moderate Pluralist? An Evaluation of His Reflections on the Place of Christianity among the Other Religions." In *The Myriad Christ:*

---

12. Smith, *Faith of Other Men*, 132–33.

Plurality and the Quest for Unity in Contemporary Christology. Ed. T. Merrigan and J. Haers. Leuven: Leuven University Press, 2000, 349–80.

D'Sa, Francis X. "The Universe of Faith and the Pluriverse of Belief: Are All Religions Talking about the Same Thing?" *Dialogue and Alliance* 11 (1997): 88–116.

Eck, Diana L. *Encountering God: A Spiritual Journey from Bozeman to Banaras.* Boston: Beacon Press, 1993, 1–44, 200–232.

———. *A New Religious America: How a "Christian Country" Has Become the World's Most Religiously Diverse Nation.* San Francisco: HarperSanFrancisco, 2001, chapters 1 and 2, and/or 6 and 7.

James, William. *The Varieties of Religious Experience.* Various editions. Lectures 2, 3, 20.

Jung, C. G. *Psychology and Alchemy.* Vol. 12 of Jung's collected works. London: Routledge and Kegan Paul, 1953, 3–37.

———. "The Spiritual Problem of Modern Man." In *Modern Man in Search of a Soul.* New York: Harcourt, Brace, 1955, 226–54.

Küng, Hans, and Karl-Josef Kuschel, eds. *A Global Ethic: The Declaration of the Parliament of the World Religions.* New York: Crossroad, 1993, 13–39.

Nasr, Seyyed Hossein. "Religion, Globality, and Universality." In *A Dome of Many Colors: Studies in Religious Pluralism, Identity, and Unity.* Ed. Arvind Sharma and Kathleen M. Dugan. Harrisburg, Pa.: Trinity Press International, 1999, 152–78.

Panikkar, Raimon. "Eruption of Truth: An Interview with Raimon Panikkar." *Christian Century,* August 16–23, 2000, 834–36.

———. "Religious Identity and Pluralism." In *A Dome of Many Colors: Studies in Religious Pluralism, Identity, and Unity.* Ed. Arvind Sharma and Kathleen M. Dugan. Harrisburg, Pa.: Trinity Press International, 1999, 23–47.

Race, Alan. *Interfaith Encounter: The Twin Tracks of Theology and Dialogue.* London: SCM Press, 2001, 1–42.

Schuon, Frithjof. *The Transcendent Unity of Religions.* New York: Harper & Row, 1975, 1–56. See also the Introduction by Huston Smith, ix–xxvi.

Toynbee, Arnold. "The Task of Disengaging the Essence from the Non-essentials in Mankind's Religious Heritage." In *An Historian's Approach to Religion.* New York: Oxford University Press, 1956, 261–83.

———. "What Should Be the Christian Approach to the Contemporary Non-Christian Faiths?" In *Christianity among the Religions of the World.* New York: Scribner's, 1957, 83–112.

Troeltsch, Ernst. "The Place of Christianity among the World Religions." In *Christianity and Other Religions.* Ed. John Hick and Brian Hebblethwaite. Philadelphia: Fortress Press, 1980, 11–31.

Further Readings on Biblical/Patristic Foundations for a Theology of Religions

Blenkinsopp, Joseph. "Yahweh and Other Deities: Conflict and Accommodation in the Religion of Israel." *Interpretation* 40 (1986): 354–66.

Denaux, Adelbert. "The Monotheistic Background of New Testament Christology: Critical Reflections on Pluralist Theologies of Religion." In *The Myriad Christ: Plurality and the Quest for Unity in Contemporary Christology.* Ed. T. Merrigan and J. Haers. Leuven: Leuven University Press, 2000, 133–58.

Dupuis, Jacques. *Toward a Christian Theology of Religious Pluralism.* Maryknoll, N.Y.: Orbis Books, 1997, chapters 1 and 2.

Els, Pieter J. J. S. "Old Testament Perspectives on Interfaith Dialogue: The Significance of the Abram-Melchizedek Episode of Genesis 14." *Studies in Interreligious Dialogue* 8 (1998): 172–90.

Gnuse, Robert Karl. "Holy History in the Hebrew Scriptures and the Ancient World." *Biblical Theological Bulletin* 17 (1987): 127–37.

Kennedy, James M. "The Social Background of Early Israel's Rejection of Cultic Images." *Biblical Theological Review* 17 (1987): 138–44.

LaHurd, Carol Schersten. "The 'Other' in Biblical Perspective." *Currents in Theology and Mission* 24 (1997): 411–24.

Malina, Bruce J. "'Religion' in the World of Paul." *Biblical Theological Bulletin* 16 (1986): 92–101.

Meagher, P. M. "Jesus Christ in God's Plan, Interreligious Dialogue, Theology of Religions, and Paul of Tarsus." *Vidyajyoti* 61 (1997): 742–56.

Perkins, Pheme. "Christianity and World Religions: New Testament Questions." *Interpretation* 40 (1986): 367–78.

Wilken, Robert L. "Religious Pluralism and Early Christian Theology." *Interpretation* 40 (1986): 379–91.

Young, Frances. "Christology and Creation: Toward a Hermeneutic of Patristic Christology." In *The Myriad Christ: Plurality and the Quest for Unity in Contemporary Christology.* Ed. T. Merrigan and J. Haers. Leuven: Leuven University Press, 2000, 191–206.

Part I

THE REPLACEMENT MODEL
"Only One True Religion"

Chapter 1

Total Replacement

In the final analysis, Christianity is meant to replace all other religions. This is the first of the Christian attitudes toward other faiths that we will be reviewing and assessing. It's also the dominant attitude, the one that generally has held sway throughout most of Christian history. Although views differed about the way this replacement was to be carried out and why it was necessary, Christian missionaries throughout the centuries have cast forth into the world with the conviction that it is God's will to make all peoples Christians. In the end — or, as soon as possible — God wants there to be only one religion, God's religion: Christianity. If the other religions have any value at all, it is only a provisional value. Ultimately, Christianity is to take over. So for this Replacement Model, the balance between the universality and particularity of God's relationship with humanity clearly comes down more heavily on the side of particularity. God's love is universal, extending to all; but that love is realized through the particular and singular community of Jesus Christ.

Still today, this Replacement Model is broadly and strongly represented within the Christian churches. That's another reason for giving it first place in our line-up of Christian theologies of religions. This model is found especially in the so-called Fundamentalist or Evangelical Christian communities. To ignore, or downplay, the strength, importance, and challenge of Fundamentalists and Evangelicals within contemporary Christianity is to cut off, or do injustice to, a large part of the Christian family. As historian Martin Marty puts it: "To look at American religion and to overlook Evangelicalism and Fundamentalism would be comparable to scanning the American physical landscape and missing the Rocky Mountains."[1]

So for the rest of this chapter, those of us who feel certain "negative vibes" on hearing the term "Fundamentalist" are asked to put their conditioned responses or stereotypes on the shelf and listen, as openly and sensitively as possible, to the way these Christians view and reach out to other religious believers. What might appear as extreme in these views flows from a deep concern for what Evangelicals hold to be the heart of Christianity — especially as that heart beats in the churches of the Reformation. To dismiss this model as outdated is to hide from the fact that these attitudes *do* represent a strong, and an increasingly louder, voice within the Christian population.

---

1. Martin Marty, *A Nation of Believers* (Chicago: University of Chicago Press, 1976), 80.

Fundamentalist/Evangelical Christians

But whom are we talking about? The terms are frustratingly slippery. The way the name "Fundamentalist" is used in the media nowadays it might refer to a Baptist TV preacher, a Hasidic rabbi, a Mormon housewife, or a soldier in the Islamic Hisboullah. And "Evangelical" might cover black Baptists, Dutch Reformed churches, Mennonites and Pentecostals, Catholic charismatics, or Southern Baptists. So if we can't really define our terms, we can at least limit them to movements that took shape within American Christianity since the beginning of the twentieth century.

Variety in the Same Family

Fundamentalist Christianity was launched and christened, one might say, when three million copies of the booklet called *The Fundamentals* were sent out free of charge (two wealthy Los Angeles businessmen picked up the bill) to ministers, evangelists, and Sunday school superintendents between 1910 and 1915. These booklets assembled the troops and sounded the charge of American Protestants in their counterattack on the way "modernity" was destroying the foundations of Christian faith and identity. These destructive inroads came in different forms: in the new science of evolution that questioned the accuracy of the Bible; in the new historical-critical approach to the Bible (coming especially from Germany) that was substituting human science and interpretation for direct listening to the Word of God; also in the new study of comparative religions that placed Christianity in the same historical basket as all the other religions. To all these temptations to sell out to the lure of modern thinking, Fundamentalists hoisted their resolute and often aggressive "no."

But this rejection of anything having to do with modernity became so resolute and so sweeping that it caused divisions in the ranks of the Fundamentalists. During the 1940s and 1950s, a number of evangelists and theologians concluded that, although they certainly shared the theological concerns of the Fundamentalists, they could not go along with what appeared to them to be the Fundamentalists' polemical spirit, their anti-intellectualism, and their lack of social concern. In 1941, these protesters formed the National Association of Evangelicals. While they were just as committed to resisting the erosion of Christianity by the waves of modernity, they "wanted no dog-in-the-manger, reactionary, negative or destructive type of organization."[2] Indeed, these reformers of Fundamentalism were convinced that "if the voice of fundamentalism would be tempered slightly, evangelical Christianity could 'win America.'"[3] Their most influential leader and voice was Billy Graham, who in 1950 founded the

---

2. Martin Marty, "Tensions within Contemporary Evangelicalism: A Critical Appraisal," in *The Evangelicals*, ed. David F. Wells and John D. Woodbridge (Nashville: Abingdon, 1975), 172.

3. George Marsden, *Understanding Fundamentalism and Evangelicalism* (Grand Rapids, Mich.: Eerdmans, 1991), 64.

Evangelistic Association. The differences between Fundamentalists and Evangelicals were clear, but they were also more a matter of style than of substance. As one specialist put it: "A fundamentalist is an evangelical who is angry about something.... Fundamentalists are not just religious conservatives, they are conservatives who are willing to take a stand and to fight."[4]

During the 1960s and 1970s further developments in the Evangelical camp took place and signaled both the strengthening and the opening of Evangelical convictions. "New Evangelicals" or "Ecumenical Evangelicals" are open to working with other Christian churches and the World Council of Churches. Also, because they hold that Fundamentalists have been too absolute in insisting on the inerrancy (total lack of error) of the Bible, the New Evangelicals prefer to speak about a "limited inerrancy." They therefore recognize that while the Scriptures are "infallible" in matters of faith and practice, there may be inaccuracies regarding historical and scientific data. Finally, many of these New Evangelicals, especially in view of the Vietnam War and the growth of the Moral Majority, have asked their Evangelical brothers and sisters whether they have been politically and socially naive and have aligned themselves too easily with nationalistic and sometimes oppressive political platforms. These protesters have formed a "New Evangelical Left" which insists that one cannot follow Jesus without being actively and politically involved in trying to bring justice to the oppressed.

To the three movements we have so far identified — Fundamentalists, Evangelicals, New Evangelicals — we might add a fourth, which is really a powerful and pervasive current within them all rather than a clearly defined group: the Pentecostals or Charismatics. As a movement, Pentecostalism began in the early 1900s in a series of revivals, especially in Los Angeles, that were based on a simple yet revolutionizing claim: if Christianity takes its origins and ongoing life from a new outpouring of the Holy Spirit, then Christians should be able to experience this Spirit. And the experience should be something they really feel, something that stirs them deeply and that they translate into exuberant worship, even into glossolalia (the speaking in tongues). Like quenching waters over dry land, the Pentecostal renewal spread quickly, and internationally. In the 1960s and 1970s it even began to pervade the mainline churches, both Protestant and Catholic, where its preferred name was the "Charismatic Renewal." Today, much of the growth of Christianity in Latin America and parts of Asia is being generated by Pentecostal churches. Differences between Pentecostals and other Evangelicals, however, are more in the intensity of their Spirit-empowered spirituality than in the content of their theology.

In fact, when it comes to their underlying beliefs and theology, there is a common foundation among Fundamentalists, Evangelicals, and Pentecostals that supports their differences in style or theological detail. This shared foundation rests on four solid pillars:

---

4. Ibid., 1.

1. For all of these Christians, the Bible is the rock-bottom guide to all that a follower of Jesus does and claims. And for the most part, despite certain differences about total or partial inerrancy, this book is to be read as it is written. That doesn't necessarily mean with blind literalness, but it does call for constant vigilance lest "what I want to hear" gets in the way of "what is said."

2. All of these believers hold that their Christian lives must be more than a verbal "I believe" in the Bible or in what the minister says. Those lives must, rather, be rooted in and inspired by a personal experience of the saving power of the living Christ and his Spirit. In various ways, they talk about being "born again" or "baptized in the Spirit" or "making a choice for Jesus."

3. So it is Jesus who makes all the difference in their lives — and in the life of the world. In their lives, in the course of history, he can make a radical difference because he *has made* a radical difference. He is Savior. They want to follow only him.

4. Because of the wonder and power of what they have found in Jesus the Christ, these Christians are committed to sharing with others the gift they have been given. They want others to see and feel what they have seen and felt. That means they do want to convert the world, not because they feel superior to others but because gifts are to be shared.

Because what they have in common transcends what makes them different — and in order to give us one name for the same perspective — throughout this chapter, we will be using, for the most part, "Evangelical" as the blanket term for all the groups that would say "Amen" to the four characteristics just mentioned.

How Many?

Having drawn a clearer focus on just who the Evangelicals are, can we say how many of them there are in the United States? A lot, even though any figures are going to be estimates. In the 1980s, Gallup Polls used a "born-again experience" as the defining quality of an Evangelical and concluded that their numbers covered 40 percent of the U.S. population. More recent studies and surveys make use of more extensive criteria and estimate that about 25 to 30 percent of the population is in the Evangelical camp. These studies, however, separated out the Afro-American Protestant population (roughly 8 to 9 percent of the total population), which is overwhelmingly Evangelical in orientation. So, if we include black churches, we're back, roughly, at Gallup's 40 percent.[5] That means almost half the Christians in the United States — further reason to take them, and their views of other religions, seriously and respectfully.

---

5. See the Website for the Study of American Evangelicals: *www.wheaton.edu/isae/defevan.html*.

Given the variety of these more conservative Christian churches, there is also a variety in their approaches to other religions. We're going to try to respect and understand those differences by dividing our analysis of this Replacement Model into two parts: what we might call total and partial replacement. As expected, the differences fall out along the lines of the variances between Fundamentalists and Evangelicals.

Total Replacement:
No Value in Other Religions

The theology of total replacement that we are considering looks upon other faith communities as so lacking, or so aberrant, that in the end Christianity must move in and take their place. As stated, this has pretty much been the Christian view for most of the church's history. It's still the attitude of many contemporary Fundamentalist, and some Pentecostal, churches. For much of the twentieth century, especially because of the influence of a particular Swiss theologian, this was the perspective that inspired most of the Protestant missionaries who went forth to preach the Gospel. This theologian was Karl Barth (1886–1968), perhaps the most influential Protestant thinker of the past century. Although Barth was not a Fundamentalist, he did lay the theological foundation for the Replacement Model for understanding other religions. We can begin our review of this model by assembling some of the main building blocks in Barth's foundation.

Karl Barth: "Let God Be God — in Jesus Christ!"

In many ways, the historical context in which the young Karl Barth tried to live his Christian life and work out his theology was starkly similar to our own. The 1920s and 1930s were a time of proliferating new ideas but just as many proliferating uncertainties and anxieties. He had studied with the leading "liberal theologians" of his times and had joined their efforts to adapt Christianity to the humanism of the Enlightenment. He was swept up by the new ideas coming from science and the study of "Oriental" religions. He used his many talents to show the neat dovetailing between human experience and Jesus' message. But it all didn't work. This he found out not in the ivory towers of a university but from the pulpit of his small church in Switzerland where he was pastor. The new liberal theology was not touching the hearts of his people, or his own heart. Rather, it seemed to "fit into" and become part of the swirl of ideas and viewpoints that were confusing people with so many possibilities and no clear direction. People weren't able to make choices, to commit themselves to something clear and firm. Also, and most frighteningly, liberal theology fizzled in the face of the reality of evil, especially as that evil was horribly embodied in the stupidity and slaughter of World War I. For Barth and for his people, "the heady wine of nineteenth century optimism, evolutionary progress, and universal brotherhood went perceptibly flat on the field of Flanders and Verdun."[6]

So in his sermons and especially in a book that he wrote in the parsonage of his congregation, Barth changed course — for himself and, as it turned out, for Protestantism throughout Europe and the United States. His *Commentary on Romans* became a revolutionizing classic. In this commentary, and subsequently in the twelve volumes of his *Church Dogmatics*, Barth's message, which he felt was the message of the Gospels and of St. Paul, thundered forth: human beings cannot get their act together by themselves. But with God, they can. Yet for this to happen, humans have to step back and let God be God.

For Barth, this message was nothing else but the Good News of the New Testament, especially as enunciated by St. Paul and the Reformers. It can be spelled out in the four "alones" that undergird and continue to inspire Protestant Christianity:[7]

1. We are saved *by grace alone:* for Barth, this was not simply something he read about in the New Testament. It was also written large and bold in his own life and in the mixed-up, violent, suffering world around him: human beings are in a mess, and they can't get out of this mess by themselves. They're stuck. Biblical or theological terms to describe this state are "original sin" or "fallen nature." In the language of twelve-step programs, if human beings are going to get out of the holes they dig themselves into, they're going to have to recognize a "Higher Power." There is such a Power. Barth, with St. Paul, called it *grace.*

2. We are saved *by faith alone:* the negative flip-side of "by faith alone" is "not by works." In order to make room for the entrance of grace, we have to step back, get out of the way, recognize our inability to guide our lives by ourselves. But we can do this only if we *trust.* And that's what "by faith alone" is all about: as the popular saying has it, we let go in order to let God. Like a small child falling into the arms of her parent, we jump off the cliff and fall into the arms of God's love and grace. This, perhaps, is the hardest part of the process, the part where humans find themselves stalled because either they're afraid or they're incapable. To trust, to do nothing else but turn oneself over completely to Someone else, is so frightening that it feels impossible — Barth would say it *is* impossible. Thus, the need for the third "alone."

3. We are saved *by Christ alone:* it is in Jesus Christ, and only in him, that God has acted and revealed the true nature of things — that God is ready to love us, affirm us, and rescue us purely out of divine love, not because we deserve it or have merited it. In fact, our trying to "do" something to deserve grace gets in the way of the outpouring of God's love. It "ungraces"

---

6. George W. Hunt, "Karl Barth — Ten Years Later," *America*, November 4, 1978, 302.

7. For what follows on Barth's views of religions and Christianity, see the well-known "Paragraph 17" of Barth's *Church Dogmatics* (Edinburgh: Clark, 1956), vol. 1/2.

grace. This is what is embodied in and made known in Jesus Christ. It's incredible news, something we could never imagine. We can know it and believe it only if we hear this news. And thus, finally, the fourth "alone."

4. We are saved *by Scripture alone:* it is in the Bible, and preaching based on the Bible, that the message and reality of Jesus are communicated to us. Here is *revelation* in the truest sense of the word — telling us something that otherwise we could not imagine, or believe, or trust. "In revelation," Barth announces, "God tells man that he is God.... In telling him this, revelation tells him something utterly new, something which apart from revelation he does not know and cannot tell either himself or others."[8]

"Religion Is Unbelief!"

On the basis of this assessment of the human condition, made known in the Bible and confirmed by Barth's reading of the world, he formulated his famous verdict on religion, which has echoed through many a Protestant church and seminary for the past century. It's a verdict that slaps us in the face and turns upside-down our normal understanding of religion. Despite all "the true and the good and the beautiful which a closer inspection will reveal in almost all religions," Barth's final judgment is "the judgment of divine revelation upon all religion":

> Religion is unbelief. It is a concern, indeed, we must say that it is the one great concern, of godless man.... From the standpoint of revelation religion is clearly seen to be a human attempt to anticipate what God in His revelation wills to do and does do. It is the attempted replacement of the divine work by a human manufacture. The divine reality offered and manifested to us in revelation is replaced by a concept of God arbitrarily and willfully evolved by man.[9]

In other words, it is precisely in religion, and because of religion, that humans don't do what they need to do: stand back, trust, and let God be God in Jesus Christ. In religion, humans try to "get into the act" with their own words and beliefs and rituals and laws — and in the end, mess up God's action. So religion is really the opposite of what it appears to be; it's a human creation rather than a divine creation. God enters our lives to rescue us not through the "works of religion" but through the immediate, personal power of grace.

Barth's verdict on religion sounds extremely harsh and utterly negative — until we realize that he leveled it not only at the "other" religions but also, and especially, at Christianity. In a sense, Barth would agree with the views we studied in the last chapter that held that "all religions are essentially the same."

---

8. Ibid., vol. 1/2, 301.
9. Ibid., vol. 1/2, 299–300.

They are, but not because they all reveal the Divine but because they all, including and especially Christianity, get in the way of the Divine. Therefore, Barth warned against making comparisons between Christianity and the religions — not because Christianity was superior or in another class, but rather, because there are no differences to compare. When you look at all the things that make up Christianity as a religion — its theology, worship, church structure, morality, art, ethics — you find the same "active idolatry and self-righteousness" that are rampant in other religions. For Barth, therefore, there is no empirical evidence to argue that Christianity is any better than any other religion in the world.

Christianity as the True Religion

And yet, even though there was no empirical evidence, Barth did have reason to argue that Christianity, after all, can be proclaimed as the one true religion among all the others. Here we enter into Barth's understanding of the paradoxical nature of experiencing God "by faith and grace and Christ alone." Christianity is the true religion because it's the only religion that knows it is a false religion; and it knows, further, that despite its being a false and idolatrous religion, it is saved through Jesus Christ. Notice that for Barth, as for all Fundamentalist/Evangelical Christians, the privileged place of Christianity has nothing to do with Christianity as a religion. It has everything to do with Jesus Christ. Barth uses the analogy of the sun: among all the untrue and false religions of the world, Christianity is the only false religion upon which the sun of Jesus Christ shines. And that makes it the only true religion, because only Christians, thanks to Jesus, clearly grasp that the good works of their religion are useless and that to really feel the power of God in their lives they must only trust and turn themselves over to the love and grace given to them in Jesus and his Spirit. Without Jesus, this grace is not available; without Jesus, this understanding and this trusting are beyond human capacity.

Given Barth's assessment of religion, what kind of a relationship is possible between Christianity and other religious traditions? Barth's answer is clear: "We have here an exclusive contradiction."[10] Certainly Barth would call upon Christians to respect the good will, the sincerity, and the religious freedom of other believers. But because the sun of Jesus Christ shines on and within only one religion, and because only in that sun can one come to live by "faith alone," in "grace alone," there really isn't much for Christians to relate to in other religions: no revelation, no saving grace, because no Jesus; and, therefore, no possibilities of dialogue. Barth even warned missionaries against searching for "points of contact" in other religions — that is, questions that help lead the non-Christian to Christian answers. All that Christians can really do is lovingly and respectfully announce the Gospel and let the light of Christ take the place of the darkness that exists without him.[11]

---

10. Ibid., vol. 1/2, 295–96, 303; see also 280–94.
11. This summary of Barth's views of other religions is taken from his early period, especially

Taking the New Testament and Jesus Seriously

In using Karl Barth's theology to assemble the foundation stones for this Evangelical theology of religions, we have to be careful. For all Evangelicals, there is always something deeper than theology, a firmer bedrock that sustains the foundation: the New Testament. Evangelical Christians resonate with Barth's theology because it is so thoroughly nurtured and normed by the biblical witness. In this respect, these conservative Christians pose a reminder and a challenge to all their fellow Christian brothers and sisters: to be Christian means to take the Bible, especially the New Testament, seriously. That's an essential, defining characteristic of all followers of Jesus, recognized by all the churches, whether they're on the far right or left of the denominational spectrum. A Christian is someone who bases her life on the New Testament witness concerning Jesus Christ. To hold a belief, to take a stance, or to move in a direction that even appears to contradict the core message of the New Testament should set off warning signs for any Christian: it may mean that he is abandoning, or watering down, the very identity he claims to bear.

And so the Christians who endorse this replacement theology of religions claim, straightforwardly and honestly, that they are simply holding to the clear message of the New Testament. One does not necessarily have to take the Bible literally to recognize that one of the most evident and central messages of the New Testament is that Jesus is the means, the only means, that God has given to humans by which they can figure out what life is all about and get out of the mess they're in. There may be different ways of looking at Jesus in the New Testament, different titles given to him, different ways of explaining how he saves and what it means to call him divine. But amid all these differences, one thing is constant, like a thread knitting all the diverse colors together: the announcement that Jesus *is* Savior, the *only* Savior, and that without him, humans can't get out of their dead-ended, sinful predicament.

It would be helpful, perhaps sobering, for some liberal Christians to review the New Testament texts which for the Evangelicals speak so clearly (whether one takes them literally or symbolically).

Texts that affirm both that Jesus saves and that others don't:

- "There is salvation in no one else, for there is no other name under heaven given among mortals by which we must be saved." (Acts 4:12)

- "For no one can lay any foundation other than the one that has been laid; that foundation is Jesus Christ." (1 Cor. 3:11)

---

from his *Römerbrief* (Epistle to the Romans), first published in 1922 by Chr. Kaiser, Munich, and from "Paragraph 17" (eighty-one pages!) of *Church Dogmatics*. Later Barth did come to speak of "other words and other lights outside the walls of the church." But it was his early views that had such broad influence on Protestant attitudes into the second half of the past century. Besides, he always insisted that the "other words and other lights" could not be heard and seen without Christ. See Paul F. Knitter, *Towards a Protestant Theology of Religions* (Marburg: N. G. Elwert, 1974), 32–36.

- "There is one mediator between God and humankind: Christ Jesus."
  (1 Tim. 2:5)

- "I am the Way, the Truth, and the Life. No one comes to the Father except
  through me." (John 14:6)

- "Whoever has the Son has life; whoever does not have the Son of God
  does not have life." (1 John 5:12)

Texts that show the lostness of humanity without Jesus:

- The first three chapters of Paul's Letter to the Romans paint the hopeless
  situation of humankind, both Jews and Gentiles, without Christ: "They are
  without excuse, for though they knew God, they did not honor him as
  God.... All, both Jews and Greeks, are under the power of sin." (Rom.
  1:21; 3:9)

Texts that insist on the necessity of hearing and believing the gospel about Jesus
in order to be saved:

- "Whoever believes in the Son has eternal life; whoever disobeys the Son
  will not see life, but must endure the wrath of God." (John 3:36)

- In Romans 10, after announcing that one must believe in Jesus to be saved,
  Paul asks: "But how are they to believe in one of whom they have never
  heard?... So faith comes from what is heard." (vv. 14, 17)[12]

Whether one agrees or not with the content of such texts, one cannot deny,
Evangelicals attest, that they are there — at the very heart-center of the New
Testament. And there is no doubt about what the early Christians understood
when they wrote and read these statements: God saves in Jesus. Don't look
anywhere else. If one is a Christian, one cannot deny, ignore, or water down
these texts. If one finds oneself in fundamental disagreement with them, perhaps
it is more honest, Evangelicals would suggest, to withdraw from the Christian
community.

And so we see how much the Evangelical view of other religions pivots on
their — and the New Testament's — understanding of Jesus. This understanding, and its implications for religions, is summarized lucidly and eloquently by
Bishop Stephen Neill:

> [Christian faith] maintains that in Jesus the one thing that needed to hap-
> pen has happened in such a way that it need never happen again in the
> same way. The universe has been reconciled to God. Through the perfect
> obedience of one man a new and permanent relationship has been estab-
> lished between God and the whole human race. The bridge has been built.

---

12. For fuller listing and commentary on such texts, see John Sanders, *No Other Name: An In-
vestigation into the Destiny of the Unevangelized* (Grand Rapids, Mich.: Eerdmans, 1992), 38–41;
R. Douglas Geivett and W. Gary Phillips, "A Particularist View: An Evidentialist Approach," in
More Than One Way? Four Views of Salvation in a Pluralistic World, ed. Dennis L. Okholm and
Timothy R. Phillips (Grand Rapids, Mich.: Zondervan 1995), 229–38.

There is room on it for all the needed traffic in both directions, from God to man and from man to God. Why look for any other?...For the human sickness there is one specific remedy, and this is it. There is no other.[13]

Does this mean that, according to this replacement theology of religions, all the followers of other religions who have never, through any fault of their own, heard of Jesus will be packed off to hell? As we will see in the next chapter, Fundamentalists and Evangelical Christians hesitate to give clear, absolute answers to that question. They don't want to play God. But what they do say, loudly and clearly, is that if anyone comes to know and enjoy God and God's salvation, it is because they have explicitly heard the message of Jesus and trusted. That's clear in the Scriptures. And that's where Evangelicals take their stand.[14]

"One Way" Makes Sense

We should not think, however, that because the Bible is the bedrock of Evangelicals' faith, it's the only source from which they draw their reasons for claiming that Jesus is the only Way and that other religions need to be replaced by the Gospel. What the Bible tells them also makes good common sense. To believe "by faith alone" does not mean to believe by blind faith. The stereotype of Fundamentalists or Evangelicals as gullible, insecure people who unplug their brains in order to believe anything and everything that is written in the Bible is just that — a stereotype. If the Bible teaches the truth, the truth will resonate with our mind's ability to ask questions and draw reasonable conclusions. So they invite us to think about the reasonableness of God providing a path for all people that is not only clear and sure but also singular.

R. Douglas Geivett and W. Gary Phillips, two respected Evangelical scholars, paint a picture of the human predicament that reflects the life experience of many people, especially college students finishing their studies and setting out on careers, marriage, family. Deciding what to do, whom to marry, and how to bring up the kids are daunting tasks. But they're all the more bewildering, if not overwhelming, in view of the huge marketplace of values and options and ultimate solutions for a truly happy life that populate our "multicultured" and "multivalued" postmodern life. How does one make sense of life? What makes for a truly satisfying way of living and relating?

When one adds to these philosophical queries further ethical questions, the job of deciding how to live becomes all the more tangled: the common belief is that to get ahead nowadays and to make a buck, you've got to be better than, smarter than, tougher than the next guy. Often you have to bump someone else's

---

13. Stephen Neill, *Crises of Belief* (London: Hodder and Stoughton, 1984), 31.

14. W. Gary Phillips, "Evangelicals and Pluralism: Current Options," in *The Challenge of Religious Pluralism: An Evangelical Analysis and Response,* ed. David K. Clark (Wheaton, Ill.: Wheaton Theology Conference, 1992), 174–89; Ronald H. Nash, "Restrictivism," in *What about Those Who Have Never Heard? Three Views on the Destiny of the Unevangelized,* ed. John Sanders (Downers Grove, Ill.: InterVarsity Press, 1995), 107–39.

wagon off the road in order to move yours forward. But is this right? What if one refuses to go along with this popular morality? Is this to take the higher road — or the dumber road?

There's no sure answer to these questions. No clear "right way to go." The uncertainty mounts when one considers the irradicable and cantankerous reality of evil in life. Yes, bad things — often lots of bad things — happen to good people. Or good people do bad things, even when they don't want to. And bad things — like sickness, violence, death — can change the substance of one's life from wondrous happiness to deepest despair in the twinkling, or the closing, of an eye. Life offers the beauty and the thrills of the high wire, but one can fall at any moment.

So Geivett and Phillips reason that in the midst of so much uncertainty, unclarity, and fear, in face of so many different and doubtful ways to go, doesn't it make eminent sense that, if there is a God, this God would provide us with a clear set of directions, a sure helping hand, an assurance that within and beyond the uncertainties, there is purpose to life and a well-defined path to walk toward it? And if God has done so, then what has been called "the scandal of particularity" (that God would offer one way to find truth) is really not that scandalous at all. "Particularism [only one way] is not scandalous to the spiritually needy person who has been looking for God's precise remedy to the specific ills of humanity."[15] What human beings need is one clear, God-given path!

All of these commonsense arguments for "one-and-only" pertain more to our personal, individual search for meaning. There are also social, even geopolitical, reasons why a God-given "one way" makes much-needed sense. Bishop Lesslie Newbigin offers a powerful statement of this argument. First, he asks a sobering question: Are we sure there are no absolute truths? If we say we're sure, we've blindly accepted "one of the axioms of our contemporary Western culture." Like any axiom, it can't be proven. Just because final truths are hard to find doesn't mean they don't exist. Newbigin draws on a comparison with science: "Physicists, faced with the problem of reconciling relativity with quantum theory, do not fall back on the supposition that reality has different natures, acts in different ways, is fundamentally incoherent. They continue with unwearied energy to seek a unified theory which will hold the whole of physics together."[16] So why can't human history, like the solar system, have one center? Today, more than ever, we humans need such a center.

We need it for a variety of contemporary reasons. On the one hand, the kinds of world-spanning, life-threatening problems that humanity faces today — nuclear war, ecological devastation, ethnic violence spilling over borders — call for unified, concerted, cooperative solutions. More than ever, humankind needs to get its act together and form one family. That doesn't mean removing diver-

---

15. Geivett and Phillips, "A Particularist View," 218; see also 219–27.

16. Lesslie Newbigin, *The Gospel in a Pluralist Society* (Grand Rapids, Mich.: Eerdmans, 1989), 161, see also 162–69.

sity; but it does require binding the diversity in a newly won unity. For this to be possible, it makes evident sense, again, that if there is a God, this God would provide the one criterion of truth, the one center of unity that can connect, and then hold, people together. But this isn't easy, mainly because there is always one nation, or people, that sets itself above all the others as the master-builder of unity. This, too, Newbigin tells us, is the reason we need not just "one truth" but "one God-given truth." A singular revelation given by God stands above all other claims to truth; that means no man-made system can put itself above God's standard. Not to recognize one God-given center is to run the risk of making one's self, or one's nation, the center for all. So Newbigin concludes: "To affirm the unique decisiveness of God's action in Jesus Christ is not arrogance; it is the enduring bulwark against the arrogance of every culture to be itself the criterion by which others are judged."[17]

But we're moving too quickly. Once the Evangelicals show that it makes sense that God would provide one source of truth and one path of salvation for all humanity, they don't automatically conclude that this source and path is Jesus. They're not just arguing from the Bible alone. All they're asking for is the right and the space to get out their message about Jesus. Once they do so, and once people really hear this Word and feel the power of the Spirit within it, Evangelicals are confident that the truth of Jesus as the only Name in which humans can be saved will prove itself. They're assured that when people see and feel how Jesus responds to the needs of the human heart and the turmoil of our present world, they will accept this one Savior as the source and strength of unity for all humankind. Such acceptance will be not just an emotional response of the heart but a rational, satisfying choice of the head. Choosing Jesus as the One who saves is something not just preachers but also philosophers can endorse. (In fact, one Evangelical scholar wrote an entire book in which he lays out the philosophical and rational case for the exclusiveness of truth and grace in Jesus.)[18]

What this Replacement Model is calling for, really, is a kind of "holy competition" between the many religions and their individual claims to have the one-and-only, or the final, truth. Such competition is as natural, necessary, and helpful as it is in the business world. You're not going to sell your product effectively if you present it as "just as good" as the next guy's. You've got to believe, and say why, you think yours is the best. So let the religions compete! In such an open, honest, nonviolent competition, Evangelicals are sure that Jesus will come out on top.

---

17. Ibid., 169.

18. Harold A. Netland, *Dissonant Voices: Religious Pluralism and the Questions of Truth* (Grand Rapids, Mich.: Eerdmans, 1991).

Further Readings

Barth, Karl. "The Revelation of God as the Abolition of Religion." In *Church Dogmatics,* 1/2, paragraph 17. Edinburgh: Clark, 1956, 280–361. Abridged version in *Christianity and Other Religions.* Ed. John Hick and Brian Hebblethwaite. Oxford: One World Publications, 2001, 5–18.

Bradshaw, Tim. "Grace and Mercy: Protestant Approaches to Religious Pluralism." In *One God, One Lord: Christianity in a World of Religious Pluralism.* Ed. Andrew D. Clarke and Bruce W. Winter. Grand Rapids, Mich.: Baker Book House, 1992, 227–36.

Crockett, William V., and James G. Sigountos. "Are the 'Heathen' Really Lost?" In *Through No Fault of Their Own: The Fate of Those Who Have Never Heard.* Ed. William V. Crockett and James G. Sigountos. Grand Rapids, Mich.: Baker Book House, 1991, 257–64.

Dayton, Donald W. "Karl Barth and the Wider Ecumenism." In *Christianity and the Wider Ecumenism.* Ed. Peter C. Phan. New York: Paragon House, 1990, 181–89.

Geivett, R. Douglas, and W. Gary Phillips. "A Particularist View: An Evidentialist Approach." In *More than One Way? Four Views of Salvation in a Pluralistic World.* Ed. Dennis L Okholm and Timothy R. Phillips. Grand Rapids, Mich.: Zondervan, 1995, 213–45.

Grenz, Stanley J. "Toward an Evangelical Theology of Religions." *Journal of Ecumenical Studies* 31 (1994): 49–66.

Harrison, Peter. "Karl Barth and the Non-Christian Religions." *Journal of Ecumenical Studies* 23 (1986): 207–24.

Hart, Tevor. "Karl Barth, the Trinity, and Religious Pluralism." In *The Trinity in a Pluralistic Age: Theological Essays on Culture and Religion.* Ed. Kevin J. Vanhoozer. Grand Rapids, Mich.: Eerdmans, 1997, 124–42.

Henry, Carl F. "Is It Fair?" In *Through No Fault of Their Own: The Fate of Those Who Have Never Heard.* Ed. William V. Crockett and James G. Sigountos. Grand Rapids, Mich.: Baker Book House, 1991, 245–56.

Huff, Peter A. "The Challenge of Fundamentalism for Interreligious Dialogue." *Cross Currents* 50 (2000): 94–102.

Jones, Michael S. "Evangelical Christianity and the Philosophy of Interreligious Dialogue." *Journal of Ecumenical Studies* 36 (1999): 378–96.

Nash, Ronald H. "Restrictivism." In *What about Those Who Have Never Heard? Three Views on the Destiny of the Unevangelized.* Ed. John Sanders. Downers Grove, Ill.: InterVarsity Press, 1995, 107–39.

Netland, Harold A. *Dissonant Voices: Religious Pluralism and the Question of Truth.* Grand Rapids, Mich.: Eerdmans, 1991, chapters 5 and/or 7 and/or 8.

———. "The Uniqueness of Jesus in a Pluralistic World." *Religious and Theological Studies Fellowship Bulletin* 5 (1994): 8ff.

Phillips, W. Gary. "Evangelicals and Pluralism: Current Options." In *The Challenge of Religious Pluralism: An Evangelical Analysis and Response.* Ed. David K. Clark. Wheaton, Ill.: Wheaton Theology Conference, 1992, 174–89.

Chapter 2

Partial Replacement

Many believers who occupy the Fundamentalist-Evangelical-Pentecostal precincts of Christianity find that the "total replacement" approach to other religions is not only clear; it is also harsh. They feel that it really allows for no value, no presence of God, in other religions, viewing them as entirely man-made, as obstacles to, rather than conduits for, God's love. In theological terms, there is neither revelation nor salvation in the world of other religions. And that means the only kind of dialogue Christians can have with persons of other faiths is one in which Christians try to get to know those faiths better in order to replace them with Christianity. Yes, this is harsh. It is so harsh that for many Evangelicals it doesn't seem to fit either the reality they see in other religious traditions or the message they hear in the Bible.

God Present in Other Religions? Yes and No

So there's another, more embracing version of the replacement perspective. It represents especially the views of those Bible-based Christians who in chapter 1 we described as the New Evangelicals — people firmly committed to the uniqueness of Jesus and to fending off any sellout of the Gospel to the modern world, but at the same time, more open, more ecumenical, more ready to find God's presence in the world. In fact, their basic criticism of the Total Replacement Model is that it misses the very real presence of God within the world of other religions.

Revelation: Yes!

The telling difference between what we are here calling the "Partial Replacement Model" and its predecessor has to do with revelation. Evangelicals who follow this more moderate viewpoint recognize and affirm, and even rejoice in, a genuine revelation of God in and through other religions. It goes by different theological names: "original revelation," "creation revelation," or, more commonly, "general revelation."[1] What the terms are getting at is an authen-

---

1. See, for instance, Emil Brunner, "Revelation and Religion," in *Christianity and Other Religions*, ed. John Hick and Brian Hebblethwaite (Philadelphia: Fortress Press, 1980), 113–32; Paul Tillich, *Systematic Theology* (Chicago: University of Chicago Press, 1951–63), 1:53–60; Bruce Demarest, "General and Special Revelation: Epistemological Foundations of Religious Pluralism," in

tic presence of God's Spirit within the persons and the structures of other faith communities. These communities represent more than groups of human beings asking questions, wrestling with the big issues of human existence. They also represent ways in which God gives answers and reaches out to the human search. This is a very big difference from the Total Replacement Model.

The first reason Christians should be open to recognizing God's revealing presence in others is very Evangelical — because that's what the Bible tells us. For example:

1. What Barth and some Fundamentalists miss in their reading of Paul in the first chapters of Romans is that God really does speak to all peoples through the power of nature and through personal conscience: "Ever since the creation of the world God's eternal power and divine nature, invisible though they are, have been understood and seen through the things God has made.... What the law requires is written on their [Gentiles'] hearts, to which their own conscience also bears witness" (Rom. 1:20; 2:15). That's pretty clear.

2. Confirming the power of nature to speak God's language, Paul told the Gentiles of Lystra: "In past generations, God allowed all the nations to follow their own ways; yet God has not left you without a witness in doing good — giving you rains from heaven and fruitful seasons, and filling you with food and your hearts with joy" (Acts 14:16). As to the Athenians, Paul announced: "God is not far from each one of us. For in God we live and move and have our being" (Acts 17:27).

3. Even more sweeping is John's announcement in the beginning of his Gospel when he tells us that the Word of God that was made flesh in Jesus is the same Word that was in the world from the beginning, giving life to the world, "and this life was the light of all people. The light shines in the darkness and the darkness did not overcome it" (John 1:1–14).

This image of the Word of God finding voice before and after the historical Jesus was taken up in the early centuries of the church by the first theologians, called the Fathers of the Church; they recognized clearly that God's ability and desire to speak cannot be limited to Christian circles. Furthermore, John Calvin, one of the original Reformers, was in basic agreement with Martin Luther when he spoke of a "sense of God" instilled into human nature so that "the knowledge of God and of oneself is connected by a mutual bond."[2] Followers of the strict Replacement Model seem to forget or neglect these indications from the Bible and early theologians.

What the Bible tells us about God speaking to all peoples is confirmed for Evangelical theologians by what they see in other cultures and religions. It's not

---

One God, One Lord: Christianity in a World of Religious Pluralism, ed. Andrew D. Clarke and Bruce W. Winter (Grand Rapids, Mich.: Baker Book House, 1992), 189–206.

2. See Brunner, "Revelation," 121–22.

so much a case of God speaking *to* people, from above or beyond; rather, God's voice is heard *within*, from the movements of the heart and through events of history. For Paul Althaus (a German Lutheran theologian who felt Barth was too narrow in his view of religions), people hear the Divine in the "Something More" that tugs at their hearts when they fall in love and decide to stay committed to another person even when it gets difficult, or when they answer a sense of social responsibility for the poor, or when they hope that good is stronger than evil even when the evidence is to the contrary.[3] Paul Tillich (who comes close to Barth as one of the best-known Protestant theologians of the past century) is more general and mystical: we feel the presence of God when we find ourselves "grasped by an Ultimate Concern" — a concern that grounds us and holds us and "qualifies all other concerns as preliminary and... contains the answer to the question of the meaning of life." Tillich found that one of the major ways in which this Ultimate Concern grasps us is when we sense or feel or just know that no matter what we are, we are *accepted*. Tillich tells us that even when we don't know clearly what is accepting us, we should "just accept Acceptance" and we are in the hands of God.[4]

Balancing these more personal and individual expressions of a general revelation, Wolfhart Pannenberg, a contemporary Protestant theologian, points to the processes of history as the stage for God's speaking to humanity. God's voice becomes audible, he suggests, through an interplay between, on the one hand, our innate need to keep searching and asking questions and, on the other, the concrete events of history. It's as if our in-built searching for greater meaning is the antenna, and the happenings and people that enter our lives are the sound waves by which we hear God addressing us. It's a process that is ongoing, never finished, and future-directed. As we look back on our lives we can sense, Pannenberg suggests, that there is a direction, a movement forward, in the course of our life's history; yet the full meaning of it all is in the future, in the final act of history. It is this acting, speaking presence of the Divine within all history that can be seen especially in the religions of the world. For Pannenberg, "the history of religions is the history of the appearing of the Divine Mystery which is presupposed in the structure of human existence."[5] This is very different from Barth and the Fundamentalists, who heard only a divine silence in the religions.

So for this Christian view of religions, it is certain *that* God speaks to other believers through their religions. When we consider *what* God has to say, this new model becomes even more positive. For these Evangelical theologians, this general revelation can make other religious believers aware not only of the exis-

---

3. Paul Althaus, *Die christliche Wahrheit,* 7th ed. (Gütersloh: Gütersloher Verlaghaus, 1966), 61–96.

4. Paul Tillich, *Christianity and the Encounter of World Religions* (New York: Columbia University Press, 1963), 4; Tillich, *Systematic Theology,* 1:153–55; Tillich, *The Courage to Be* (New Haven: Yale University Press, 1952).

5. Wolfhart Pannenberg, ed., *Revelation as History* (London: Macmillan, 1968), 3–21, 125–58; Pannenberg, *Basic Questions in Theology* (Philadelphia: Fortress Press, 1971), 2:112.

tence of the Divine but that this Divine is a "you" — personal, loving, calling.[6] Further, the voice of God in other traditions can also make clear to them their need for redemption — that is, that humans are caught in their own selfishness and that if they are going to be freed from this prison, God is going to have to step in. "The need for human and world redemption is the theme of all religions."[7] In this Evangelical model, therefore, other religions are not just "human manufacture," as Barth held; rather, they are *willed by God;* they are God's "representatives," God's "tools" by which God carries out the divine plan.[8]

From all this, it seems we can conclude that these Evangelicals view other religions as paths leading to God and salvation. But such a conclusion, as we will now see, would be much too hasty.

Salvation: No!

When the question shifts from whether there is *revelation* in other religions to whether there is *salvation*, the theologians we are considering in this model show a sudden change of tone and direction. That is, they have no problem in recognizing that God speaks through other faiths. But they do not, because they feel they cannot, affirm that God also brings other believers to what Christians call salvation — that is, to unity with God, to a sense of being loved, affirmed, forgiven, and held by God, and to the assurance of eternal life after death. While these theologians say clearly that God reveals in other religions, they just as clearly declare that God does not save in other religions.[9] And they do this for what they think are two very good reasons: it is what the New Testament makes clear, and it is what is evident to anyone who studies other religions.

1. *The New Testament.* In appealing to the New Testament, these theologians are, again, simply doing what Christians naturally do: they listen first to God's Word. And on the issue of salvation in other religions, the message is pretty clear: "There are no unambiguous instances in Scripture of persons who become true believers through responding to general revelation alone." Or: "This much is perfectly evident: general revelation is totally insufficient as a vehicle of salvation."[10] When we dig deeper into just why Scripture rules out salvation through other religions, we're back at the pillars of Protestant theology: the "by

---

6. Wolfhart Pannenberg, *The Idea of God and Human Freedom* (Philadelphia: Fortress Press, 1973), 111–15.

7. Carl Heinz Ratschow, "Die Religionen und das Christentum," in *Der christliche Glaube und die Religionen*, ed. C. W. Ratschow (Berlin: Töpelmann, 1967), 118–20, 123–24.

8. Althaus, *Die christliche Wahrheit*, 137–39; Millard J. Erickson, *How Shall They Be Saved? The Destiny of Those Who Do Not Hear of Jesus* (Grand Rapids, Mich.: Baker Book House, 1996), 157–58.

9. See, for instance, Calvin E. Shenk, *Who Do You Say That I Am?* (Scottdale, Pa.: Herald Press, 1996), 117–20.

10. Erickson, *How Shall They Be Saved?* 158; Harold Lindsell, *A Christian Philosophy of Mission* (Wheaton, Ill.: Van Kampen Press, 1949), 107; see also Carl Braaten, "Hearing the Other: The Promise and Problem of Pluralism," *Currents in Theology and Mission* 24 (1997): 398–99.

faith alone through Christ alone." For Evangelicals, there are two rock-bottom truths contained in two "alones."

a. Salvation is brought about by Jesus Christ and only by him. In more technical terms, this is called "the ontological necessity" of Christ. It means that both the actuality and the very possibility of God reaching out to embrace humans and to bring them to happiness in this life and the next have been made real in and through Jesus. In the image of traditional Protestant theology, the "fall of humanity" in Adam and Eve brought about a rift, a breakdown, between God and humanity; humans sinned, rebelled, and therefore something has to be done to mend the rift, to bridge the gap. That something, thanks to God's freely given love, has been done in Jesus. He, and only he, "fixed things." God has built, as we already heard, one bridge. Only by making use of and crossing this one bridge can humans reach the Divine. Only by coming somehow into contact, real personal contact, with Jesus can people be "at-oned with" God — that is, saved.

Contrary to views we shall encounter in coming chapters, this Evangelical model of understanding religions does not hold up Jesus as an expression or illustration or symbol of God's saving love, as if that love were already active in the world and Jesus enables us to really see it. As Carl Braaten, a well-known contemporary Lutheran theologian, states lucidly: "Christ is not merely *expressive* of a divine salvation equally available in the plurality of religions; salvation is constituted by the coming of God in the concrete history of Jesus of Nazareth."[11] That means: without Jesus, no salvation to begin with. This is what is contained in the Evangelical insistence on "by Christ alone." It's an insistence that is crystal clear in those "one-and-only" texts of the New Testament that we reviewed earlier.

Therefore, Braaten speaks from the heart and deepest convictions of Protestant Evangelical theology when he states:

> In the texts of the New Testament and early Christian traditions Jesus is depicted not as a savior but as *the* Savior, not as a Son of God, one among many in a pantheon of gods and half-gods, but as the one-and-only Savior of the World, God's only begotten Son. This exclusivity claim is part of the kernel of the gospel, not so much husk that can be demythologized away [that is, interpreted as only symbolic]. . . . Jesus is the one-and-only Savior, or he is not Savior at all.[12]

Pannenberg offers a further and deeper reason why Christians must insist that all salvation depends on, and comes from, Jesus. It's not just because the early Christians experienced Jesus in this way and then made such claims about

---

11. Carl Braaten, *No Other Gospel: Christianity among the World's Religions* (Minneapolis: Fortress Press, 1992), 74.

12. Braaten, "Hearing the Other," 398; Braaten, "The Uniqueness and Universality of Jesus Christ," in *Faith Meets Faith: Mission Trends No. 5,* ed. Gerald H. Anderson and Thomas F. Stransky (New York: Paulist Press, 1981), 74–75.

him. It's what Jesus himself thought and said about himself! Pannenberg bases this assertion on one of the surest things we can know about the historical Jesus: that he thought himself to be what is called "the eschatological prophet." This means he knew that he was the "last" of God's prophets and that God's Reign — or, God's salvation — was now being offered in and through him. As Pannenberg puts it: "Since the impending future of God was becoming present through him [Jesus], there is no room for other approaches to salvation besides him. . . . The presence of God in Jesus was not first a matter of Christian experience, but a claim of Jesus himself and this claim involved eschatological finality."[13] To allow for "other Saviors" is to contradict Jesus himself. And that would contradict what a Christian is all about.

But this Partial Replacement Model for a theology of religions says more about why Jesus is necessary. Not only is salvation brought about by Jesus, but also:

b. Salvation is made known only by Jesus. Again in more technical terms, this is called "the epistemological necessity" of Christ. It makes the connection between the "by Christ alone" and the "by faith alone": only in Christ can we realize that we are saved only by faith. Without Christ, we just don't get it — nor would we dare it. To imagine, much less believe, that the infinite offense against God by human sin and selfishness is removed by an infinite act of love (God's Son stepping in to make amends) — and even more, to imagine that all God expects of us is to trust this act of love, nothing more — is, according to Evangelical Christians, "contrary to all evident reality," "unseen, unheard of, impossible," a "pure miracle." The only way we humans can know that this is what God does and, having known it, trust that this is what God does is through Jesus Christ. That's why salvation, for Evangelical Christians, is not simply a deep experience of oneness with God or a sense of inner peace and purpose. Rather: "Salvation is union with Christ; it is receiving the righteousness of God through faith on account of Christ."[14]

Therefore, for anyone to be "saved," to know and truly feel the power of God's love and presence, they have to somehow come into contact with Christ. And the means by which contact is made is, for Evangelicals, the preaching of the Gospel. Braaten is explicit: "Outside of Christ and apart from the preaching of the Gospel there are no known historical alternatives that may be theologically accepted as divinely authorized means of salvation. If traditionally Roman Catholic theology taught that 'outside the church there is no salvation,' Lutheran theology has taught that 'outside of Christ there is no salvation.'" Or better, "outside of the Word about Christ there is no salvation." Without this Word, without the Gospel, the religions of the world, even though they are bearers of real revelation from God, can't bring this revelation to fruition. Again, Braaten

---

13. Wolfhart Pannenberg, "Religious Pluralism and Conflicting Truth Claims," in *Christian Uniqueness Reconsidered: The Myth of a Pluralistic Theology of Religions*, ed. Gavin D'Costa (Maryknoll, N.Y.: Orbis Books, 1990), 100–101.

14. Braaten, "Hearing the Other," 399.

draws the hard but necessary conclusion: "No religion, therefore, is capable of generating the freedom to let God be God, which only faith can do....Thus the religions themselves fall under the wrath and judgment of God despite all the good and truth that they also undeniably have given to human experience and history."[15]

2. *Evidence from the religions themselves.* Such a final verdict on the religions — namely, that without Christ they can't arrive at the realization that a true experience of God's love comes by faith alone — is not based only on the Bible. It is also verified, according to Evangelicals, by what is evident when one takes a close look at the teachings and workings of other religions. Pannenberg speaks for many Evangelicals when he even maintains that such verification by "the facts of the science of religion" is necessary for a Christian theology of religions. Anything a Christian says about other religions, while it is first of all based on the Bible, also has to be confirmed by "an unprejudiced understanding of the total process of the universal history of religions."[16] So what do these Christians see when they take an unprejudiced look at the history of religions?

First, they discover that despite all that the other religions know about the existence and love of God through general revelation, despite all their good will and sincere efforts, followers of other faiths end up, in one form or another, to one degree or another, trying to *save themselves.* They don't really trust. They don't let go and let God. Despite all that they may know of their own need of redemption and of the Divine's generosity, they end up trying to do something, to prove something, to know something so that they can feel that God indeed is with them. They don't give up on "good works." As one theologian puts it, while for Christians good works *follow* God's love ("consecutively"), in other religions, good works try to *win* God's love ("constitutively"). Or, more clearly: in all "non-Biblical religions, humans seek themselves, their own salvation; even in their surrender to the Deity, they want to find their own security."[17]

Evangelical Christians also observe in other religions something that is related to this stubborn attempt to find one's own security: an ever-recurrent effort to put God, or the Ultimate, in a box. This means that in one form or another, the religions set up an idol in place of God. They can do this in different ways:

- Either they *personalize* God into a divine fellow (or fellows) whose actions they can then predict or dictate; or they *depersonalize* God into some kind of an abstract principle that they can grasp with their reason. In either case, the essential mystery and transcendence of God are stuffed into the container of human thought or desire.

- Or, according to Paul Tillich, all the religions keep forgetting that their words, all their rituals, and all their institutions are *symbols* of the Divine, not the Divine itself. Religious symbols are supposed to point to,

---

15. Braaten, *No Other Gospel,* 78, 76.
16. Pannenberg, *Basic Questions,* 69–70.
17. Brunner, "Revelation," 122–25.

embody, and make real the Divine; but they are not the Divine itself; they can never capture all that God is or wants to reveal. Forgetting this, the religions make themselves divine, or they make their teachings and laws more important than God. And so they end up taking the place of God. Again, we have idolatry. (For Tillich, the only symbol of the Divine that really points to the Divine but at the same time points away from itself is Jesus.)[18]

- Pannenberg basically agrees when, from his study of other religions, he notes that all of them fail to realize what is so clear to Christians and Jews — that God is always a *God of the future*. God never gives us the full picture, the full meaning of God's self. Like history itself, what God is up to in the world is a "work in progress." God has given us a one-and-only "preview" of the goal of history in Jesus, but even Jesus points to something more to come. Some religions think they have the full picture in the past, in some original golden age; then they keep trying to recapture this past through "primordial myths." Other religions try to pin the future down in the present by finalizing or absolutizing their teachings or refusing to change and expand them. It all comes down to putting limits on the mystery of God and the future that God wants to reveal.[19]

Christianity's Relationship with Other Religions

On the basis of this Evangelical approach to other religions, which proposes both that God is speaking in other religions (revelation) but not saving in them, what kind of relationship can Christians have with persons of other religious families? Contrary to the Total Replacement Model which we studied earlier and which could not find in other faiths anything to relate to, Evangelical Christians do speak of dialogue with other religions.

Harold A. Netland, a respected Evangelical theologian, describes both the motive and the content of such a Christian dialogue with persons of other faiths. Dialogue is a way "to take the other person seriously as a fellow human being." It's a mark of "humility, sensitivity, and common courtesy to followers of other faiths." After all, whatever the theological judgment on these persons regarding their state of salvation, they are children of God whom Christians are called upon to love and respect. So what to talk about? Netland lists a variety of topics: the dialogue can deal with the nature of dialogue (that is, Why does each of the religions want to talk? and What are the presuppositions they bring to the conversation?). Also, the dialogue can be a matter of trading information about each other, especially to correct false notions they have of each other; this kind of dialogue can be a major means to dissolve the poisons of prejudice, mistrust, and conflict between religions. More practically, the conversation can take up

---

18. Tillich, *Systematic Theology*, 2:91–111, 136–59, 191–208.
19. Pannenberg, *Basic Questions*, 113, 107–10.

common social or environmental or even political concerns so that the different religions can cooperate with each other in making their shared social or political space a more peaceful place to live.[20]

But eventually, the dialogue is going to have to get around to facing the real differences between Christianity and other religions. Given the Evangelicals' general assessment of the religions, there are going to be many more differences than similarities. And here, according to Pannenberg, we have the real stuff of dialogue: "It is precisely the conflicting positions and truth-claims of the religions that have to become the subject of dialogue." Persons from different religions can best help each other by talking about their disagreements — where they think the other is wrong; why each party believes that its view is superior to others (for example, why they think that without their truth and Savior, the others are not really going to be able to put their lives together and be saved). This is where the dialogue becomes interreligious, when religious people are not just trading information or working on social matters but talking about what really matters to them: God's truth. And this is where the dialogue becomes, as we've already heard from the Fundamentalists, a holy competition. It's a competition in which each religion tries to prove itself "superior in illuminating the people's experience of their life and world" — that is, superior in answering the innermost questions and needs of the human heart and the needs of our messed-up, selfish, violent world.[21]

Evangelical Christians insist that this dialogical competition must always be carried out with genuine respect for the dignity, intelligence, and religious freedom of the other believers. Such dialogue should be evangelism (persuading, inviting, attracting), not proselytizing (coercing, cajoling, condemning). If the conversation with others is carried out in this way, and if everyone really listens and opens their hearts, Evangelicals are certain that Jesus will prove himself to be what the New Testament proclaims him to be: the "one Name" in which people really hear and find God.

So in the end, in this competitive dialogue, Christians do relate with other religions. They don't just discard these other beliefs as the Fundamentalist Total Replacement Model does. The religions do prepare the way for the Gospel. But it's a negative preparation: they provide questions, or indicate directions, which only Jesus can answer and guide. The religions therefore can serve "as a base from which to start because Jesus fulfills the truth which the religions have sought in vain." Evangelicals would affirm the image E. Stanley Jones offered for India and its Hindu religion: India is "the land of the almost." Only Jesus brings the "almost" home. Another image Evangelicals use for Jesus is that of headlights: "We can only read road signs at night when headlights shine on

---

20. Harold A. Netland, *Dissonant Voices: Religious Pluralism and the Question of Truth* (Grand Rapids, Mich.: Eerdmans, 1991), 297–300.

21. Wolfhart Pannenberg, "The Religions from the Perspective of Christian Theology," *Modern Theology* 9 (1993): 286–87; Pannenberg, "Religious Pluralism" (see note 13), 103.

them, so when the light of Christ shines on other religions, we see meaning there which we would not understand without Christ."[22]

Once again, we can turn to Carl Braaten to summarize the relationship of Christianity to other religions in this Evangelical model: "Religions are not systems of salvation in themselves, but God can use even them to point beyond themselves and toward their own crisis and future redemption in the crucified and risen Lord of history."[23] So God can "make use of them." They're not totally rejected. But in the end, they do have to face their own "crisis." That's why we have called this Evangelical theology of religions one of *partial displacement.*

The World Council of Churches: Dialogue, Yes! — Theology, No!

Given the Protestant focus that is evident in our description of the Replacement Model for a theology of religions, we should also ask how the World Council of Churches lines up with this model. Founded in 1948, the WCC embraces some 400 million Christians in 330 churches, denominations, and fellowships from 100 countries and territories throughout the world. Although the majority of those Christians would probably locate themselves in what in the United States are called the "mainline" Protestant churches, the voices of Evangelical and Orthodox Christians are also present and powerful in the meetings and projects of the WCC. Because the WCC truly contains an ecumenical blending of Protestant and Orthodox churches, we shouldn't be surprised that its positions are not totally consistent. And the fluctuation sometimes seems to move beyond the borders of the Replacement Model. A quick historical review will show this back-and-forth, and this push beyond.[24]

During the early decades of the twentieth century, the Protestant missionary movement had a very open — you might even say progressive — attitude toward (and theology of) the religions that the missioners were meeting in Asia and Africa. At the International Missionary Conference in Edinburgh in 1910, and in Jerusalem in 1928, missioners called for dialogue and cooperation with them. One might say the Protestants were actually ahead of the breakthroughs in Catholic attitudes toward the religions that came in the Second Vatican Council, which we will look at in the next chapter. But given the growth of the Fundamentalist and Evangelical churches that we noted in the previous chapter, and especially given the widespread influence of the theology of Karl Barth in Protestant churches and seminaries, the World Missionary Conference took on very different tones in its meeting in Tambaran, India, in 1938. At this meeting, there were still calls to work with other faiths in overcoming the dangers of fascism

---

22. Shenk, *Who Do You Say?* 142, 155.
23. Carl Braaten, *The Flaming Center* (Philadelphia: Fortress Press, 1977), 109.
24. For a lucid, insightful review of the WCC's attitudes toward other religions, see Kenneth Cracknell, "Ambivalent Theology and Ambivalent Policy: The World Council of Churches and Interfaith Dialogue 1938–1999," *Studies in Interreligious Dialogue* 9 (1999): 87–111.

that were then looming on the horizon. But the ultimate goal or outcome for such encounters with other believers could only be conversion, for the Tambaran conference described the relationship between Christianity and other religions as an either-or, never a both-and. Conversations between the Gospel and other religious paths may find points of similarity, but ultimately any similarities would give way to a more fundamental dissimilarity, or what was called discontinuity. *Replacement*, understood generally as total replacement, has the final word.

It was this model of total replacement that colored, if not defined, the attitudes of the WCC toward other religions at its inception in 1948 and for the first three decades of its life. Around the early 1970s, however, such attitudes started to fluctuate. Perhaps it was because of the breakdown of colonialism and the resurgence of self-awareness of non-European nations and religions; perhaps it was also the example of the Catholic Church's new openness to other faiths in Vatican II, but at meetings of WCC specialists in Beirut and then Zurich in 1970, "the breaking of the Tambaran log jam" occurred.[25] Then, in 1971, the Sub-unit on Dialogue with People of Living Faiths was set up within the WCC; its explicit purpose was to promote greater respect for and dialogue with persons of other faiths. After a historic meeting of the sub-unit in Chiang Mai, Thailand, in April 1977, the WCC issued two years later its *Guidelines on Dialogue*. It was heralded as "a historic turn," a "landmark in the development of the dialogue debate in the ecumenical context."[26] Admonishing Christians that they should not approach dialogue from a "position of superiority," the *Guidelines* also urged all followers of Jesus not to consider dialogue only a luxury or a pleasant pasttime; rather, dialogue with persons of other faiths is a necessary "means of living out our faith in Christ in service of community with our neighbor."[27] As we noted, here the WCC seems to be pushing beyond the borders of even the Partial Replacement Model.

But if there was such a push, it was not grounded and sustained with any clear theological support. If the WCC was loud in its calls for dialogue of religions, it barely whispered a theology of religions. As one commentator put it: in the *Guidelines*, there was a "deliberate eschewing of any kind of theological statement about the status before God of men and women of other faiths."[28] Not only did the *Guidelines* hold back from talking about salvation through the religions; it had to explicitly question whether there was any real "self-disclosure of God" (revelation) through other faiths. So while the WCC was pushing dialogue beyond the Replacement Model, its theology was still located in a perspective of *total* replacement. This theological ambiguity, amid calls to dialogue, was required to respect the convictions of most member churches, especially the Evangelicals and Orthodox.

---

25. Stanley Samartha, quoted in ibid., 97. Samartha is one of the WCC's pioneers in dialogue.
26. Stanley J. Samartha, "Guidelines on Dialogue," *Ecumenical Review* 31 (1979): 155, 157.
27. World Council of Churches, *Guidelines on Dialogue with People of Living Faiths and Ideologies* (Geneva: WCC, 1979), 11–12.
28. Cracknell, "Ambivalent Theology," 101.

Theological ambiguity made for further fluctuations in official WCC statements. At the World Assembly in Vancouver in 1983, "the older exclusivist [total replacement] position was reasserted" and led to a final "formulation which denies the presence of God in other religious traditions."[29] Yet calls to dialogue with persons of other faiths remained. To try to resolve the ambiguity and the tensions between dialogue and theology, the WCC sub-unit on dialogue assembled a group of specialists representing the full spectrum of theological views in Baar, Switzerland, in 1990. Their task: to lay a more coherent theological groundwork for WCC dialogue with other religions. They ended up with a rather bold statement that explicitly affirmed the presence of God, in the Holy Spirit, revealing and saving in and through other religions. This was indeed pushing beyond given models for a theology of religions. Perhaps that was part of the reason why at the General Assembly in Canberra in 1991 (and in subsequent General Assemblies) the Baar statement was quietly but effectively ignored.

And that's where things seem to remain within the WCC: strong appeals to Christians to engage persons of other religions in serious dialogue and cooperation, but theological positions that retain their roots in the Replacement Model — either total or partial. Still, the appeals for dialogue remain vigorous, so do the calls for further theological reflection. As Konrad Raiser, general secretary of the WCC, has put it: "Like all religions today, Christianity is challenged to reassess its long standing exclusivist claims and to contribute to building a new culture which includes and sustains plurality."[30] Given where it's come from and where it seems to be going, maybe we should locate the theology of religions of the WCC somewhere between the Replacement Model and the other models we will be exploring.

Are the Other Believers "Lost"?

But if, as we have seen, the Replacement Model, in either its total or partial expression, insists that no one can be saved unless they come into an explicit contact with Jesus and his Gospel, the nagging question continues to nag: Does that mean a loving God sends off to hell all the people who don't know about Jesus? Evangelicals do not run away from that question. In the 1992 World Assembly of the World Evangelical Fellowship, this representative gathering of Evangelicals from all over the world made a telling admission: " 'Can those who have never heard of Jesus Christ be saved?' ... We did not achieve a consensus on how to answer this question. More study is needed."[31] This lack of consensus signals both a discomfort and a division within the Fundamentalist-

---

29. Ibid., 102, 88.
30. Konrad Raiser, *To Be the Church: Challenges and Hopes for a New Millennium* (Geneva: WCC, 1997), 23.
31. The WEF's Manila Declaration, in *The Unique Christ in Our Pluralist World*, ed. Bruce J. Nicholls (Grand Rapids, Mich.: Baker Book House, 1994), 15.

Evangelical ranks. They all agree that salvation is to be found nowhere else than in Jesus Christ. But if someone lives in the remote mountains of Nepal and has so never heard of Jesus, does that person therefore end up in hell? Something seems wrong with that conclusion.

For some Fundamentalists, there's nothing wrong with it at all. Harold Lindsell, speaking out of the total replacement perspective, is consistent and straightforward: "If they [non-Christians] die without knowledge of Jesus Christ, they perish."[32] Others point out that if non-Christians perish, there's no blame on God's part. We forget that we are *all* sinners. People, whether Christian or otherwise, end up in hell because they have rebelled against God; they have trusted in themselves rather than in the Divine. What is presumed here is the reality of what we called general revelation: all people do know enough about God to rebel against God. And they *do* rebel. Everyone. "No man who has never heard of Jesus Christ is condemned for rejecting Christ; all men are condemned for their revolt against the light that they have."[33]

Still, for many Evangelicals, this remains too harsh and too inconsistent — for how can you say that non-Christians are properly condemned because they didn't make good use of general revelation when, according to Evangelical theology, no one can make good use of general revelation without Christ? It still seems that people are ending up in hell just because they had the bad luck to be born in areas Christian preachers never got to. So, many Evangelicals, perplexed by this question, invoke a kind of *Christian agnosticism:* they don't know. And they can't know, because the Bible has not provided any clear answers to the question of what happens to people who never hear about Jesus. What the Bible does make clear is that whenever a person experiences God in a way which "saves" them, it's because of Jesus. After that, all we can say is: "God is not bound to save everybody. God is free to save anybody."[34] Better to be silent.

Still, even in this silence people take different positions — some are called "pessimistic agnostics" and others are referred to as "optimistic agnostics." The pessimists, stressing that God is not bound to save everybody, find in the Bible "a sufficient number of reasonably clear biblical texts" that indicate that "the gate is wide and the road is easy that leads to destruction, and there are many who take it" (Matt. 7:13). Therefore, "with a great sense of sorrow," these Evangelicals suspect that few are going to make it to heaven. Others, the optimistic agnostics, don't find the biblical evidence that unambiguous and stress that if God is free to save anybody, God's love will move in the direction of forgiveness. Yet they don't want to say for sure, or how. That would be going beyond the Bible. But they hope.[35]

---

32. Harold Lindsell, "Missionary Imperative: A Conservative Evangelical Exposition," in *Protestant Crosscurrents in Mission: The Ecumenical-Conservative Encounter,* ed. Norman A. Horner (Nashville: Abingdon, 1968), 57.

33. Carl Henry, cited in John Sanders, *No Other Name: An Investigation into the Destiny of the Unevangelized* (Grand Rapids, Mich.: Eerdmans, 1992), 47.

34. Braaten, "Hearing the Other," 400.

35. For this discussion on agnosticism, see Dennis L. Okholm and Timothy R. Phillips, eds., *More*

In fact, the number of Evangelicals who so hope seems to be growing. Since the 1990s, as one peruses the books and journals of Evangelical theology, it is clear that what was once a rather taboo topic is now being vigorously debated.[36] What follows is a sketchy review of how the optimists are trying to move out of agnosticism and explore ways in which they can affirm both that there is no salvation without being somehow linked with Christ and also that those who in their lifetimes have not heard the Gospel can still enter eternal life.

The last-minute solution. For those persons of other religions and cultures who have sincerely done what they could in following their conscience and leading a moral life, God will send messengers, either human or angelic, before the actual moment of death to tell them about Jesus Christ and to give them a chance for a last-minute decision. This is a suggestion offered originally by Thomas Aquinas and intended for, as he put it, good pagans living "in the forests" without a chance to learn about Christ.[37]

The after-death solution. This is similar to the previous viewpoint, but it pushes the opportunity to hear the Good News and to make a decision about it beyond the portals of human lifetime. Either during the mysterious interval between death and what follows, or perhaps at the end of human history as we know it, an opportunity for a "final option" will be provided those who did their best with the limited resources and knowledge they had. During the last two or three decades, this view has been growing in popularity among Evangelicals.[38]

The election solution. This one is a bit philosophical. It's based on what is called "the middle knowledge" of God — that is, the knowledge that God has of what would have happened had circumstances been different. Thus, God knows those persons of other religions who, if they would have had the chance to hear about Jesus, certainly would have followed him. These persons are given entrée into heaven. Therefore, "God may be working in undreamt ways among people who do not stand within the stream of Judeo-Christian history."[39]

The exception solution. Just as we know from the Bible that God made exceptions for the "holy pagans" of the Jewish Bible (Enoch, Job, Melchizedek, Jethro), so we can expect God to continue making exceptions among the holy, sincere people of other religions. Such persons, like the holy pagans of the Bible, are saved in anticipation of Jesus' saving death and resurrection.[40]

The universalist solution. This is definitely a very minority viewpoint. Karl Barth, for all his negativity about religion, strongly suggested it, but he never

Than One Way? Four Views of Salvation in a Pluralistic World (Grand Rapids, Mich.: Zondervan, 1995), 20–21; Netland, *Dissonant Voices,* 268–69.

36. Sanders, *No Other Name,* 21–22.

37. See ibid., 152–56; Netland, *Dissonant Voices,* 275–77.

38. Erickson, *How Shall They Be Saved?* 159.

39. Robert H. Culpepper, "The Lordship of Christ and Religious Pluralism: A Review Article," *Perspectives in Religious Studies* 19 (1992): 320; see also Sanders, *No Other Name,* 167–70.

40. Gary W. Phillips, "Evangelicals and Pluralism: Current Options," in *The Challenge of Religious Pluralism: An Evangelical Analysis and Response,* ed. David K. Clark (Wheaton, Ill.: Wheaton Theology Conference, 1992), 178–82; Netland, *Dissonant Voices,* 270–74.

clearly affirmed the position. It, too, is an idea that goes back to the early church — that at the very end of history, because Jesus did die and rise *for all people*, there will be a "universal restitution" in which all will have the opportunity to choose Christ and his salvation, and, perhaps, all people will make the choice. And so the "Lord of history" will prove himself to be "also Lord of the world's religions."[41] But proponents of this viewpoint are cautious. They warn their fellow Christians not to bank on it or use it as an excuse to slacken off on the necessity of announcing Jesus and the Gospel to all peoples.

The wider mercy solution. This is not only a relatively new perspective among Evangelical theologians; it also boldly treads where most Evangelicals would never think of entering. Two of its boldest spokespersons are Clark Pinnock and John Sanders.[42] This solution, often called "inclusivism," is carefully defined by Pinnock: "Inclusivism believes that, because God is present in the whole world (premise), God's grace is also at work in some way among all people, possibly, even in the sphere of religious life (inference). It entertains the possibility that religion may play a role in the salvation of the human race, a role preparatory to the gospel of Christ, in whom alone fullness of salvation is found."[43]

Because this perspective is so controversial, we need to sort out the ingredients in that definition. It starts with a belief that is rock-solid for all Christians: "God's boundless mercy is a primary truth that cannot be compromised." God's desire to save all people is *just as central* to Christian consciousness as is God's decision to do so only through Jesus. And then Pinnock and Sanders draw what would seem to be a necessary conclusion: if God's desire to embrace all people is not to be compromised in the case of those who have not heard about Jesus, then Christians must "recognize that God can save outside of the visible boundaries of Christianity." But how? Proponents of this wider mercy solution offer what should be an easy answer for Christians: through the universal presence and activity of the Holy Spirit. And if the Holy Spirit is active outside the visible boundaries of Christianity, so is real *revelation*. When they say "real," they mean a revelation that can both reveal and save. To say that God offers a saving revelation to Christians and a nonsaving revelation to everyone else is, in Sanders's opinion, to speak of "two different Gods." Pinnock and Sanders are even ready to go a further step and recognize the possibility that the Holy Spirit can make use of other religions to carry on this revealing-saving work. But they're cautious on this point, reminding themselves that, really, if anyone feels

---

41. Braaten, *The Flaming Center,* 118. On Barth's universalism, see Donald W. Dayton, "Karl Barth and the Wider Ecumenism," in *Christianity and the Wider Ecumenism*, ed. Peter C. Phan (New York: Paragon House, 1990), 181–89.

42. See Clark Pinnock, *A Wideness in God's Mercy: The Finality of Jesus Christ in a World of Religions* (Grand Rapids, Mich.: Zondervan, 1992); and Sanders, *No Other Name.* Handy summaries of their positions, which form the basis for the overview in this chapter, can be found in Pinnock, "Acts 4:12 — No Other Name under Heaven," in *Through No Fault of Their Own: The Fate of Those Who Have Never Heard*, ed. William V. Crockett and James G. Sigountos (Grand Rapids, Mich.: Baker Book House, 1991), 107–15; Pinnock, "An Inclusivist View," in *More Than One Way?* 95–121; Sanders, "Inclusivism," in *What about Those Who Have Never Heard?* 21–55.

43. Pinnock, "An Inclusivist View," 98.

the saving power of God, it is through faith, not works — that means, through trusting in God's love, not through practices of religion.

The final ingredient in the wider mercy perspective is the most important and the one that makes sure it does not compromise the heart of Christianity: whatever saving presence of the Spirit or real revelation we may find in other religions, it's there *because of Jesus Christ.* That means it both comes from and leads to Jesus, the Gospel, and the church. Jesus remains the criterion for whatever truth there is in other religions and the only and final end where this truth can be fulfilled. Whatever good there might be in other religions, it is there as a preparation for Christ.

As we will see, all the essential ingredients of this Evangelical wider mercy solution can be found in the Roman Catholic/Mainline Protestant Fulfillment Model we will be examining in Part II. This exemplifies what we have already said — that models are slippery. While they're useful for describing general approaches and attitudes, they almost never perfectly fit an individual theologian; they're fluid and often spill into each other.

Further Readings

Braaten, Carl. "Hearing the Other: The Promise and Problem of Pluralism." *Currents in Theology and Mission* 24 (1997): 393–400.

———. *No Other Gospel! Christianity among the World Religions.* Minneapolis: Fortress Press, 1992, chapters 2, 3, 4.

Brunner, Emil. "Revelation and Religion." In *Christianity and Other Religions.* Ed. John Hick and Brian Hebblethwaite. Philadelphia: Fortress Press, 1980, 113–32.

Cracknell, Kenneth. "Ambivalent Theology and Ambivalent Policy: The World Council of Churches and Interfaith Dialogue 1938–1999." *Studies in Interreligious Dialogue* 9 (1999): 87–111.

Demarest, Bruce. "General and Special Revelation: Epistemological Foundations of Religious Pluralism." In *One God, One Lord: Christianity in a World of Religious Pluralism.* Ed. Andrew D. Clarke and Bruce W. Winter. Grand Rapids, Mich.: Baker Book House, 1992, 189–206.

Fackre, Gabriel. "Divine Perseverance." In *What about Those Who Have Never Heard? Three Views on the Destiny of the Unevangelized.* Ed. John Sanders. Downers Grove, Ill.: InterVarsity Press, 1995, 71–95.

Foerster, John. "Paul Tillich and Inter-religious Dialogue." *Modern Theology* 7 (1990): 1–28.

Mitchell, Mozella G. "Discovering Christian Resources for a Theology of Interfaith Relations from the African Methodist Episcopal Zion Church." In *Grounds for Understanding: Ecumenical Resources for Responses to Religious Pluralism.* Ed. S. Mark Heim. Grand Rapids, Mich.: Eerdmans, 1998, 157–74.

Newbigin, Lesslie. *The Gospel in a Pluralist Society.* Grand Rapids, Mich.: Eerdmans, 1989, chapters 13–14.

Pannenberg, Wolfhart. "The Religions from the Perspective of Christian Theology and the Self-Interpretation of Christianity in Relation to Non-Christian Religions." *Modern Theology* 9 (1993): 285–97.

Pinnock, Clark. "An Inclusivist View." In *More Than One Way? Four Views of Salvation in a Pluralistic World*. Ed. Dennis L. Okholm and Timothy R. Phillips. Grand Rapids, Mich.: Zondervan, 1995, 95–123.

Quebedeaux, Richard. "Interreligious Dialogue: Next Step for Conservative Protestant Intellectuals?" In *Christianity and the Wider Ecumenism*. Ed. Peter C. Phan. New York: Paragon House, 1990, 233–46.

Rock, Jay T. "Resources in the Reformed Tradition for Responding to Religious Plurality." In *Grounds for Understanding: Ecumenical Resources for Responses to Religious Pluralism*. Ed. S. Mark Heim. Grand Rapids, Mich.: Eerdmans, 1998, 46–68.

Sanders, John. "Inclusivism." In *What about Those Who Have Never Heard? Three Views on the Destiny of the Unevangelized*. Ed. John Sanders. Downers Grove, Ill.: InterVarsity Press, 1995, 21–55.

Thompson, Nehemiah. "The Search for a Methodist Theology of Religious Pluralism." In *Grounds for Understanding: Ecumenical Resources for Responses to Religious Pluralism*. Ed. S. Mark Heim. Grand Rapids, Mich.: Eerdmans, 1998, 93–106.

Tillich, Paul. *Systematic Theology*. Chicago: University of Chicago Press, 1951–63, 1: 137–44, 218–30; 2:78–88; 3:98–106.

———. *What Is Religion?* New York: Harper and Row, 1969, 56–97.

Volf, Miroslav. "The Unique Christ in the Challenge of Modernity." In *The Unique Christ in Our Pluralist World*. Ed. Bruce J. Nicholls. Grand Rapids, Mich.: Baker Book House, 1994, 96–108.

"The World Evangelical Fellowship Manila Declaration." In *The Unique Christ in Our Pluralist World*. Ed. Bruce J. Nicholls. Grand Rapids, Mich.: Baker Book House, 1994, 14–27.

Yong, Amos. " 'Not Knowing Where the Spirit Blows . . . ': On Envisioning a Pentecostal-Christian Theology of Religions." *Journal of Pentecostal Theology* 14 (1999): 81–112.

Chapter 3

The Replacement Model
Insights and Questions

With a basic understanding of what this Evangelical Replacement Model is say-ing about other religions and how its deep commitment to Christ and the Bible animates all that it says, we want to stand back in these final reflections to ask: What can be learned and what can be questioned? In a sense, through this concluding evaluation (and its coming counterparts for the other models), the issue of Christian dialogue with other religions becomes the arena for Chris-tian dialogue with other Christians. At the end of each part of this book, after we've tried to paint as accurate a picture as possible of each of the models for a Christian theology of religions, we will try to carry on this inner-Christian dialogue. We'll do this by asking: What can other Christians learn from this model? And what might be the further questions or disagreements that other Christians have with it? What are its basic insights, and what are its possible inadequacies?

Insights

The Centrality of Scripture in Christian Life

Even though not all Christians agree with the way the Evangelicals interpret the Bible or with the way some of them lift up the Scriptures as the sole source of God's revelation, still, all Christians have much to learn from the way the Bible, especially the New Testament, animates, sustains, and directs the life and self-identity of Evangelical communities. They remind all Christians that this is part of the self-definition, or the job description, of a follower of Jesus Christ: Christians are people who draw not just truth but life from the Spirit that they find present in the written Word of God. So we're not just talking about ortho-doxy — holding true to what the Bible tells us. Rather, it's a matter of life and empowerment and carrying on the vision and mission of Jesus, which is made possible by listening — that is, opening oneself to — the truth and power that reside in this book that is more than a book.

Christians believe that the New Testament is the witness of the first followers and communities of Jesus about what he meant to them and how he transformed their lives. Christians believe that this witness is not just a historical record;

50

it is also a vision that both excites the mind with a new way of looking at life and at the same time empowers one's whole being to live that way. This witness, therefore, is normative both for preserving the vision and maintaining the power. "Normative" means that the New Testament sets the goal as well as the parameters to get to the goal. It both defines and confines. Fidelity to this witness requires both holding to the vision and avoiding anything that would lead us astray from it.

So Evangelicals remind their fellow Christians that — in trying to answer the new challenge of religious pluralism, as summarized in chapter 1 — Christians must always be sure they are grounding their new theologies of other religions and their efforts to dialogue with other believers on the witness of the New Testament. That means that any theology of religions that wants to call itself a Christian theology will have to be guided by the Bible, especially the New Testament. And this means that a Christian will not first work out his views of other religions and then try to square them with the Bible. Instead, among the many things that provide fundamental building materials for a theology of religions, the Bible enjoys a qualitatively superior position. From that follows the corollary: a theology of religions grounded in the Bible will not contradict the biblical witness. If there are blatant contradictions, for instance, between what the Bible affirms about Jesus and what a new theology is asserting, then this new theology has problems. It has to do its biblical homework better.

Summarizing this first insight and challenge from the Evangelicals: any Christian theology of religions worth its name has to be biblical. If it's not, it may make for a good philosophy of religions, but it can't be called Christian.

The Reality of Evil and the Need for Help

The message that evil is real and that we therefore need help came through crisply and persistently in our review of the Replacement Model. In their understanding of "by faith alone," Evangelicals are telling us something about humanity that we can forget only at our peril, something that, because it is so uncomfortable, many Christians, humanists, scientists, and New Agers tend to sweep under the rug of consciousness: as things stand presently, there is something wrong with us and the world. It seems that all the religions of the world have words or symbols by which they try to get at this "something's wrong": "original sin," or "suffering" (*dukkha*), or "ignorance" (*avidya*), or "forgetfulness," or "imbalance." Philosophers prefer more sophisticated language: evil, finitude, radical limitation, illusion, angst. Wherever it comes from, however it works, whether and how it can be removed (important questions with importantly different answers from the religions and philosophers), it is there. In fact, here the philosophical tag might apply: it's *ontological* — it's given in the very machinery of the way things are and work.

Many people may be uncomfortable with Evangelical or biblical language used to point to this state of affairs. But to recognize that we are "sinners" or "fallen" is to recognize that there are limits to the human condition and that sound reason and good will of themselves do not automatically ensure progress; as Marx and Freud have reminded us, we have to be "suspicious" of all our noble projects, for they well may be self-centered and harmful to others. To ignore this reality of evil or destructive selfishness or ignorance is to compound the problem. Psychologically, it can lead to reality-avoidance and to a false image of a limitless self. Politically, as we heard, it can lead to what Marx called ideology and Christianity calls idolatry — one nation thinking it has the flawless, the perfect, political or economic system, which it all too eagerly then imposes on others.

The further conclusion that the Evangelicals draw from their understanding of "by faith alone" also seems to ring true for many contemporaries: by ourselves, even with our always inventive, ever-expanding human powers, we can neither figure out nor do anything to really fix the problem. Again, to use philosophical language, if there is an ontological problem (the machinery is broken), we also have an epistemological problem (we can't figure out, or agree on, what the problem is). Simply stated: there are limits, frightening and dangerous limits, to human knowing and achieving. That's the bad news. The Evangelicals immediately add the good news — echoed in most religious traditions — that there is a Higher Power, a Divine Reality, that can help us, perhaps rescue us, and enable us to reach beyond our own limits. But they insist that to experience this Power we have to first admit our own insufficiency — our own inability to understand why Humpty Dumpty keeps falling off the wall and our inability to put him back together again. We must open ourselves, let go and trust ("only by faith"!) this Reality. Only then will we feel our minds enlightened and our efforts empowered.

To experience this Higher Power does not mean renouncing our own responsibility to use our own powers. It's not a magical, immediate fix for our struggles. We have to do our part. But "our part" is only possible when it is connected with this "larger Part." While God's reality and grace will always be experienced as within and part of us, they can never be reduced to us. The Evangelicals insist on a real, a qualitative, difference between God and humanity — "an element of radical mystery, which anyone hoping to understand the Christian God should at some point recognize."[1] To forget this radical mystery, this God who is really different from us but always with us, is to violate the Christian message and impoverish humanity.

But radical *mystery* includes the possibility of radical *surprise*. Perhaps this mysterious, always beyond-us God has surprises for us that we never would have dreamed of by ourselves. This brings us to the third central lesson that the Evangelicals have to offer their fellow Christians and all humanity.

---

1. David Tracy, *Blessed Rage for Order* (New York: Crossroad, 1975), 28.

Jesus as the One and Only

For many of our postmodern contemporaries, as we saw in chapter 1, and for many critical Christians, as we will see in coming chapters, the claim that Jesus is the one-and-only Son of God and Savior is highly dubious and highly audacious. But the Evangelicals request that such critics reconsider whether it really is so dubious and audacious. Is it not *possible* that Jesus of Nazareth constitutes something thoroughly surprising, thoroughly exceptional and unique in the history of humanity? Even if critics don't like the sometimes brittle literalness with which Evangelicals read these claims of uniqueness in the New Testament, don't they — if they themselves want to maintain their valued open-mindedness — have to admit that what the Evangelicals are saying about Jesus *can* be true? Not to admit that possibility would be intellectually dishonest.

To deny this, say the Evangelicals, fatally dilutes the Christian tradition. For this is precisely the heart, the power-point, of the Christian message — what Christianity, for all its long life, has claimed. To deny this claim, or to so water it down that it no longer means what it says, is to violate what, they say, is the one clear and consistent theme within all the different traditions that make up the New Testament: that in Jesus, God has surprised humanity, that God has provided one clear, coherent path through the tangled, violent maze of history. For many, this will be the "scandal of particularity." But if God be God, especially if God be radical Mystery full of surprises and unable to be boxed within human expectations, isn't it inconsistent, overly hasty, and dangerous to rule out such a "scandal"?

And from what we heard earlier in this book, from Barth to the contemporary Evangelicals, given the state of our world, such a unique, particular act of God in Jesus may not be that scandalous after all. If one basically agrees that there is "something profoundly wrong" with the human condition that keeps humans from living peacefully and justly with each other, then doesn't it make sense, maybe eminent sense, that God would do something very clear and precise to help humans remedy their situation? (Call it an "ontological fix.") And if one agrees that by themselves humans cannot figure out and come to a consensus about what is at the bottom of the problem and about a solution, doesn't it, again, make sense that God would reveal and make known what needs to be done? (This would be the "epistemological fix.") Or, more concretely and geopolitically, humanity stands at a juncture in its history that perhaps it never faced before. Given the ever-mounting ecological strangulation of the life-giving and life-sustaining capacities of the earth, given the threat not just of violence but of planet-destroying nuclear violence, given the increasing poverty and maldistribution of wealth that are fueling ever more violence within cities and between nations — humanity stands in dire need of one clear source of truth and empowerment that will enable it to find a common solution for these common problems. Humanity now needs not just many truths but one truth that will unite people in a common vision and hope. Humanity needs not many solutions but one solution that will energize all to do what otherwise has been impossible. And here, the Christian message about the one revelation and the one salvation offered in the one Jesus, who is the one Son of God and Savior, may be just what people need and, in their heart of hearts, are looking for.

The best representatives of Evangelicalism make this claim not imperialistically and arrogantly but humbly and dialogically. Christians will present to others what for them personally and for their community historically is held to be *certain:* that in Jesus we find God's answer to all the questions that humans harbor in their hearts. Evangelical Christians offer this claim as an invitation — to see what it means and how it feels and fits the human quest. If other religions wish to make similar claims, so be it. Evangelical Christians will respect and try to listen to them. But they are firm, totally committed to what they hold to be true. The exchange between religions becomes, then, as we have heard, a religious competition in which no one cajoles but in which Christians hold to their certitudes about Jesus.

A highly regarded Evangelical theologian, Miroslav Volf, clarifies what kind of certitude and what kind of claims Christians can bring to their relationship with other believers. He speaks of a "provisional certitude" that paradoxically is as certain as it is provisional:

> Jesus Christ is the way, the truth, and the life. As Christians we will assert this as the truth. But we cannot assert it as *absolute knowledge,* we cannot assert it *as* the *final* truth. Short of becoming God, humans cannot possess the final truth.... All Christian beliefs are *our* beliefs, *human* beliefs and as such always *provisional beliefs*. We assert that they are true; but we make this assertion provisionally. I call this *provisional certitude*. There is, if you want, an absoluteness about our beliefs: we cannot relinquish our standpoint but rather assert that it is true. So the ground on which we stand as we act and reflect is firm. Yet we assert our standpoint as true in a provisional way: *we believe* our beliefs to be true. This hinders us from becoming arrogant and oppressive.[2]

What Christians are certain about — the uniqueness of Jesus — will be made known and, as it were, established as "absolute" only in the future. In the meantime they are provisional: deeply committed to Jesus and to announcing him as God's one-and-only final truth, but at the same time, aware that things still have to be worked out and that what they believe still has to be proven. In this meantime, they will be respectful of other religions. As Volf adds: "If we understand our views as provisionally true, we will have to understand the views of others as *possibly* true."[3]

In all this, Evangelicals are suggesting and showing their fellow Christians that it is possible to proclaim Jesus as the only Savior and to view other re-

---

2. Miroslav Volf, "The Unique Christ in the Challenge of Modernity," in *The Unique Christ in Our Pluralist World,* ed. Bruce J. Nicholls (Grand Rapids, Mich.: Baker Book House, 1994), 103.
3. Ibid.

ligions as having to be replaced by Christianity and at the same time engage other religions in a friendly dialogue of competition.

Beware of Religion

A final lesson that other Christians might learn from this replacement theology of religions has to do with Karl Barth's assertions about "religion as unbelief." Barth is getting at what others have called "the Protestant principle" — the ever-moving searchlight that the Reformation trains on all religion as it warns that religion may be as dangerous as it is necessary. There is a worm within all religion — Tillich called it "the demonic element" — by which it tries to domesticate God and capture deity in the security of human knowledge. All religion is in daily need of reformation because all religion, in both blatant and subtle ways, seeks to make itself and its creeds, codes, and cults more important than the revelation and experience it is meant to serve and pass on.[4] Only the blind or the "too well established" will miss this demonic element in the history of every religious tradition. We can thank Freud and Marx and Nietzsche for laying bare its sometimes latent presence in the way religions tend to provide too much security and so end up becoming "crutches" or "opium" — or "secure jobs."

It is important to bring this "Protestant principle," this alertness to one's own corruptibility, to any theology or dialogue of religions. In both assessing other religions and in actually encountering them, we must constantly ask ourselves the difficult question: Am I listening or speaking out of an openness to the Divine wherever it may speak or lead, or out of a resolve to further or simply hang on to the power or comfort that my religion gives me? Barth warned us that religion keeps getting in the way of what God may want to tell us in revelation, and it also can get in the way of what God may be saying to us in dialogue with others.

But the Protestant principle is necessary for interreligious dialogue in a more general way. It calls on all religious people, as they sit down to talk with each other and to promote what in the introduction we called a new "community of communities," not to forget the record of religion throughout the centuries. The reality, which looms both in the past and still in the present, is that religion has brought as much pain to humanity as it has inspired peace. In fact, in light of the religious wars and violence that have ravaged history and still rage in India, Sri Lanka, the Middle East, Yugoslavia, and Ireland — the data convince some that religion has spewed out more hatred than love. This record and these challenges have to be remembered in any encounter of religions. Otherwise, dialogue can all too easily become a sugary irenicism in which the religions of the world come together to tell each other how wonderful they are.

---

4. Paul Tillich, *Systematic Theology* (Digswell Place, England: James Nisbet, 1968), 3:104–13.

Questions

Sources for a Christian Theology of Religions?

A first question that we might ask of this Replacement Model is directed primarily to the Evangelicals, but it touches all Christians. It has to do with the place of the Bible in a Christian theology of religions. More broadly, it asks about the *sources* for such a theology: What are the primary "materials" out of which Christians build their understanding of other religions? Are the books of the Bible the only source of a theology of religions? Or must Christians, in order to formulate their attitude toward others, also make use of the books of other religions — that is, study the teachings and converse with the followers of other faiths?

We saw that for Barth and the Total Replacement Model, the Bible is the one-and-only Word of God and therefore the only lens by which they view other religions. But we also witnessed how other Evangelicals felt that this approach led to a much too narrow view of others and missed the "general revelation" that shines in them. So these Evangelicals, especially those agreeing with Wolfhart Pannenberg, recognized that while the Bible is their primary source for understanding others, it is also necessary to listen to and study what the others have to say. The Bible itself calls for this insofar as it tells us that God speaks, in general revelation, to other traditions.

It's precisely here that our question comes into focus: What do Evangelicals do when there is a clash between what the Bible tells them of other religions and what other religions say about themselves? We heard from Evangelical theologians that despite the general revelation that shines in other traditions, all other believers end up, in one form or another, trying to save themselves. They never really grasp or practice the total trust inherent in the Christian understanding of "by faith alone." They're always trying to squeeze the Mystery of God into their own boxes. They try to identify the God of the future in the clarities of the present. But Buddhists and Hindus and Muslims might well find it difficult to recognize themselves in these descriptions. For instance, what Christians call "negative theology" (one that recognizes that God is always more than we can ever know) seems to run through most of Asian religions — the Hindu reminder of *neti, neti* (God is not this, not that), the Buddha's noble silence before any attempt to define or even describe Nirvana, Zen's insistence that all religious language is but a finger pointing to the moon, never to be identified with the moon. Also, even St. Francis Xavier, when he encountered the Japanese Pure Land form of Buddhism with its call to trust Amida Buddha and do nothing else, thought that Martin Luther had beat him to Japan! Pure Land Buddhism preaches the very same message of "trust alone," without "good works"! Such data from other religions seem to contradict what Evangelicals see in these religions.

Might they be seeing what they want to see, or what they think the Bible requires them to see? This raises the very thorny and battered question of how it is possible (whether it is possible?) to walk in someone else's moccasins — to really see the world as they see it. Using imagery employed earlier, to see the universe as a Buddhist does, I have to look through the Buddhist telescope. But does this mean that in order to see what the Buddhist sees, I have to forget what I see through mine? Is that really possible? Can I really make use of someone else's telescope? Can I really see what they see? Won't I always understand whatever it is that I "see" through their telescope according to what I am accustomed to seeing through my own? Or more simply: I always see and understand other worlds from the viewpoint of my own. I can never totally abandon my own viewpoint. I can't crawl out of my Christian body and take on a new Buddhist body. (We'll sort out these issues more carefully in Part IV.)

These are indeed complex matters. But they help us identify more precise questions or suggestions for the Evangelicals. It seems that Evangelical Christians have to take a more careful look at other religions, a look that is more direct, less colored by what the Bible tells them (or by what they think the Bible is telling them). The religions themselves have to be a real source for their theology of religions — that is, for what they think about religions. Does this mean that Christians have to set aside the Bible when they study other traditions or talk with other believers? No. It seems that would be impossible, for we always bring who we are and all our conditionings to any new encounter. But we have to be ready to change what we *bring to* the encounter in the light of what we *discover in* the encounter. And this seems to require that Christians be ready to clarify, correct, even change what they know from the Bible in the light of what they learn from other religions. This will probably be a matter not of "correcting what the Bible says" but of correcting what they thought the Bible said.

So to sum up this question for Evangelicals: Isn't it necessary for Christians to recognize that there are two sources for any Christian theology of religions — both the Bible (including Christian tradition and experience) and what Christians learn from studying other traditions and talking with other believers? Each source has to be balanced by the other. Both have to enter into a kind of dialogue with each other in which each side stands ready to be clarified or corrected by the other. Evangelicals will insist that the Bible is always primary for Christians. And they are right. But primary doesn't have to mean absolute.

Jesus the One-and-Only?

This is the more difficult and delicate question, one that will be pursuing us throughout our exploration of these different Christian theologies of religions. We have heard, and perhaps agreed with, the Evangelical insistence that the proclamation of Jesus as the "one-and-only" Son of God, Word of God, and Savior runs like a powerful electrical current through all the books of the New Testament. We have heard Evangelicals' conclusions that therefore Jesus Christ is necessary (ontologically) for repairing or redeeming the disconnect between God and humanity; he is also necessary (epistemologically) for enabling people to understand and to act on God's gift of grace through faith alone. But many Christians, from their study of and dialogue with other religions, feel that such assertions trigger a number of questions.

The first question is so fundamental that it might be forgotten: Just how do Christians *know* that Jesus is the one-and-only Savior? Does their own personal experience tell them this? Or do they know it only because the Bible tells them so? Clearly and repeatedly, the Bible does say this. But is the Bible's message confirmed in the Christian's own experience? The answer would seem to be both yes and no: yes, a Christian who experiences the Spirit of Christ through the Word of the Bible and in the sacramental life of the community knows, in her own heart and mind, that this living Christ has enabled her to feel the love of God, to trust that love wholeheartedly, to experience the deep peace that it brings, and to hope that this peace will endure after death. And she feels, too, that this gift of God that she has experienced in Christ is meant not just for her, or her Christian church, but for all peoples of all times. In other words, then, the Christian's own experience confirms for her that Christ is *truly* a Savior meant for all.

But it seems that the Christian's experience does not say clearly and certainly that Jesus is the *only* Savior meant for all. To experience Jesus as the only Savior would require experience and knowledge of other religions to the extent that one could say that in no other religion do believers make similar claims about their founders or teachers, or that in no other tradition are there religious figures who affect people's lives similarly to the way Jesus has transformed Christians' lives. A comparison with marriage may help: on the basis of a person's experience of their spouse, they can say that this is the man or woman they *truly* want to marry; but on the basis of this experience they cannot say that this is the *only* man or woman they might marry.

If this is true, if it is only on the basis of the Bible and Christian tradition that Christians know that Jesus is the one-and-only Savior, then a further question arises: What do Christians do when their experience of other religions does tell them that indeed other religious people do make claims about their founders or teachers that sound very similar to what Christians say about Jesus? They may not use terms such as "Savior" or "Son of God" (though some of them do), but they speak about these individuals as the means by which they have heard God's saving Word (Muhammad), or as the teacher by whom they have come to enlightenment and Nirvana (Buddha), or as the Glorious One who loves them and affirms them just as they are (Krishna, Amida Buddha). Granted, we have to be very careful about making too facile comparisons and using our Christian telescope to interpret the universe of peoples of other religions. But as Raimon Panikkar asks, if Jesus, Buddha, Muhammad, and Krishna are not "analogous" (expressing the same idea or vision), are they not "homologous" (carrying out the same role or function)?

The new and disconcerting question being asked of Evangelicals and of all Christians is whether Jesus is the only means by which God "fixes" what is wrong with the human condition and brings people to the peace of God's self. We can still hold to what the Bible and our own experience seem to tell us so clearly: that something is wrong, that we can't mend it by ourselves, that we must let go and let God. But now we are asking, Might there be other means by which humans can "let God"? Are there other ways in which God steps in to do what no human alone can do: to understand what's wrong and feel empowered to do something about it? Are there other ways besides Jesus in which people might experience "grace alone" by "faith alone"?

This question pushes a little further: Is the Evangelical understanding of salvation through grace and faith alone perhaps not the only way to grasp and experience how the Divine touches and transforms humans? Might Evangelicals be imposing one particular way of experiencing God, as found in the Bible, on other religions? For example, could the Muslim experience of "submission to Allah," or the Buddha's message of enlightenment, or the Hindu sense of *moksha* as total oneness with Brahman the Ultimate, or the Chinese sense of living in the harmony of yin-yang — might these also be different ways to experience and talk about how Something More enters into, or emanates from, the human being in order to change the individual and the world?[5]

If there are other ways by which the Divine "saves" and transforms, other ways that are important not just for their own people but for all humankind, then the dialogue is not just a "holy competition" in which the various "one-and-only" claims try to find out who is right. It will be a dialogue in which, yes, the religions do have to confront and correct each other; but it will be one in which they cooperate rather than compete. If God is revealing and saving in many religions and not just in one, then the dialogue will be one in which the religions, by listening to each other, learn more of this God who is always more than any one of them could ever know.

And yet, to be sensitive to Evangelical convictions about the centrality of the Bible, we have to remind ourselves of the apparent clash between all this talk about other ways and saviors and the clear New Testament language about Jesus as the one-and-only. This brings up a final question, which will face us again in coming chapters: If we grant that there are two sources for a Christian theology of religions — both the Bible and the dialogue with other religious believers — then we can, or must, ask whether it is possible to understand this one-and-only language differently than Christians have in the past. For there is also an uncomfortable clash between such biblical one-and-only language and what many Christians experience in the dialogue. Christians meet Buddhists, Jews, Hindus, Muslims, and Native Americans who not only *say* that they have found peace and happiness and a sense of oneness with the Divine in their own religions but also show in the way they live their lives that this is very much the

---

5. As we will see in chapter 11, there are experts who on the basis of what is said here would conclude that there are different ways of experiencing not the same salvation but different salvations!

case. These are people who are happy, at peace, and committed to loving each other and improving our world. They sure look "saved."

Evangelicals recognize this clash when many of them insist that they don't want to designate as lost all those who don't know Jesus. These Evangelicals are trying to better balance the *particularist* texts of the Bible that proclaim Jesus as one-and-only with the *universalist* texts also found in Scripture that announce that God is a God of love who wills to bring all people to happiness and salvation. But to be honest, for many Christians, some of the solutions that the Evangelicals offer and that we reviewed seem to be more the fruit of theological imagination than biblical vision. The "last-minute" or "after-death" solutions, for instance, seem somewhat "invented."

Are there better ways to reconcile the tension between the biblical language about Jesus as one-and-only and the biblical language about God reaching out to all? Are there better ways to resolve the clash between the New Testament's claims that there is "no other name" and all the other names that Christians are meeting in their dialogue with other believers? In coming chapters we will explore some of these other attempts to reinterpret the New Testament's understanding of Jesus.

Part II

THE FULFILLMENT MODEL
"The One Fulfills the Many"

Chapter 4

The Breakthrough
at the Second Vatican Council

The model for a Christian theology of religions that we explore in this part represents a move from seeing Christianity as the "replacement" to the "fulfill-ment" of other religions. It seeks to affirm the insights of the previous model, but also to answer questions posed of it. In doing this, it represents what it considers a step forward in Christian efforts to come to a balanced understanding of other religious traditions. It offers a theology that will give equal weight to the two foundational Christian convictions we have already heard about: that God's love is *universal*, extending to all peoples, but also that God's love is *particular*, made real in Jesus the Christ. The way this Fulfillment Model carries out this balancing act is distinctly different from the way the Replacement Model does so. This model represents something really new in the history of Christianity.

It also speaks for the majority of what are called "the mainline Christian churches." If the Replacement Model, as we saw, held sway over most of Christian history, the Fulfillment Model embodies the majority opinion of present-day Christianity. If the Replacement Model represents the voice of the Evangelical and Fundamentalist churches, the Fulfillment Model characterizes the teachings of the "mainline" churches: the Lutheran, Reformed, Methodist, Anglican, Greek Orthodox, and Roman Catholic churches. This means not only that this perspective is to be found among these churches' theologians, but also, and more importantly, that it describes what most theologically informed Christians in these churches think about other religions, even when their ideas run below the surface of their consciousness. They believe that other religions are of value, that God is to be found in them, that Christians need to dialogue with them and not just preach to them. These new attitudes are based on new experiences and call for a new theology of religions. That's what the Fulfillment Model represents.

But if this model constitutes something new within the Christian communi-ties, it also marks a limit. The balancing act between affirming God's presence in other religions and God's special presence in Jesus can't get any finer. They seem to say, "We can't stretch things any further without losing the uniqueness of Jesus. To venture beyond it may mean losing one's Christian identity."

In order to focus our study of this model, we're going to give center stage to the Christian community that first developed it. Surprisingly for some, the church that prides itself in moving slowly and often lags behind innovations in other churches has been on the forefront of new theological thinking about religions: the Roman Catholic Church. So while we spent most of the previous section looking through a Protestant telescope, in this one, we'll try to view other religions with a Catholic telescope.

And to understand just how this telescope has recently been strengthened (some would say reconstructed) in order to see even farther, we will first take a look backward, at different kinds of Catholic telescopes that have been used through the ages to try to view other religions. A quick review of the history of Christian attitudes toward other religions will enable us to understand and appreciate how new this model really is.

Looking Back: A Historical Review

A bird's-eye view of Catholic attitudes toward other faiths shows that the balancing act that is part of all Christian theologies of religions really has been a kind of teeter-totter. There's been an up-and-down movement between the universal side (God loves and wills to save all people) and the particular side (God saves through Jesus) of the teeter-totter. Sometimes the universal side was weightier and so it predominated; sometimes it was the particular side that held sway. It also seems, for Catholics, that the "particular" they're talking about is not just Jesus. It is also the church. For Catholics, a real, full, saving encounter with Jesus is had only in the church. Jesus continues carrying on his mission of bringing people to God and to each other in and through his community called church. The insistence that Jesus and the church are necessary to really know God and be saved seems, for much of Catholic history, to have had greater prominence than belief in God's universal love for all.

But it wasn't that way in the very beginning. The writers of the New Testament books, and the different communities for whom they were written, did not have to deal that much with "other religions." Their primary concern was more inner-family: their relationship with their mother religion, Judaism. But during the second century, this situation changed quickly as the communities of Jesus-followers moved deeper, both physically and culturally, into the Greco-Roman world. In this new Gentile (or "pagan") context, Christians were a minority, often an endangered minority. They had to explain, to themselves and to their neighbors, how they as Jesus-followers understood and related to this broader culture, with its many philosophies and religions.

During the first three centuries, one of the principal ways in which early Christian theologians (called the Church Fathers — if there were any Church Mothers, we have no historical record of them) tried to figure out the meaning of this broader "pagan" culture was by means of a central theme of the New Testament: the Word of God. In the church language of the time, they coined a new expression (or better, symbol): the *logos spermatikos*. Literally, *logos* means word, and *spermatikos* means seedlike. All Christians experienced that the Word of God was "made flesh" in Jesus. Now they were saying that before Jesus, and still throughout the Greco-Roman world, this same Word of God was scattered like seeds. Concentrated in Jesus, it was also thrown to the winds of history. This universally sown Word is "the Word of whom all humankind partakes." One of the Fathers, Justin Martyr, could even say that anyone who hears God's call in this Seed-Word and tries to follow its lead is really already a Christian, even though she never heard of Jesus! Tertullian made the same point even more strongly when he declared that because of God's universal presence and call, the spirit of every single man and woman is "naturally Christian."[1] Although all these early Christians went on to insist that the Seed-Word in other cultures and religions needs to be clarified and fulfilled in the fully embodied Word in Jesus, this was still a strong affirmation of God's saving presence beyond the church. The universal side of the teeter-totter was well weighted.

But that was soon to change. Quite drastic — and for Christians, welcome — historical developments shifted the weight from a stress on God's universal love and presence to a stress on the particular importance of the church. After Emperor Constantine and under Emperor Theodosius (379–95), the often-persecuted minority community of Christians suddenly became the official state religion. The bishop of Rome became the "Pontifex Maximus" — the high priest who now wielded not only spiritual but political power. The welfare of the church was now wedded to the welfare of the state, which meant that the enemies of the state became the enemies of the church. Those enemies were non-Romans and non-Christians. Understandably, though regrettably, attitudes toward those "outside" the church began to change.

These changes were greatly influenced by one particular theologian and later saint: Augustine. From his reading of St. Paul, as well as from his own experience of the difficulty of wrenching himself out of the clutches of his earlier high and loose lifestyle, Augustine realized and insisted throughout his preaching and writing that we are saved *only by grace*. Without it, in this life and the next, we are lost. And he saw clear examples of this lost humanity in the "barbarian" tribes who were threatening the Roman Empire and, with it, the church. (The Visigoths captured Rome in 410 and were laying siege to Augustine's own city of Hippo as he lay dying in 430.) Gradually, Augustine came to the conviction that such saving grace is found not beyond the church but only within it. He worked out his teaching of "double predestination": God, from all eternity, predestines some to salvation within the church; the rest — "the damned masses" — end in perdition.[2] One of his pupils, Fulgentius of Ruspe (d. 533), made clear what this meant for the "heathen" religions: "There is no doubt that not only all heathens, but also all Jews and all heretics and schismatics who die outside the

---

1. Justin, *I Apologia*, 46; *II Apologia*, 10, 13; Tertullian, *Apologia*, 17, 4–6; Clement of Alexandria, *Stromata*, 1, 13; 5, 87, 2; *Protreptikos*, 6, 68, 2ff.; Origen, *Commentarium in Joannem*, 1, 39.

2. Augustine, *Enchirideon*, 107.

church will go into that everlasting fire prepared for the devil and his angels."[3] The teeter-totter was clearly weighted on the side of the church.

And it pretty well stayed there until around the sixteenth century. For all of this period, the fundamental attitude toward followers of other religious paths was encapsulated in the famous dictum, "Outside the church, no salvation." The force of this declaration, when it was first wielded by theologians like Origen (d. 254) and especially Cyprian (d. 258), was not aimed at outsiders. Rather, it was originally meant for persons already within the church as a warning that if they had any thought of leaving, it was at their eternal risk. After the fifth century, however, and through the Middle Ages, this proclamation was directed at non-Christians to tell them that those who are not in the church are out of heaven. Certainly, this ranking of other believers as "heathen," right alongside "the devil and his angels," was confirmed for most Christians by the fact that the only other believers they knew (besides the Jews) were the Muslims, who happened to have taken over the "Holy Land" and were at the walls of Europe. The Muslims were not just "other believers"; they were political foes, military enemies. Instead of dialogue, there were the Crusades.

So we hear the condemnatory tones of "Outside the church, no salvation" ringing through the centuries. And not just from pulpits or in lecture halls, but in the solemn and official declarations of popes and councils of bishops. The Fourth Lateran Council (1215) repeated the familiar words but added an emphatic adverbial phrase: "Outside the church, no salvation *at all* (*omnino*)." Pope Boniface VIII, in his bull *Unam Sanctam* (1302), gave another rendition of this sentence but clarified further that to belong to the one church and enjoy salvation, one also had to accept papal authority. Then, in 1442, the Council of Florence repeated almost verbatim the condemnation of Fulgentius given above and added: "No persons, whatever almsgiving they have practiced, even if they have shed blood for Christ, can be saved, unless they have remained in the bosom and unity of the Catholic Church."[4] It would seem that the boundless love of God for all people was bounded by the borders of the church.

But the teeter-totter was about to swing up-down again. Fifty years after the Council of Florence, Christopher Columbus landed in what he thought was India but what turned out to be a whole new world. This "new world" unleashed a flock of new theological questions and clues. As historians point out, the uncompromising insistence on the "Outside the church, no salvation" principle was both historically and psychologically conditioned. Historically, Christians thought that the Gospel had been preached to the ends of the earth. Psychologically, they could not imagine that in hearing it, anyone could not see its overwhelming truth and beauty; to refuse the truth of the church could come

---

3. Fulgentius of Ruspe, *De Fide ad Petrum,* 38, 79.
4. H. Denzinger and A. Schönmetzer, *Enchirideon Symbolorum Definitionum et Declarationum,* 802, 870–72, 1351.

only from ill will and the devil.[5] Well, the masses of new peoples in the Americas soon shook the staying power of those conditioning convictions. These peoples and tribes had, evidently, never heard of Jesus. And many of them, upon hearing (and seeing the behavior of the colonizing Christians), preferred their traditional ways. And so it was that the Council of Trent (1545–63), with the help of theologians like Robert Bellarmine and Francisco Suarez, came up with a formula — baptism of desire — that tried to place more weight on the "universal-love-of-God side" of the teeter-totter, without, however, denying the necessity of the church. If pagans could not be baptized with water, they could be baptized "through desire." This meant that if they followed their conscience and lived morally, they were implicitly expressing a desire to join the church and could thus get through the doors of heaven.[6]

With this swing of the teeter-totter we have something really new for attitudes of the time, but also a return to the view of the "seeds of the Word" scattered through history. It meant a shift from *"Outside the* church, no salvation" to *"Without the* church, no salvation." People could be outside, but if they followed God's voice in their conscience, they were somehow also inside, or related to the church. This more positive attitude toward persons of other religions was repeated and expanded by popes from the seventeenth century right up to the middle of the twentieth century. The basic message was: "The church is necessary for salvation, but..." Theologians tried to explain the "but." Especially during the first half of the past century, they devised all kinds of concepts by which they could include *within* the church any "holy pagan" *outside* the church. All Hindus or Buddhists or Muslims who followed their conscience and loved their neighbor belonged to the "soul" of the church; or, they were "attached," "linked," "related to" the church; or, they were "imperfect," "tendential," "potential" members of the church.[7] These were all sincere, and extremely imaginative, efforts to affirm God's love of everyone, but at the same time, to hold to the necessary role of the church. They were trying to balance the teeter-totter.

Whether or not the teeter-totter was really balanced or still weighted to one side can be argued back and forth. But one thing that is clear — and very important to point out in this review of history — is that all these efforts, from the sixteenth to the twentieth century, to come to a more positive attitude toward people outside the church never included a more positive attitude toward *their religions.* Throughout all this time, with very few exceptions,[8] theologians and church leaders and we can presume ordinary Catholics never imagined — or never dared to imagine — that God could make use of other religions to offer grace, revelation, and salvation. Even the Church Fathers, in recognizing that the

---

5. Francis A. Sullivan, *Salvation outside the Church? Tracing the History of the Catholic Response* (New York: Paulist Press, 1992), 199–204.

6. Denzinger-Schönmetzer, *Enchirideon,* 1524, 1542.

7. See Maurice Eminyan, *The Theology of Salvation* (Boston: St. Paul Editions, 1960), 167–81.

8. Among such exceptions were Nicholas of Cusa and perhaps Raymond Lull. See Jacques Dupuis, *Toward a Christian Theology of Religious Pluralism* (Maryknoll, N.Y.: Orbis Books, 1997), 105–9.

"Seed-Word" was scattered through history, never said that the religions could be the fertile fields for this Word. If the Word or Spirit of God was growing and touching people's lives beyond the boundaries of the church, it was happening privately, through some kind of personal or mystical experience. Because there was only one true Savior, there could be only one true religion. God could not make use of any other religion than Christianity. That was taken for granted. Until the 1960s.

A Theological Pioneer: Karl Rahner

That the Catholic community, during the second half of the past century, took a radical turn — some would say, made a giant leap forward — in its way of understanding and relating to persons of other faiths is crystallized in the writings of Karl Rahner, a German Jesuit. Rahner is arguably the most famous and influential Catholic theologian of the twentieth century[9] — a pioneer in exploring uncharted religious terrain. Though he spent most of his life in Germany, though he never studied other religions or talked much with other believers, his study of the Christian tradition, and his own deeply spiritual life, convinced him that God's world was much bigger than the Christian world. A large piece of Rahner's creative and prodigious writings was aimed at adding new lenses to the Christian telescope so that it could detect the active presence of God both deep within the being of every human and throughout the expanse of history. Around the beginning of the 1960s, he turned that telescope to the "non-Christian religions." What he saw few Christians had ever seen. In a lecture first given in 1961, he laid out a carefully crafted theological case in which he took standard Catholic doctrines and used them as building blocks for a truly revolutionary theology of religions.[10] What follows is a brief review of that case.

Nature Is Graced

The centerpiece of Rahner's revolutionary theology of religions is the same centerpiece of Christian life and belief that we have heard a lot about so far in these pages: *God is love.* But Rahner unpacked this belief and stretched its implications. To say that God is love in 1 John 3:8 means that God wants to reach out and embrace all people and beings. In other, more traditional, words, God really does want to save all people. But, Rahner reminds us, what God wants, God does. So if God really *wants* to save all people, God will *act,* will do whatever is necessary, to make this possible. If we don't recognize that, we really don't believe that God is love. But what does this "acting" or "doing" mean? It means, Rahner goes on, that God communicates or reveals God's self to every human being. God makes God's self present, and so enables every person to *feel* the

---

9. I admit bias on this statement: he was my teacher!
10. Later published as Karl Rahner, "Christianity and the Non-Christian Religions," in *Theological Investigations* (Baltimore: Helicon Press, 1966), 5:115–34.

reality — the peace, the affirmation, the tug, the lure — of God's presence. The catechism word for all this, a word that for many Christians has lost its edge, is *grace*. God gives saving grace to every single human being. Otherwise, God really doesn't love every single human being.

Unpacking further the meaning of God's love and trying to stir Christian minds and imaginations, Rahner draws a consequence: therefore, our human natures are not just "natural." If we could really feel what it's like to be a natural woman or man, we would feel something more than our human nature. We would feel our *graced nature*. We would feel the presence, the power, the warmth, and the peace of the Divine. With a theologian's penchant for heavy-duty language, Rahner tried to get at what he was talking about by calling it our "supernatural existential." Translation: our very existence is more than nature — it is "super-nature" — much, much more than what we think we are. Rahner used to say that there is no such thing as "just nature" (*natura pura*): by being human, we are more than human. More simply: to touch and feel what we really are is to touch, or be touched by, the Divine, the Spirit of God. One might even say that human nature is of a piece with divine nature.

Throughout his career, Rahner tried to describe the manifold ways in which "grace" or the Divine makes itself felt within our natures. Always, it announces itself as a deep feeling, vibrating within our most human activities, because, as Rahner stressed, "grace" is not like a suit that we put on to look like God's children; rather, it is like the electricity that lights up a light bulb to make it what it really is. Or, God's love does not just embrace us; it enters into us, fills us, and enables us to live and act differently. Grace *informs* us, Rahner said, something like the way the spirit informs the body.[11] Among the many particular examples that he gives of how we can feel this divine presence within us, the most basic is what he called, in German, the *Vorgriff*. Signifying something built into our human nature, it means, loosely, "reaching for more." In all that we reach out to, we are always reaching for more than what we try to, or do, grasp.

For Rahner, this is most evident in the way we know and love. The human being is a being that needs to know and to love/be loved. No matter how much we succeed in knowing, there always is a further question that leads to more answers, but also more questions. This is even more the case when it comes to love. Our need to be embraced by the love of another and to respond with a self-giving embrace of the other is tremendously satisfying — but never really *satisfied*. In the love we feel from, or give to, another (or others), we feel the tug of a greater Love. Actually, it is in loving and being loved by finite others that we love and are loved by the infinite Other. Truly, Rahner concludes, we are "finite beings capable of the Infinite." Within the mortal limits of who we are, we hear the voice of that which is beyond — and yet, already within — those limits. Indeed, our natures are graced.

Rahner's Catholic view of the human condition is quite different from the

---

11. Technically, he called this "quasi-formal causality."

view we encountered in the Protestant Evangelicals. He would consider it a balance, perhaps a correction, for their understanding of our "fallen nature" and "sinful condition." Yes, to deny or water down the reality of sin or selfishness or evil in our world is both blissfully and dangerously naive. But Rahner would remind his Protestant brothers and sisters of what St. Paul realized after wrestling with his own sinfulness and limitations: "Where sin increased, grace abounded all the more" (Rom. 5:20). That's precisely the "Good News." If we've fallen into a deep ditch, we've also been given the means to crawl out of it. If selfishness and greed are, as we hear so often, simply "part of human nature," the ability to love and care about others is even a deeper, more powerful and satisfying part of human nature. This is what Rahner intended when he declared himself an "optimist about salvation." By this he meant not only that the number of people outside of Christianity who truly find God are greater than the number who don't. More fundamentally, he was expressing his conviction that good and evil do not have a fifty-fifty chance. Good (or grace) is stronger than evil (or sin). Our potential to be "saved" is greater than our reality as "fallen." And we don't have to wait until heaven to realize this and live it. God's presence and God's offer of love and strength are givens, now, in our very human nature.

In insisting that people can truly experience God and find salvation outside of the boundaries of the church, Rahner was confirming a trend in Catholic theology since the Council of Trent. But he went well beyond that trend when he added the next piece of this theology of religions.

Religions Are "Ways of Salvation"

Rahner went on to make a claim that, for most Christians, was startling: God's grace is active in the religions. God was offering the gift of God's self in and through the other religious beliefs, practices, and rituals. The reason Rahner gave for such an audacious claim was, again, another key ingredient of Catholic experience and theology.

Catholic theology has always taken seriously what contemporary anthropology and psychology insist on — that human beings are *embodied* and *social* beings. Everything that we are and know and believe and commit ourselves to has to come to us through our bodies and through other people. Whatever is real is real because we have heard it, seen it, felt it, smelled it, touched it — with and from others. What we know or trust is not just injected into us through some kind of a spiritual transfusion. It first has to take some kind of physical, material form. If this is true of us as human beings, it is also true of us as religious beings. It has to be the way God or the Spirit will deal with us — through our bodies and through other people. Therefore, Rahner's conclusion — *grace must be embodied*. God's presence has to take some kind of material shape.[12]

---

12. The discussion and quotations in the following paragraphs are from Karl Rahner, *Foundations of Christian Faith* (New York: Crossroad, 1978), 178–203, 318.

This is where and how Rahner draws his stunning conclusion: among the many "bodies" that God's presence can assume in human history, we can expect that one of the foremost and most effective will be the religions of the world. After all, it is precisely in the religions that humans carry on their search for deeper meaning, their efforts to reach out through ritual and symbols and stories to that which is more. If we believe that God acts and breathes throughout human history, and if we believe that that breath has to take visible, material shape, then the religions are the first areas we should investigate for clues of that divine breath or Spirit. For anyone who would deny or doubt this, Rahner had a teasing Catholic question: Catholics insist on the necessity of the church precisely because they believe that God meets us in physical, social forms. They call such forms "sacraments," the church itself being the "primary sacrament." Well, a general truth for Catholics is a general truth for others. If Christians need sacraments, so do Buddhists and Hindus. They find these "sacraments" (in the broad sense of embodiment of God's grace) especially in their religions.

Rahner drew his conclusion in one crisp, powerful statement, which for many Catholics at the time was both startling and liberating: the religions therefore can be "ways of salvation." God is drawing people to God's self in and through the beliefs and practices of Hinduism, Buddhism, Islam, and indigenous religions. In Rahner's own careful, often complex words: the non-Christian religions can be "a positive means of gaining the right relationship to God and thus for the attaining of salvation, a means which is therefore *positively included in God's plan of salvation.*" "Positively" willed by God! Catholics had heard before that Buddhists can be saved through baptism of desire. Rahner was saying that they also have their own "baptism" within Buddhism. They are saved not *despite* their Buddhism, as had previously been said, but *because of* their Buddhism.

But we should say "can be saved." With this new theology, Rahner was not throwing a blanket seal of approval over all religions. His carefully constructed case establishes the possibility, not the *reality,* of the divine presence in other traditions. Whether the possibility is a reality has to be a further conclusion from the concrete study of, and dialogue with, persons of other faiths. Rahner was just opening a possibility — but one that never before was open for Christians.

And yet when one follows the tightly interlocking steps of Rahner's theological argument, he really is establishing not just the possibility but the *probability* that God is speaking other languages than "Christian." Such a probability is in no way weakened, Rahner added, by the undeniable reality of error and corruption in the other religions. If corruption were a gauge for how much God can make use of a religion, Christianity might receive an even lower ranking than many others. Here, individuals bear the responsibility of using their own intelligence and conscience to recognize and reject for themselves what is rotten or broken in their community. One never has to buy the whole religious package of truth *and* error in order to belong to a particular religion. That a religion gives growth to weeds does not mean that it cannot also produce wheat (Matt. 13:29–30).

Rahner used an analogy to invite Christians to a new way of approaching persons of other faiths. A Christian missionary, Rahner recommends, should not begin a conversation about the Divine with a Hindu in the same way a teacher takes up a discussion of Australia with a Bavarian first grader! The first grader has never heard of Australia; the teacher is starting from scratch. That's probably not the case with the Hindu, Rahner insists. God has been present to and making God's self known to the Hindu long before the missionary arrives. And the missionary should prepare herself to be surprised by what God has already been doing through Hinduism — surprises that may have a thing or two to teach the missionary. Rahner's theology of religions, therefore, calls for a different kind of relationship between Christianity and other religions than the one we encountered in the Replacement Model: it's not a matter of other religious persons having the questions for which Christians have the answers. There are questions and answers on both sides.

But would Rahner say that the answers on each side can balance out — that Christians may have as much to learn from Hindus as vice versa? To respond to that complex issue, we have to follow Rahner on the next step of his theology of religions.

Anonymous Christians

If grace, or God's loving presence, is part of our very human natures (step 1), and if this grace must always be embodied (step 2), Rahner adds another essential Christian belief (step 3) to his theology of religions that assures that this is a *Christian* theology: *all grace is Christ's grace.* With this final step in his case for God's presence in the broader religious world, Rahner provides both further depth but also new limits. The limits are required by what Christians have always said about Jesus and what Catholics have always said about the church.

If God's grace — that is God's loving presence — pervades our nature and history, it is because of Jesus Christ. This is certainly a motif we heard repeated throughout the previous part of this book. It's central to Christianity. Christians believe that Jesus is *the cause* of whatever "salvation" or healing Spirit there is in the universe. But Rahner explains how Jesus is the cause of salvation in a manner that both clarifies and offers further possibilities of interpretation. (We'll indicate such interpretations in the final chapter of this part.) He does so, again, using theological shop-talk which, translated, can be helpful. Jesus is not the *efficient cause* of salvation; he is, rather, its *final cause.* Efficient causes produce something that wasn't there to begin with. Final causes represent the goal of what is being produced and so make possible and guide the entire production. A carpenter is himself the efficient cause of the table he makes. The idea in the carpenter's head, representing the table's purpose and therefore how it should be constructed, is the final cause. Jesus, says Rahner, is not the efficient cause of God's saving love. Such love has always been there, a given part of God's very nature. But Jesus is the final cause of this love insofar as in him we see what God is up to, what God intends to bring about in giving the Divine Spirit to all people. Jesus' message about human society as God's reign of love, peace, and justice, as well as Jesus' very person showing what a child of God is really like, represent the intent and direction of every breath of God's Spirit that blows within humankind.

As the embodiment of the final goal, the real possibilities, of history, Jesus satisfies what Rahner felt was one of the deepest and most complicated needs of the human heart. Rahner's abstract theological language may not be the best for expressing what he's getting at, but it makes his point: humans need and are looking for an "absolute savior." Translated: in order to make a full commitment to living a Godlike life of love and justice, we need to know, clearly and surely, that God has committed God's self to us. Such assurance God has provided in Jesus. That's what "final cause" and "absolute savior" mean: Here, in this man, we have God's clearest and final Word that God is truly *with us* and is so irrevocably. Jesus is, therefore, our "absolute guarantee," "the greatest support and source of confidence" that it is possible and worthwhile to live a life like Jesus'. With him, we know where we're going. And we know we can get there, in this life and in the next.

All this makes for significant differences between the ways the Replacement Model and Rahner's Fulfillment Model understand the necessity of Jesus. Both affirm this necessity, but for the Evangelicals, it's the necessity of an efficient cause, which means that anyone who does not know Jesus cannot really know and experience God's embracing, saving love. For Rahner, it's the necessity of a final cause, which means that those who do not know Jesus can still experience the saving love of God, but they don't yet see clearly just where it's leading, what its true purpose and possibilities are. There are big differences between the two models — between being or not being saved.

From his understanding of Jesus as the reason why God pours out divine love over all creation in the first place, Rahner drew a further conclusion: therefore, any Buddhist or Hindu or Aboriginal Australian who experiences the grace of God's love in their religion is already connected with and oriented toward Jesus, because Jesus represents the ultimate goal of God's gift of love and grace. Further, since the continuing presence and power of Jesus are found in the community that carries on his message through history, those people who are "graced" in and through their own religions are also oriented toward the Christian church. They are, in a sense, already Christians and experience what Christians experience and are directed toward what Christians have in Jesus. But they don't realize it yet. They're Christians without the name of Christian. They are *anonymous Christians*.

We must immediately remind ourselves that Rahner proposed this vision of anonymous Christians only for his fellow Christians. He did not write for Buddhists and Hindus. His purpose was to liberate Christians from their negative views of those outside the church and to enable them to realize that God is much greater than they are. God can be forming followers of Christ wherever and whenever God wants. Rahner did not want Christians to go out and tell their Buddhist or Muslim friends that they were already on the Christian side.

Limits for the Church and for the Religions

Such an understanding of just how God saves through Jesus makes for new insights, as well as new limits, for both the Christian religion/church and other religions. For the church and its mission, Rahner painted a picture that could both frighten and inspire his fellow Christians: the church was no longer to consider itself an island of salvation and truth in the midst of a sea of perdition and error. Missionaries no longer go forth to rescue people from the clutches of the devil. Rather, in Rahner's language, the church should consider itself "the historically tangible *vanguard* and the historically and socially constituted explicit expression of what the Christian hopes is present as a hidden reality even outside the visible Church."[13] Another and perhaps better word for what he meant is *sacrament*. The church embodies and brings to clearer, living color what is already there. This means that the purpose of the church is not to rescue people and put them on totally new roads (although sometimes that will be necessary); rather it is to burn away the fog and enable people to see more clearly and move more securely.

But won't such a picture of the church and its purpose also burn away missionary zeal? That's a question and objection that Rahner soon had to face. Pagans don't need to be saved any longer. They're probably not even "pagans"! Why then should missionaries "go forth" any more? For reasons, Rahner responded, that are still motivating, but also more mature. In sharing their Good News, Christians work *with* people, not just *for* them, in order to help them become more fully aware of, and thus more committed to, what they really are: children of God, called to live in their own lives the love and justice seen in Jesus. In his earlier writings, Rahner thought that becoming a Christian made things easier, offering "a still greater chance for salvation." Later, he stated that it actually makes things more demanding. In becoming a follower of Jesus one assumes a "greater responsibility" for others rather than a greater advantage for oneself.[14]

But if Rahner's theology of religions set limits for the church, it did likewise for the religions. In the end, no matter how fruitful the work of the Spirit might be in other religious traditions, no matter how many genuinely holy people are found within them — persons walking along other religious paths do not really know where they are going; they don't really know who they are. This is because for Rahner, as for the Evangelicals, there is an *only* in his theology: only Jesus Christ is the final cause of salvation. Only here has God shown what God is

---

13. Rahner, "Christianity and the Non-Christian Religions," 133.
14. Karl Rahner, *Schriften zur Theologie* (Einsiedeln: Benziger, 1970), 9:513–14.

truly up to. Only here has God marked the goal of creation. Only here has God provided an "absolute savior."

Therefore, other religions, with all their possible truth and goodness, are to serve, as it were, the role of John the Baptist: to prepare the way, to make people ready to take the last step and join the Christian community, and thus, finally, to realize the meaning of the riches they had already been given. Rahner even placed a certain time-limit on this process. Once these other religions truly encounter Christianity, once the Gospel is really announced to them (but Rahner admitted that so much of the announcing is still so European that people in other cultures can't hear it), then the religions, like John the Baptist, have to step aside and make way for Jesus the Christ. Before Jesus, all other religions lose their previous validity — or better, they *fulfill* it.

As we will see, Rahner's trail-blazing new ideas have provided the master plan for the efforts of contemporary Catholic theologians to develop a new theology of religions. More significantly, his revolutionary approach to other believers was taken up and, for the most part, officially affirmed by what might be called the past century's broader revolution in the Roman Catholic Church: the Second Vatican Council.

Vatican II: A Milestone

If Rahner was the first to explore the path toward a new Christian theology of religions, the Second Vatican Council (1962–64) set out on it. The council stands as a milestone in the history of what the Christian church has said about other faiths and about itself in relation to them. Never before had a church, in its official pronouncements, dealt so extensively with other religions; never before had it said such positive things about them; never before had it called upon all Christians to take these religions seriously and dialogue with them. Compared to the "Outside the church, no salvation" view that held sway from the fifth to the sixteenth centuries, Vatican II is not just a milestone, but a fork in the road. Rahner himself later remarked that many of the bishops of the council didn't fully realize how new and demanding this direction was.[15] If they had, they might have moved more slowly.

"Precious Things Both Religious and Human"

What the council had to say about other religious believers is contained mainly and most boldly in its Declaration on the Relationship of the Church to Non-Christian Religions (*Nostra Aetate* [*NA*]). Though the document was to be a historic "milestone," it was also a providential afterthought. Originally, the bishops intended only to produce a statement on the Jews that would help confront and correct the way Christian attitudes had fostered anti-Semitism; a new

---

15. *Schriften zur Theologie* (Einsiedeln: Benziger, 1967), 8:357.

theological perspective on Judaism was needed. But when other bishops, representing areas where Christians lived their lives alongside other religions, saw such doors opening, they also wanted to open them to religions beyond Judaism. Thus, what was first intended as an appendage to the council's Decree on Ecumenism turned out to be a "declaration" on its own.

The declaration's statements about religious people outside the church are set against the backdrop of the council's re-endorsement of what had been taught since the Council of Trent: that God's love and saving presence can't be locked within the walls of the church. (In fact, Vatican II went even further and explicitly taught that even avowed atheists who follow their conscience are really, though unknowingly, following the voice of God and so are "saved" [Dogmatic Constitution on the Church (*Lumen Gentium* [*LG*])] 16.) For the first time in church history, the Declaration on Religions offers specific descriptions of just how each of the major historical religions seeks to respond to "those profound mysteries of the human condition." It summarizes briefly the basic beliefs and practices of Hinduism, Buddhism, and Islam and makes positive reference to "other [primal] religions to be found everywhere." The declaration expressly recognizes and applauds the "profound religious sense" animating all these traditions. It affirms that their teachings and practices represent what is "true and holy" and "reflect a ray of the Truth that enlightens all people." And then the declaration goes on to deliver an "exhortation" to all Catholics that they had never received from their pastors before: "prudently and lovingly" to "dialogue and collaborate" with other believers and so "in witness of Christian faith and life, to acknowledge, preserve, and promote the spiritual and moral goods found among these people" (see *NA* 2).

The Declaration on Religions is not the only council document with good things — which are new things — to say about other religions. The Decree on the Church's Missionary Activity (*Ad Gentes* [*AG*]) lifts a phrase directly from Rahner's 1962 essay when it recognizes in the religions "elements of truth and grace" (*AG* 9). It also applies the ancient and rich expression of the Church Fathers in affirming that in the religions one can find "seeds of the Word," the same Word embodied in Jesus (*AG* 11, 15). These seeds of the Word give rise to genuine "seeds of contemplation" (*AG* 18), a "sort of secret presence of God" (*AG* 9). Indeed, in the religions there are "precious things, both religious and human" (Pastoral Constitution on the Church in the Modern World [*Gaudium et Spes* (*GS*)] 92). One can imagine that for a Pope Boniface VIII or the Council of Florence, such language would have sounded very strange, if not down right heretical.

Are "Rays of Truth" "Ways of Salvation"?

As is evident, what Vatican II has to say about other religions resonates with Rahner's new theology — with two significant exceptions. To the satisfaction of many, the council did not take up Rahner's notion of other believers as "anonymous Christians." It was too controversial among Christians, too uncomfortable for non-Christians. But to the disappointment of others, the council did not follow Rahner in expressly concluding that the religions are to be viewed as possible, or probable, "ways of salvation" — instruments by which God draws people to God's self. This is a key ingredient in Rahner's new vision of the religions. Why didn't the council endorse it? That question provides the tinder and sparks for a rather heated debate among Catholic theologians.

Some theologians say the bishops didn't go as far as Rahner because they realized it would have jeopardized the value of what God has done in Jesus. According to these interpreters, Vatican II really is closer to the Protestant perspective we studied earlier: there is genuine revelation in other traditions — "rays of Truth"; but they're just that — "rays," not enough to enable the full sunlight of God's saving grace to be felt.[16] So, revelation through the religions, yes; salvation, no. Other theologians hold that the Council Fathers did agree with Rahner, but implicitly. After all, they say, to affirm that there is "truth," "holiness," "grace," and a "secret presence of God" available in other religions implies that people are being touched by, and so can respond to, the reality of the Divine. That means they feel the presence of God. Isn't that what "being saved" is all about? Also, the council did affirm the thoroughly Catholic conviction that grace, or God's self-offering, must be socially embodied: "The universal design of God for the salvation of the human race is not carried out exclusively in the soul of people with a kind of secrecy" (*AG* 3). If it is not just secretly in their soul, then it is socially in their religions, these theologians conclude.

For Bishop Piero Rossano, who for years worked in the Vatican's Secretariat for Non-Christian Religions, "Vatican II is explicit on this point" — salvation does "reach or may reach the hearts of men and women through the visible, experiential signs of the various religions."[17] For the always cautious Karl Rahner, however, the jury was still out: "The essential problem for the theologian has been left open [by Vatican II]. . . . [T]he theological quality of non-Christian religions remains undefined."[18] The bishops, in other words, neither affirmed nor denied that the religions might be the actual conduits by which the Spirit flows into the lives of peoples beyond the church. And perhaps the reason they didn't decide this question is that they deliberately chose not to. Vatican II, from the very start, was defined by Pope John XXIII as a pastoral, not a doctrinal, council. That means it wanted to speak to the people, not to the theologians. Regarding the other religions, its intentions were "to foster between them and Christianity new attitudes of mutual understanding, esteem, dialogue, and co-

---

16. A recent case arguing that Vatican II refused to call the religions ways of salvation is made by Gavin D'Costa, *The Meeting of Religions and the Trinity* (Maryknoll, N.Y.: Orbis Books, 2000), 101–9.

17. Piero Rossano, "Christ's Lordship and Religious Pluralism in Roman Catholic Perspective," in *Christ's Lordship and Religious Pluralism*, ed. Gerald H. Anderson and Thomas F. Stransky (Maryknoll, N.Y.: Orbis Books, 1981), 102–3.

18. Karl Rahner, "On the Importance of the Non-Christian Religions for Salvation," in *Theological Investigations* (London: Darton, Longman, and Todd, 1984), 18:290.

operation."[19] Trying to pass judgment on controversial theological issues could well get in the way of this pastoral, personal agenda.

"Preparation for the Gospel"

But there was a further point that the council did make clear, and, in doing so, it echoed Rahner's final ingredient in his theology of religions. In the words of the Dogmatic Constitution on the Church (*Lumen Gentium*): "Whatever goodness or truth is found among them [the religions], it is considered by the Church as *a preparation for the Gospel*" (*LG* 16). Once again, we have a swing in the teeter-totter of Catholic attitudes toward other religions. Having lifted up the truth and grace and beauty of other religions, Vatican II, in order to remain faithful to its own identity and experience, now must lift up the uniqueness of what God has done in Jesus, and continues to do in the church. Because it is only Jesus "in whom people find the fullness of religious life and in whom God has reconciled all things to Himself (2 Cor. 5:18–19)" (*NA* 2), the religions can find their fullness only in Christ. And for Catholics, that means the church. And so, besides singing the praises of other religions as never before, the bishops of Vatican II also could repeat the old Christian refrain that "the church is necessary for salvation." Evidently, they mean "for the *fullness* of salvation": for "it is through Christ's Catholic Church alone, which is the all-embracing means of salvation, that the fullness of the means of salvation can be found" (*LG* 14; *UR* [*Unitatis Redintegratio* = Decree on Ecumenism] 3). So the bishops see all the goodness and truth within other religions as something like a compass needle that naturally points north: because the Spirit of God is present in these other communities, they are "oriented toward" (*LG* 16) their fulfillment in Christ and the church.

What, then, is the real purpose of dialogue with other believers? Although Christians will undoubtedly learn much from their interreligious dialogues, the ultimate outcome of the conversations is to bring other believers to their completion and true identity in the church. The council's decree on missionary activity tries to balance both ingredients of dialogue: "[T]hrough sincere and patient dialogue they [Christians] will learn what treasures the bountiful God has distributed among the nations. At the same time they should strive to illumine those riches with the light of the Gospel, to liberate them and bring them under the dominion of God the Savior" (*AG* 10).

Vatican II, therefore, does stand as a milestone in Christian attitudes toward other faiths. But it wants to be a "faithful" milestone. While it certainly pointed in directions never before explored by Christians, it also wanted to make sure that those directions did not lead away from the heart of the Gospel and the special place of Jesus Christ in expressing God's love for all.

---

19. Dupuis, *Toward a Christian Theology,* 158, see also 169–70.

After the council, the Catholic community — laity, theologians, and pastors — were to continue that exploration and expand even further Vatican II's vision of other religions.

Further Readings

Beinert, Wolfgang. "Who Can Be Saved?" *Theology Digest* 38 (1991): 223–28, 303–8.

D'Costa, Gavin. "Karl Rahner's Anonymous Christian: A Reappraisal." *Modern Theology* 1 (1985): 131–48.

Dupuis, Jacques. *Toward a Christian Theology of Religious Pluralism.* Maryknoll, N.Y.: Orbis Books, 1997, 84–129 for historical overview of Christian attitudes toward other religions; 130–70 for the context and teaching of Vatican II.

Fitzgerald, Michael. "Other Religions in the Catechism of the Catholic Church." *Pro Dialogo* (Vatican) 85–86 (1994): 165–77.

International Theological Commission (Vatican). "Christianity and World Religions." *Origins* 14 (1997): 150–66.

Lamadrid, Lucas. "Anonymous or Analogous Christians? Rahner and von Balthasar on Naming the Non-Christian." *Modern Theology* 11 (1995): 363–84.

Nostra Aetate (Declaration on the Relationship of the Church to Non-Christian Religions). In *The Documents of Vatican II.* Ed. Walter M. Abbott. Piscataway, N.J.: America Press, 1966.

Pawlikowski, John. "Vatican II's Theological About-face on the Jews: Not Yet Fully Recognized." *The Ecumenist* 37 (2000): 4–6.

Pontifical Council for Interreligious Dialogue. "The Attitude of the Church toward the Followers of Other Religions." *Bulletin Pro Dialogo* 19 (1984): 126–45.

Rahner, Karl. "Christianity and the Non-Christian Religions." In *Theological Investigations.* Baltimore: Helicon Press, 1966, 5:115–34.

———. "Jesus Christ in Non-Christian Religions." In *Theological Foundations: An Introduction to the Idea of Christianity.* New York: Crossroad, 1978, 311–21.

Ruokanen, Miikka. "Catholic Teaching on Non-Christian Religions at the Second Vatican Council." *International Bulletin of Missionary Research* 14 (1990): 56–61.

Schmalz, Mathew N. "Transcendental Reduction: Karl Rahner's Theory of Anonymous Christianity." *Vidyajyoti* 59 (1995): 741–52.

Stinnett, Timothy R. "Lonergan on Religious Pluralism." *The Thomist* 56 (1992): 97–116.

Sullivan, Francis A. *Salvation outside the Church? Tracing the History of the Catholic Response.* New York: Paulist Press, 1992, 3–43, 141–81.

Wong, Joseph H. "Anonymous Christians: Karl Rahner's Pneuma-Christocentrism and an East-West Dialogue." *Theological Studies* 55 (1994): 609–37.

Chapter 5

Greater Openness and Dialogue

It's often said that if anything changes in religion, it comes from the bottom, from the grassroots, not from the top, from church leaders and bureaucrats. In the case of the further growth in Catholic attitudes toward other religions after Vatican II, that's not entirely true. Certainly the council opened Catholics' minds, then hearts, to other believers and so churned up waves of interreligious dialogue on the local level. But further stimulus, and new ideas, were also churning in the minds and public statements of the pastors in the central offices of the Catholic Church in Rome. One of the main generators of repeated calls to dialogue was the Vatican Secretariat for Non-Christian Religions, established already in 1964 by Pope Paul VI in order to take the council's new attitude toward other religions seriously. As a result of pursuing that vision and experiencing what happens when one actually gets to know and talk with persons of other faiths, the secretariat eventually realized it needed a name change. In 1989, the secretariat became the Vatican Commission for Interreligious Dialogue. The negatively defined "Non-Christians" became Hindu, Buddhist, and Muslim dialogue partners.

But perhaps the strongest and most persistent "top-down" call for greater openness to other faiths since Vatican II has come from the pope who was in office for most of those years, John Paul II. Although Pope Paul VI had been called "the pope of dialogue," it seems that he never moved beyond the conviction that "there is only one true religion, the Christian religion," and that only in the Christian church can one realize "an authentic and living relationship with God."[1] John Paul II went beyond this. This is evident, as we shall see, both in what he had to say, but more so in what he has done. He has continually reached out to persons of other faiths, from his bold gathering of different religions in Assisi to pray together for peace in 1986, to the journey he made toward the end of his papacy when he traveled, ailing and feeble, to Palestine/Israel to foster greater communication with and between Muslims and Jews, and to ask forgiveness for Catholic sins of the past.

Perhaps the primary source of energy for the pope's journey of dialogue has been his understanding, and experience, of the Holy Spirit. Some have called this focus on the Spirit John Paul II's "singular contribution" to the growing

---

1. See *Ecclesiam Suam*, in *Acta Apostolicae Sedis* 56 (1964): 655; and *Evangelii Nuntiandi* 53.

body of Catholic theology of religions.[2] For John Paul, the fundamental reason why there are such spiritual treasures in the religions of the world, why beneath the surface of their vast differences there is an undercurrent of unity, why dialogue among these religious families is so necessary and so promising is the reality of the one Spirit alive and active, before Christ and after him, within the religious searchings and findings of humankind. This Spirit, the pope reminds his fellow Christians, is full of surprises, for s/he "blows where [s/he] will" (John 3:8).[3] There are many religions, but there is one Spirit seeking to bear fruit in them all.

Three Steps Forward

If we try to sift through what the Vatican, in its public statements, under the leadership of John Paul II, has been saying about other religions over the past decades, three themes stand out. All of them represent genuine steps forward along the path that Vatican II opened.

1. *The religions can be considered "ways of salvation."* Here the Vatican has dislodged the theological log-jam resulting from controversy about whether Vatican II did or did not view other religions as genuine conduits of grace. The pope himself began the process in his encyclical on missionary work, *Redemptoris Missio* (The Mission of the Redeemer [*RM*]), when he talked about the Holy Spirit indwelling "the very structure" of the human condition, and then added that this divine Breath is to be found "not only in individuals but also in society, and history, peoples, cultures, and religions" (*RM* 28). This saving Spirit also indwells the religions. Furthermore, the pope in this same encyclical uses technical language to state that God can reach out to draw people to God's self through "participated forms of mediation of different kinds and degrees" (*RM* 5). These "forms of mediation" participate in Christ's central mediatory role, but they are *other than* Christ's role. Evidently, they will be found in the religions.

But even if for some it is not so "evident" that the pope is affirming other religious traditions as carriers of saving grace, another Vatican statement, issued right after this encyclical, removed the ambiguity. In *Dialogue and Proclamation* (*DP*), issued jointly by the Commission on Interreligious Dialogue and the Congregation for the Evangelization of Peoples in 1991, spokespersons for the Catholic Church talked about other faiths as never before. They explicitly recognized "the active presence of God through His Word" and "the universal presence of the Spirit" not only in persons outside the church but also in their religions. Therefore, it is "in the sincere practice of what is good in their own religious traditions... that the members of other religions correspond positively to God's invitation and receive salvation." Even more unambiguously,

---

2. Jacques Dupuis, *Toward a Christian Theology of Religious Pluralism* (Maryknoll, N.Y.: Orbis Books, 1997), 173.

3. *Redemptoris Hominis* (1979) 11; see also John Paul II's encyclical on the Holy Spirit, *Dominum et Vivificantem* (1986).

DP concludes that the religions of the world play "a providential role in the divine economy of salvation" (*DP* 29, 17). "Correspond positively... divine economy..." — this is theological language for saying that *in and through* other religions, people truly can find and connect with God. Making such forward steps even more resolutely, the official Vatican International Theological Commission issued a statement on the religions in 1996 in which this distinguished body clearly affirmed that other traditions have a "saving function" and therefore can be "a *means* [the original Italian is *mezzo*] which helps for the salvation of their adherents."[4]

In this step, the church teaches that other religions can be bearers not just of "truth and goodness" but of the saving presence of the Spirit.

2. *The church must be dialogical.* The first theme, that other religions are truly ways of salvation, is very important but is more a matter of theological clarification. This second theme touches the way Christians go about trying to be Christian. The leaders of the Catholic Church have, in effect, been telling their fellow members that on the list of a Christian's job description is a new item: dialogue with persons of other faiths. To be a Christian requires seeking conversation with people who are different. The Catholic Church, in order to be catholic, must be a dialogical church.

We already heard this call to dialogue in Vatican II. But that was an "exhortation" — something one might do after taking care of the essentials. In recent statements, especially the two already referred to — *Redemptoris Missio* and *Dialogue and Proclamation* — dialogue moves from the periphery to the center. This move is embodied in the two words "dialogue" and "proclamation." Both of these activities, Catholics are now told, are intrinsic elements in carrying out "the mission of the church." The word "mission" stands for "purpose" — why the Christian religion actually exists, what it's supposed to be doing in the world. That mission is described as two activities that are really one: Christians are to let people hear the Good News of God and by doing so "transform humanity from within, making it new" (*DP* 8). (Notice, the real purpose of the church is not to take the Good News and go inward, in warm protected communities, but to take it and reach outward, to change the world; if Christians gather inward in their churches, it's only to be able to move outward into the world.)

Now, what these recent documents are saying is that in order to carry out this mission and achieve this purpose, Christians must not only proclaim — they must also dialogue.[5] And this is something genuinely new. Both proclamation and dialogue are "component elements and authentic forms" of the one mission of the church (*DP* 2; *RM* 55). "There can be no question of choosing one and

---

4. International Theological Commission, "Christianity and the World Religions" (1997), 84, 87, in *Origins: CNS Documentary Series*, August 14, 1997.

5. Though we are concentrating on the more extensive statement of *DP*, this inclusion of dialogue into the essential mission of the church was first proclaimed in the 1984 declaration of the then Vatican Secretariat for Non-Christian Religions, "The Attitude of the Church toward the Followers of Other Religions."

ignoring or rejecting the other" (*DP* 6). "They are intimately related, but not interchangeable" (*DP* 77). To make sure that Catholics get this new point, they are reminded that proclamation is "only one aspect" of the church's mission (*DP* 8). If Christians, in other words, only talk and never listen, they're not very good Christians.

This new message becomes all the more challenging when we take a closer look at what the pope and the Vatican congregations mean by dialogue. Dialogue is not just a matter of casual conversation; nor is it to be a sly means of softening up the audience in order to convert them. Rather:

- Dialogue is "a method and means of mutual knowledge and *enrichment*" (*RM* 55, *DP* 9; emphasis added). Notice, the pope says *mutual* enrichment. Both sides have something to learn and gain.

- In the dialogue, both sides must be ready to be "questioned," "purified," thoroughly "challenged" (*DP* 32, 49; *RM* 56). In other words, to be shaken up. Dialogue is not chit-chat.

- Having been challenged and questioned, Christians engaged in dialogue with other believers must also be prepared to be changed and ready "to allow oneself to be transformed by the encounter" (*DP* 47).

- *Dialogue and Proclamation* goes an amazing step further: the change or transformation can actually lead to *conversion*. Christians must be ready for that. But what kind of conversion? Yes, "a deeper conversion of all toward God." But even more: "In the process of conversion, the decision may be made to leave one's previous spiritual or religious situation in order to direct oneself toward another" (*DP* 41). They're talking here about the possibility not only of a Buddhist becoming a Christian but of a Christian becoming a Buddhist.

This is dialogue in the fullest sense of the term: an encounter in which all sides speak boldly but also, just as much, *listen boldly* (here Christians might need some practice).

3. *The church is in service of God's Reign.* The third advance in Catholic approaches to other religions that has been made by the Vatican is more indirect. It has to do with the role of the church in God's dealings with humankind. We've already heard how that role is understood. Even after official Catholic teaching admitted that there is salvation outside the church, it continues to speak of the church as "necessary" for salvation. This is due, in large part, to the way Catholic teaching has *identified* the church with the Reign of God. The "Reign" or "Kingdom" of God, Scripture scholars tell us, is the master-symbol, or the heart, of Jesus' own understanding of his mission and message. It represents the historical process of transforming this world and bringing it, inch by inch, closer to Jesus' vision of how people will live with each other and construct their societies when they really take God's message seriously. Wherever people truly love God by loving their neighbors as themselves, there the Reign of God is taking

shape. And up until the second half of the past century, Catholic theology had taught that this takes place only in the church; it identified Reign and church. And by "church" it generally meant the "Roman Catholic" one. (Not until Vatican II did the Catholic Church recognize clearly that Protestant churches were really Christian, that is, authentic churches.)

In Vatican II, things began to change. In many of the conciliar documents, the bishops recognized that the Reign of God and the church have to be distinguished; they cannot simply be identified. This admission goes beyond saying that "grace" operates outside the walls of the church. I think it is not too much to say that the church teaches that the goals and purpose of Jesus himself — the specific mission given to him by God — are realized also in and through other religions.

But these recent developments in official Catholic teaching go even further. Not only do they recognize that the Reign of God is larger than the church; they also acknowledge that this Reign is *more important* than the church. Or expressed more positively, the church of Jesus is meant to be a servant of the Reign that Jesus proclaimed and himself served. "The church is effectively and concretely at the service of the kingdom" (*RM* 20). The church's mission is "to foster the 'Kingdom of our Lord and his Christ' at whose service she is placed" (*DP* 35, also 59). So, the pope tells us, "the church is not an end unto herself, since she is ordered toward the kingdom of God of which she is seed, sign, and instrument" (*RM* 18). This would all imply that the first and foremost purpose of the church is to promote God's Reign, not itself. As the pope says, the church is a "sign" of — a pointer toward, a sacrament for — the Reign of God. But the Reign itself is larger. And it is taking form in other places, finding other signs as well.

A Necessary Balance

If we place these recent developments in official Catholic theology of religions on our symbolic balance between "the universal" and "the particular," the universal side of God's love rises higher than ever before in Christian history. It can be said that no other Christian church has so clearly and so officially affirmed the positive value of other religions and the need to dialogue with them. But Catholic theology does not leave it there. It balances this assessment of the value of religions and dialogue with what Christians have experienced and believe God to have done in Jesus of Nazareth. Not to do this would be to lose the core of Christian identity. What God is doing in the religions has to be seen in relation to what God did and is doing in Jesus. The attempt to achieve this necessary balance is characteristic of the official Catholic pronouncements we have been reviewing. Again, we can note three ingredients.

1. *Jesus is the only Savior of all humanity.* Whether a proper balance will be achieved depends, primarily, on a proper understanding of Jesus and his role. The pope and Vatican congregations echo what we already heard from Karl

Rahner and what they feel has been the living faith of Christians through the centuries:

- If God's saving love fills the universe, its pipeline is Jesus, only Jesus. In the pope's words: "Christ is the *one* savior of all, the *only* one able to reveal God and lead to God.... [S]alvation can come *only* from Jesus Christ.... In him and *only* in him, are we set free from alienation and doubt" (*RM* 6; emphasis added).

- Jesus, therefore, is both "history's center and goal" (*RM* 6; *DP* 22, 28) (sounds like Rahner's notion of "final cause") and he who "reconciles" or repairs the "rupture in the relationship between Creator and his creation ... after original sin" (echoes of efficient cause).[6]

- Given this role, Jesus contains the *fullness* of what God wants to make known to humanity. "Jesus revealed *completely* the Father and his plan of salvation.... He also *fully* reveals man to himself.... [He is] the *definitive* manifestation of the mystery of the Father's love for all."[7]

- Therefore, if the pope could talk, as we saw, about other "mediations" or vehicles of God's love and grace, these others "acquire meaning and value *only* from Christ's own mediation and they cannot be understood as parallel or complementary to his" (*RM* 5; emphasis added). As the "one mediator," Jesus must be "clearly distinguished from the founders of other great religions."[8]

2. *Dialogue must have limits.* The amazingly open dialogue to which Catholics are obliged also has to make room for this unique role of Jesus. That means that although the Vatican may have shaken up many a missionary by announcing that both proclaiming and dialoguing are essential components of the missionary's job, in the end, the proclaiming component holds a "permanent priority" over dialogue, for it makes up "the missionary activity proper" (*RM* 44, 34). So although proclamation and dialogue are both necessary, they are "not on the same level," for dialogue must always "remain oriented toward proclamation" (*DP* 77, 75). Even more clearly: "Dialogue should be conducted and implemented with the conviction that the Church is the ordinary means of salvation and that she alone possesses the fullness of the means of salvation" (*RM* 55; also *DP* 19, 22, 58). With such a conviction, the dialogue that Christians carry on with other believers remains not only "oriented toward proclamation" but oriented toward *conversion.* Although, as we heard, Vatican statements recognize that conversion can be a two-way street, John Paul II also makes clear that the conversion sought after by Christians is one that will result in the formation of new Christian communities; and that means a conversion that leads to baptism.

---

6. From the pope's November 1999 apostolic exhortation *Ecclesia in Asia* 11.
7. Ibid., 13–14; emphasis added.
8. Ibid., 2.

This, the pope states clearly, "is a central and determining goal of missionary activity" (*RM* 47–49).

3. *The Reign of God and the church are distinguishable but not separable.* In *Redemptoris Missio*, the pope expressly warns that if Christians stress the new distinction between the Kingdom of God and the church too much and make their understanding of dialogue and mission too "kingdom-centered," they run the risk of losing hold of the central meaning and role of the church. So the pope balances his recognition that the Reign of God is larger and more important than the church with the reminder that, in this case, what is *distinguished* should not be *separated.* "The Kingdom cannot be detached either from the Christ or from the Church" (*RM* 18). "The Kingdom is inseparable from the Church, because both are inseparable from the person and work of Jesus himself" (*DP* 34). Therefore, while the church is always the servant of the Kingdom, its servant role is both *necessary* for that Kingdom to really take shape in the world and *unique* among all the other possible servants of the Kingdom. Without the church, as without Jesus, our hopes for really changing this world into God's Reign of love and justice would be without foundation and nourishment. Yes, the Reign of God is taking shape beyond the borders of the church, but out there it is "an inchoate reality, which needs to find completion through being related to the Kingdom of Christ already present in the Church" (*DP* 35).

That last sentence explains clearly why we are calling this Catholic view of other religions the Fulfillment Model. Karl Rahner, Vatican II, and Pope John Paul II all made unexpected, some would say revolutionary, breakthroughs toward a more positive, a more dialogical, relationship of Christians with other believers. They all recognized the reality and richness of the Spirit in these religions. But because they believe that God has also done something extraordinary and special in Jesus the Christ, they want to *add to* — not deny or subtract from — the richness of other traditions. This addition will be a *fulfillment:* "Christ is thus the fulfillment of the yearning of all the world's religions and, as such, he is their sole and definitive completion" (*RM* 6).

Recently, a number of Catholic theologians have been attempting to move through the openings made by Rahner and the Vatican in order to extend even further Christianity's outreach to other religions. These theologians, in general, try to avoid the language of fulfillment and prefer that of dialogue or witness or relationship. In what follows we will review some of their efforts.

Expanding the Dialogue

Many of the present-day attempts to stretch Catholic outreach to others even further, without breaking lifelines with past tradition, are marked by a "turn to the Spirit." This is seen especially in two of the most prominent voices in the Catholic discussion: Gavin D'Costa and Jacques Dupuis, S.J.[9] Both of them

---

9. Other Catholic theologians for whom the Spirit is key to their approaches to other religions are Michael Barnes, *Christian Identity and Religious Pluralism* (Nashville: Abingdon, 1989), 135–

want to follow the lead of John Paul II and try to show that with the Spirit as their starting point and center, Christians can be both more open to others and more faithful to the Gospel.

A Turn to the Spirit: Gavin D'Costa

Born of Indian parents, raised in Kenya, educated and presently teaching in England, Gavin D'Costa brings a multicultured sensitivity to his work as a theologian. As he focuses that work on other religions, two concerns seem to animate and guide him: to show the dangerous excesses of the so-called pluralist Christians (who seem to advocate the equality of religions) and to draw on the rich, dialogical potential of traditional Christian belief. The pluralists, D'Costa maintains, end up mistreating both Christianity and other religions. In their efforts to affirm all religions, they level all religions — that is, they miss their real differences in general, and the real difference of Christianity in particular. (We'll be hearing more of such criticisms in Part III on the Mutuality Model.) Pluralists, he says, forget what is a fact of interreligious, multicultural life: we can never crawl out of our own cultural, religious skin. We always view "the other" from our own given perspective. Or, to stretch the image we've been using, even when a Christian tries to look through a Hindu's telescope, what she sees is still colored by what she's used to seeing with her own Christian telescope. (This insistence on the cultural-conditioning of all knowledge is the launching pad for the Acceptance Model that we will be examining in Part IV.)

D'Costa wants to make a virtue out of necessity. If we're always viewing other traditions through our Christian telescope, he wants to refocus that telescope so we can see more. More precisely, he wants to give it a Trinitarian focus. Christians, he reminds us, are not monotheists in exactly the same way Jews or Muslims are, for they believe in a God who is Trinitarian — threefold. In Christian experience, the Divine relates to the world in really different ways — so different that we must conclude that there are differences within the Divine itself! Different symbols for these differing relationships have been used:

- Parent (or Father) to express the Divine as creative, the source of all.

- The Word or Child (or Son) to indicate the Divine as reaching outward to communicate God's truth and restoring power, especially and particularly in Jesus of Nazareth, the incarnate Word and Son of God.

- The Spirit, who is the very life breath of God, carrying on the message of God's Child-Jesus but pervading all of creation with God's life-giving energy.

59; Joseph DiNoia, "Christian Universalism: The Nonexclusive Particularity of Salvation in Christ," in *Either/Or: The Gospel or Neopaganism,* ed. Carl E. Braaten and Robert W. Jenson (Grand Rapids, Mich.: Eerdmans, 1993), 37–48.

D'Costa suggests that this third way of relating within God — the Spirit — should, so to speak, be the lens in the telescope that Christians use to look at, and dialogue with, other religions. Viewing others from the perspective of the Spirit, Christians know that the reality of the Divine cannot be contained only in the activity of the Creator-Parent or of the Savior-Word, but that the Divine is also Spirit infusing other religions.[10]

So their particular belief in the Holy Spirit leads Christians to affirm the universality of God in all cultures and religions. And D'Costa warns Christians that to believe in the Spirit means that they should be ready for surprises and challenges. They cannot know in advance just what "fruits of the Spirit" they will find growing on the religious trees of other cultures. Because of their beliefs in the Spirit, Christians are predisposed to find God's truth in other religions, but they cannot predetermine what that truth will be.

But the predisposition is also an obligation. Believing in the presence of the Spirit in other traditions, Christians not only will admire these traditions but will also have to listen to and learn from them. Here D'Costa injects greater vigor into the message we heard from the Vatican — that the Christian church must be a dialogical church. He is even more pointed: without listening to other religions, the church can't really be church. "The church stands under the judgment of the Holy Spirit, and if the Holy Spirit is active in the world religions, then the world religions are vital to Christian faithfulness.... Without listening to this testimony [of the Spirit in other religions], Christians cease to be faithful to their own calling as Christians, in being inattentive to God."[11] It's like saying to a married couple: in order to be faithful to each other, you need to make friends with others. This need that Christians have of other religions is not just so that they can marvel at what the Spirit is doing in other religious backyards. D'Costa points out that the other religions are necessary for helping Christians clean up their own yards — to keep them from "ideologies" (using religion for one's own gain) and "distortions" (bending religion into a tool to take advantage of others).

In a Spirit-based approach to other religions, D'Costa adds, Christians have to be careful about the way they use the word "fulfillment." "Fulfillment, historically, does not work in only one direction."[12] In fact, in the dialogue with other religions, the Christian "church is laying itself open to genuine change, challenge, and questioning."[13] So if theologians are going to speak of "fulfillment," D'Costa prefers to make it *mutual fulfillment*. Here, it seems, he is not just following, but stepping beyond, what we heard from the Vatican.

But since D'Costa is urging a Trinitarian theology of religions, and since

---

10. For concise statements of D'Costa's Trinitarian/Spirit–based theology of religions, see his book *The Meeting of Religions and the Trinity* (Maryknoll, N.Y.: Orbis Books, 2000), chapter 4.

11. Gavin D'Costa, "Christ, the Trinity, and Religious Plurality," in *Christian Uniqueness Reconsidered: The Myth of a Pluralistic Theology of Religions,* ed. G. D'Costa (Maryknoll, N.Y.: Orbis Books, 1990), 23. See also D'Costa, *The Meeting,* 114.

12. Gavin D'Costa, "Revelation and Revelations: The Role and Value of Different Religious Traditions," *Pro Dialogo* 85–86 (1994): 161.

13. D'Costa, *The Meeting,* 134.

Christians believe that the three "persons" are deeply interrelated, he has to make an addition to this Spirit-focused view of other believers. This free-ranging, full-of-surprises Spirit is not entirely free. The Spirit is related, intensely and in its very nature, to the Word in Christ; relationships always bring some kind of restrictions. And that means that what the Spirit speaks in other religious languages has to be brought into resonance with the Word spoken in Jesus. In the following sentence, D'Costa tries to balance the universal outreach of the Spirit with the particular content of the Word in Jesus: "The riches of the mystery of God are disclosed by the Spirit and are measured and discerned by their conformity to and in their illumination of Christ.... Jesus is the normative criterion of God, while not foreclosing the ongoing self-disclosure of God in history, through the Spirit."[14] The disclosure of the Spirit can never be foreclosed; but it has to be "measured" by its "conformity" to God's Word in Jesus, for that Word is "normative" for all other words of the Spirit. This seems to imply that while the Spirit certainly reaches beyond Jesus in *extent*, it cannot go beyond Jesus in *content*. Such seems to be the implications of D'Costa's distinction: "There is no independent revelation through the Paraclete [another name for the Spirit], but only an application of the revelation of Jesus."[15]

For some, there may be tensions in what D'Costa is saying about how the universal activity of the Spirit is related to the particular Word of God in Jesus. Such tensions, D'Costa would say, are unavoidable for the Christian.

Beyond Fulfillment: Jacques Dupuis

Jacques Dupuis, S.J., deals with those tensions differently — perhaps more co-herently — than does D'Costa. Dupuis, a Belgian Jesuit who has spent most of his long life in India, is one of the most cited and respected contemporary Catholic theologians exploring the world of other religions. In his research and in his actual experience of dialogue in India, he has felt tensions in much of contemporary theology of religions. In fact, for Dupuis, the tensions often seem to be out-and-out contradictions. The problems, for him, stem from the fulfillment agenda of most Christian approaches to other faiths. He notes that no matter how much "truth and goodness" may be found along other paths, they all have to lead to the one goal of Christianity: that is, they have to function as preparations for something else. In Dupuis's estimation, such an attitude has produced three unhappy outcomes. First, it places limits on what God may be doing in other religions, for it allows only that kind of truth and goodness in them that can be fulfilled in the church. Second, it ends up making the church more important than God, also more important than Christ and his vision of the Reign of God. Third, it's an obstacle to real dialogue because it doesn't allow for the

---

14. D'Costa, "Christ, the Trinity, and Religious Plurality," 23.

15. D'Costa, *The Meeting*, 122. D'Costa is here quoting C. K. Barrett. Elsewhere, D'Costa states that the activity of the Spirit in other religions "does not confer independent legitimacy upon other religions" — that is, independent of Jesus Christ (*The Meeting*, 113).

level playing field that dialogue requires. If other believers are told — or for that matter, if Christians are told — that no matter how beautiful a hand God may have dealt Hinduism or Buddhism or Islam, God always reserves the trump card to Christianity, the game cannot be taken seriously. So Dupuis, in his magisterial and much-acclaimed book *Toward a Christian Theology of Religious Pluralism*, has attempted to move beyond a fulfillment perspective to a theology that would truly allow for dialogue by allowing the Divine free rein.

Dupuis, at the outset, states clearly what is at stake in his, and in every, effort to work out a new Christian theology of religious pluralism: "the very credibility of the Christian message for the future."[16] In our imagery, if Christians don't achieve a better balance on the relational scale of the universal and the particular, Dupuis says, people will find that Christianity no longer speaks either to their head or to their heart. For Dupuis, a theology of religions that will register as "credible" has to be one that will promote authentic dialogue, a theology that will truly respect other religions and recognize their validity. And to do this, Christians have to move beyond the Fulfillment Model, which sees other religions only as "stepping stones" or "seeds" or as a "preparation" for the goal, the end result, the final act — Christianity (204, 388).[17] For Dupuis the only theology that will be credible is one that will ground the possibility of real complementarity between religious believers engaged in dialogue. And he spells out boldly just what he means: " 'Complementarity' is not understood here in the sense of the fulfillment theory, according to which Christian truth 'brings to completion' — in a one-sided process — the fragmentary truths it finds sown outside" (326). Repeating but advancing on what we just heard in D'Costa, Dupuis wants a theology that will truly, not just in words, make possible a "mutual complementarity," a "mutual enrichment and transformation" (326) — one in which the intended final outcome is not for your side to convert to my side but, rather, "a more profound conversion of each to God" (383).

The foundation for his efforts to move beyond the constrictions of the Fulfillment Model and to fashion a truly dialogical theology of religions is the Holy Spirit. Dupuis wants to lay out what theologians call a pneumatological — Spirit-based — theology of religions.[18] In this, he harmonizes with the pope and other theologians: the Spirit is alive and active throughout history, especially in religious communities, before and after Christ. But Dupuis adds a melody not heard so clearly in the voices of other theologians — what the Spirit is about in other religions may be genuinely different from what one finds in God's Word in Jesus — never *contradictory to,* but really *different from.* To affirm the Spirit

---

16. Jacques Dupuis, " 'The Truth Will Make You Free': The Theology of Religious Pluralism Revisited," *Louvain Studies* 24 (1999): 261.

17. Since most of the references in this section will be to Dupuis's *Toward a Christian Theology,* page numbers will be given in the text.

18. We should also point out that although the Holy Spirit occupies a pivotal place in Dupuis's theology of religions, he also holds to the continued action of the Word of God, the second person of the Trinity, throughout history, beyond the incarnational presence of the Word in the humanity of Jesus. See Dupuis, *Toward a Christian Theology,* 220–23.

within other cultures and religions implies, therefore, that God has more to say to humanity than what God has said in Jesus. This is why Dupuis can so readily agree with Edward Schillebeeckx, in a claim we heard in chapter 1 — that "more divine truth and grace are found operative in the entire history of God's dealings with humankind than are available simply in Christian tradition" (388).

For some Catholics, such Spirit-based conclusions seem to go too far. Dupuis grounds them in classical Trinitarian theology, where Christians insist that there are real distinctions between the three persons of the Trinity (called "hypostatic distinctions"), which means that one person of the Trinity cannot be reduced to or subordinated to another. For Dupuis, if there is "real differentiation and plurality" between the Word of God in Jesus and the Spirit of God in other religions, we can expect that the religions are going have "different" and "new" things to tell Christians — things that they have not yet heard (and, of course, vice versa) (206, 197–98). Christians, therefore, do not "possess a monopoly of truth" (382).

Dupuis takes a further step that moves him into new territory. On the basis of the Spirit's abiding presence in the religions, he says Christians need to recognize that these other paths have a "lasting role" and a "specific meaning" in what God hopes to achieve with humanity (211). In other words, God does not intend all people to find their fulfillment in the Christian church. The many religions exist not just as a "matter of fact" but as a "matter of principle." Plurality reflects the way things are, the way God wills them to be (201). Having sounded such a bold claim, Dupuis goes a step further: this means that if Christians are going to take other religions seriously and dialogically, they have to move beyond the lingering "ecclesiocentrism" (church-centeredness) that clouds their theologies of other religions. He warns against an "ecclesiological inflation" that so blows up the necessity of the Christian church as to diminish or discount the value of other religions. Forthrightly and courageously, Dupuis chides viewpoints that Catholics usually hesitate to criticize: "the narrow ecclesiocentric perspectives of *Redemptoris Missio* must be regretted" (371).

But if Dupuis holds that theology must be wary of being too "church-centered," he admits and affirms that any Christian view of other religions must remain *Christ-centered*. If God and God's Reign are at the center of Christian life, it is Jesus Christ who leads to that center (191). And this is the point of Dupuis's new theology where he begins the delicate balancing act that we have observed throughout this chapter. He realizes that Christ-centeredness has led to the same kind of inflation of Christianity and deflation of others as has church-centeredness. He proposes a more dialogical understanding of Jesus Christ.

On the one hand, Dupuis lays his cards clearly on the table: "The Christian faith cannot stand without claiming for Jesus Christ a constitutive uniqueness" (304). "Constitutive uniqueness" means that Jesus, and only Jesus, "opens access to God for all human beings" (387). This, for Dupuis, is the marrow in the bones that engendered the Christian body from the start (286, 295, 350). And the reason why Jesus alone opens the door to the Divine for all people is that while all of us are children of God, Jesus is the Son of God like no one else. His "personal identity" is that of the very Word of God, the Son of God — the second person of the Trinity (155, 296–97). And, therefore, Christians believe, and must believe, that in Jesus, God has delivered the fullness of revelation.

On the other hand, Dupuis wants to take these essentials of Christian belief and understand them in a way that does not diminish other religions and allows for real dialogue with them. To do this, he makes some razor-sharp distinctions that call for razor-sharp attention on the part of his readers. The "fullness" of God's truth in Jesus is "qualitative," not "quantitative." What he means by that is so nuanced that it bears direct quotation: "This plenitude...is not...one of extension and all-comprehension, but of intensity....It does not — it cannot — exhaust the mystery of the Divine" (382). Perhaps another way of putting what Dupuis is getting at is to understand the "fullness of truth" in Jesus not as giving us the whole picture (quantitative) but as so focusing the picture we have (quali-tative) that we know what it is all about and can understand any further additions to it. It's a fullness of focus, of intensity, rather than one of detail and totality.

Dupuis therefore explicitly admits that the fullness of God's truth in Jesus is "relative" (that is, limited — a word that few Christian theologians would dare to use); but he prefers the more positive adjective: "relational." The fullness of what God wants to make known to humans is focused in Jesus; but to increase the depth of the picture, Christians have to *relate* what they have in Jesus to what the Spirit is doing in other religions. Indeed, Christians don't really know the fullness of God's message in Christ unless they talk with others.

With such a relational understanding of Christ's uniqueness, Dupuis holds that Christians can open themselves in authentic dialogue with others — without diminishing or jeopardizing who Jesus is for them and for the world. Dupuis can repeat, and truly mean, familiar Christian language: Jesus stands among other religious leaders as "the deepest and most decisive engagement of God with humankind" (388). "No revelation...either before or after Christ can either surpass or equal the one vouchsafed in Jesus Christ, the divine Son incarnate" (249–50, see also 318, 204).

As for the relationship between what God speaks in Jesus and what God speaks in the Spirit, even though Dupuis warns that one should not be subor-dinated to the other, he also clarifies: "Christ, not the Spirit, is at the center as the way to God." Whatever God has to say in the Spirit through other religions has to be understood "in view of" Christ; it does not take the place of Christ (197). Thus in the mutual enrichment and transformation that Dupuis envisions as the goal of dialogue, Christians may discover that other religions have seen "certain dimensions of the Divine Mystery" more clearly than Christians have. And in their dialogue with others, Christians may see "at greater depth" what they already possess in the fullness of Christian revelation (382–83, 388).

So even though Dupuis wants to plot a course that will steer Christians away from attitudes that regard other religions as "stepping stones" to Christianity, he also tries to adjust course so that Jesus as the Christ maintains his place at the center and as the final goal of all God's dealings with humanity. Occasionally he makes use of language that is tinged with tones of fulfillment. He describes, for instance, other religions as "incomplete 'faces' of the Divine Mystery...to be *fulfilled* in him who is 'the human face of God' [Jesus]" (279). Other religious paths are "integral parts of one history of salvation that culminates in the Jesus-Christ event" (303). At the very end of his path-finding book, he suggests that this "fulfillment" or "culmination" of other religions in Jesus will take place only (or completely) at the very end of history when, according to Ephesians 1:10, the entire body of creation, including all religions, will find its identity and perfection under Jesus as its one head and heart (389). In the meantime, the religions maintain their validity and identity, together with Christianity.

We've tried to take as careful and complete a look as possible at Dupuis's case for a new Christian theology of religions since for many it represents as far as one can go and still remain within the borders of orthodoxy. In particular, he tries to push Christian belief in the centrality of Jesus beyond the limits of the Fulfillment Model that characterizes official Catholic teaching. A selective sampling, in the next section, shows that other Catholic theologians are walking along the path that Dupuis has mapped — and are trying to make it smoother and more inviting.

Other Catholic Views

Like Dupuis, other Catholic theologians recognize that if a Christian no longer places Jesus Christ at the heart of what God is up to in all of history, she's no longer really a Christian. "The Christian faith collapses if the definitive claim for Jesus Christ is denied."[19] They say this because this is what Christians have known in their hearts throughout the centuries. Jesus stands at the center of their lives because he stands at the center of God's plan; his name is "above all other names" (Phil. 2:9); he is so special that Christians naturally feel bewildered or offended when he is placed on a level with others. This is a pastoral-personal reason why many Catholic theologians and ministers shy away from views that suggest that Jesus may be one among many saviors. In the words of Hans Küng, to say such things would offend their people and put themselves at "the risk of parting company with their own faith-communities."[20]

Theologians point out that one of the key words in this personal experience of Christ is "decisive." In their experience of Christ, Christians have felt empowered to turn themselves around, to cut themselves away from what has dragged them down or stifled their hope (that's what *de-cidere* means — to cut away).

---

19. Monika Hellwig, "Christology in the Wider Ecumenism," in *Christian Uniqueness Reconsidered: The Myth of a Pluralistic Theology of Religions,* ed. G. D'Costa (Maryknoll, N.Y.: Orbis Books, 1990), 109.

20. Hans Küng, *Global Responsibility: In Search of a New World Ethic* (New York: Crossroad, 1991), 101.

They've been enabled to take a stand, a stand on which they can build their individual lives and pursue their dreams of making this world a better place in which to live and love. In other words, in Jesus Christians know that God *has* provided a final word and a firm place. No matter how many wars, no matter how many broken relationships, no matter how much hatred, no matter how sick one's past — in Christ, in the example he sets and the Spirit he imparts — one can hope, and one can act on that hope.[21] Thus, as Monika Hellwig observes, while there have been a variety of Christians throughout the centuries who have denied the church's understanding of the divinity of Jesus, "none have denied that Jesus Christ as savior makes the definitive difference."[22]

Other Catholic theologians point out, further, that the "definitive" or "last-word" quality of Jesus is necessary in Christian experience not just to pursue Jesus' vision of what the world can be like but also to resist the evils that are so entrenched in the world as it is. To stand up in Jesus' name against the powers that be, to hold firm to the values of God's Reign when most of the world is going in the opposite direction, to be able to be one of the "good guys" who always finish last or get stepped on, one needs to know, these theologians claim, more than that this is one choice among many. One needs to know that one is taking a stand where God has taken a stand, where God has drawn a bottom line. This is the meaning of traditional claims that Jesus is God's final word. As Hans Küng puts it, only with such an assuring word can one remain *steadfast.*[23]

But to make such a "definitive difference" and to be truly assuring, the theologians go on, God's word in Jesus must be *singular.* For God to have given many "final words" would undermine the reliability of all of them. This is precisely what enables a person to commit himself totally and to hang in there with this commitment even to the point of the final giving: one knows that this is the truth which cannot be questioned or qualified by any other. To stand before the executioner resolved to die for God's truth only to be told that God has issued other very different but equally valid truths cannot but put into question, and so weaken, one's resolve. As Karl-Josef Kuschel puts it: "If there were besides or outside of Christ other possible incarnations or revelations of God just as complete as that of Christ, then God would remain in the final analysis an impenetrable riddle whose credibility would still be undecided."[24] This harks back to what we heard from Karl Rahner — the natural human need to give oneself fully and definitely to what is true and good calls for a full and definitive expression of truth and goodness — or what Rahner calls "an absolute savior." And absolutes come in singulars.

But what has been said so far has been said by theologians about Christians,

---

21. See, for example, Edward Schillebeeckx, *The Church: The Human Story of God* (New York: Crossroad, 1990), 26–27.

22. Hellwig, "Christology in the Wider Ecumenism," 109.

23. Küng, *Global Responsibility,* 94–101.

24. Karl-Josef Kuschel, "Christologie und interreligiöser Dialog: Die Einzigartigkeit Christi im Gespräch mit den Weltreligionen," *Stimmen der Zeit* 209 (1991): 398–99.

for Christians. This is not necessarily the way Christians will talk about Christ, or represent Christ, to followers of other religions. In fact, Kuschel insists that Christians can, and must, give witness to their belief in Christ in such a way as to communicate "finality without exclusivism and definitiveness without superiority."[25] How? It all hangs on the way Jesus is God's "final and definitive" gift. He is the last and unsurpassable Word on God because he is a Word of love. This is what Jesus makes clear: God is love, and we know God and are one with God when we love. But to love truly, the example of Jesus tells us, we must give of ourselves, empty ourselves. This is why St. Paul speaks so much about God in Christ *emptying* God's self (*kenosis*) (Phil. 2:6–8). And this is how Christians will speak about Jesus as God's full and final communication: in a loving, truly emptying way. There's a paradox at play here: Jesus, and Christians trying to follow him, reveals his fullness through his emptiness, his uniqueness through his service, his excellence through his humility. So if Christianity "fulfills" other religions, it does so through this self-emptying Word of love; and that means by respecting, embracing, and learning from them.

Monika Hellwig makes a practical suggestion on how Christians can make their claims about Jesus to other religions in a loving, self-emptying way — through what she calls "a friendly wager." It's a wager "that Jesus is indeed at the heart of the mystery of existence and destiny." In other words, they bet that in Jesus God has done and offered something really unique, something that can truly turn things around in the messed-up lives of individuals and societies. When they propose their wager to others, they don't argue from what the Bible says, or even from what they have felt in their own hearts and communities. Rather, they appeal to "what can be observed in what Jesus has done and how he has influenced and continues to influence people." Look carefully at Jesus' message and his own life — and at what happens when people take him seriously and live that message. Hellwig summarizes carefully why she thinks that this is a "good bet" and why others might see it in the same way:

> We as Christians see the possibility of meeting the evident human need for redemption from selfishness, bullying, discrimination, and exclusion in and through the person of Jesus Christ because of the beginning he has made and the further developments among his more dedicated followers. We know from our cumulative experience that where people implement the possibilities he opened up there is growth toward *fuller life, hope, community, and happiness.*

Hellwig makes this statement "as a friendly wager against all who would say otherwise," but then she adds immediately: "without denying the salvific actual or potential role of other savior figures."[26]

---

25. Ibid., 401, 396.
26. Hellwig, "Christology in the Wider Ecumenism," 111–16.

This is a wager that challenges both believers in other traditions and Christians themselves. Whether it proves itself to be a good bet depends not only on who Jesus is but on how well Christians try to live his message.

Uneasy Voices from Asia

So far in this section on efforts to expand the dialogue, we have heard mainly from theologians who try to listen to and guide the needs and questions of the Catholic community. In this final section, we will listen directly to the voice of the Asian churches in the official pronouncements of the Federation of Asian Bishops' Conferences (FABC) and in the preparations for and reactions to the Asian bishops' synod in Rome in April 1999.[27] We detect further efforts to expand the dialogue that go beyond (perhaps stand in tension with) what we've heard from the Vatican and from mainstream Catholic theologians.

First, the Asian bishops, in the very first meeting of the FABC in 1970, made it clear that the Asian churches must be dialogical churches: "We pledge ourselves to an open, sincere, and continuing dialogue with our brothers and sisters of other great religions of Asia, so that we may learn from one another how to enrich ourselves spiritually and how to work more effectively together on our common task of total human development."[28] The Indian bishops, in their preparatory statements for the 1999 synod, were even more clear and energetic: "Dialogue is not merely one ecclesial activity among many. It is a constituent dimension of every authentic local church.... After Vatican II, to be church means being a faith community-in-dialogue."[29] To cut off possibilities of dialogue with the religions of Asia is to cut off much of the air the Christian churches of Asia breathe.

In carrying out this necessary dialogue, the Asian bishops have clearly and repeatedly endorsed a "Kingdom-centered" understanding of the Catholic Church — the church's whole purpose is to serve this broader Reign of God, not to control or dominate it.[30] Therefore, conversion to the church is not on the top of their dialogical agenda: "Sincere and authentic dialogue does not have for its objective the conversion of the other; for conversion depends solely on God's internal call and the person's free decision.... Dialogue aimed at 'converting' the other to one's own religious faith and tradition is dishonest and unethical; it is not the way of harmony."[31] The kind of dialogue envisioned by the bishops can best take place in what they call "basic human communities,"

---

27. The chief documents of the FABC are found in Gaudencia B. Rosales and C. G. Arévalo, eds., *For All the Peoples of Asia: Federation of Asian Bishops' Conferences Documents from 1970 to 1991*, vol. 1 (Maryknoll, N.Y.: Orbis Books, 1992), and Franz-Josef Eilers, ed., *For All the Peoples of Asia: Federation of Asian Bishops' Conferences Documents from 1992 to 1996*, vol. 2 (Maryknoll, N.Y.: Orbis Books, 1997).

28. Quoted in Sebastian Painadath, "Theological Perspectives of the FABC on Interreligious Dialogue," *Jeevadhara* 27 (1997): 272.

29. Quoted in the *National Catholic Reporter*, April 10, 1998, 16.

30. Rosales and Arévalo, *For All the Peoples of Asia*, 1:252.

31. Ibid., 120; see Painadath, "Theological Perspectives," 280–82.

gatherings of faith-based peoples. But "faith" here includes not just Christians but persons from other religious traditions. What draws such communities together, and what makes up the substance of their dialogue, is their concern for the well-being of everyone in their broader communities. The well-being of all, rather than conversion from other religions to Christianity, is the focus of Asian dialogue.[32]

But how do the Asian churches balance this bold openness of dialogue with the proclamation of the uniqueness of Jesus? The bishops first make perfectly clear their faithful and happy endorsement of Christian tradition and what Pope John Paul II has insisted on for the mission of the church — that Jesus Christ is Savior of the world. *That* this is so is for the Asian communities no problem. *How* it is so, or *how* they are to announce it to their Buddhist and Hindu and Muslim friends, is a problem they feel more acutely, they suggest, than do many Vatican bishops and theologians. What has become clear for the bishops is that the traditional way of talking about Jesus as the one-and-only Savior doesn't work in Asia. Why? Because it creates animosity between the many religious communities of Asia. Thus the Japanese bishops say: "If we stress too much that 'Jesus Christ is the One and Only Savior,' we can have no dialogue, common living, or solidarity with other religions." The Sri Lankan bishops have said: "The uniqueness of Jesus and of the Church has been a perennial problem and poses its own distinctive difficulties for authentic dialogue."[33] "When various religious groups lay absolute claims to truth, aggressive militancy and divisive proselytism follow, and in their wake, bitter religious divisions."[34]

The Asian bishops go on to ask, How can we understand and talk about Jesus differently than has been the case in the churches of Europe and America? Here the Asian bishops have no easy answers. They suggest, in general, that "in the tradition of the Far East, it is characteristic to search for creative harmony rather than distinctions." Truth is much more a matter of "both-and" rather than "either-or." Thus, the truth of Christ must relate to and include other truths rather than exclude or absorb them. Maybe even, if Jesus is unique, so are other religious leaders. As for what is distinctive about Jesus, the Asian bishops stress Jesus' message of self-emptying love, or radical service of others. Jesus is in the center precisely because he "de-centers" himself, empties himself, refuses to "rule over." This is a message that other religions can hear with open mind and heart.

But in stressing the distinctiveness of Jesus as the self-emptying servant, the Asian bishops are even more precise — Jesus is particularly the servant of *the poor.* His example of love of neighbor certainly includes everyone as neighbor,

---

32. See Cardinal Julius Darmaatmadja, "A New Way of Being Church in Asia" *Vidyajyoti* 63 (1999): 887–91.

33. The statements in this paragraph and the next are drawn from the Asian bishops' responses to the Vatican "lineamenta" (proposals) sent to the bishops in preparation for the synod. They can be found, together with the Vatican proposals, in *The East Asian Pastoral Review* 35, no. 1 (1998).

34. Rosales and Arévalo, *For All the Peoples of Asia*, 1:300.

but it especially includes those neighbors who have been taken advantage of, marginalized, and therefore suffer the violence of poverty. This is the kind of dialogue that the Asian bishops want to promote with particular urgency — a dialogue of liberation and of action. They believe that a mutual concern for the poor not only can become a common theme for interreligious dialogue in Asia but can also prove itself to be a means of carrying on a much deeper and rewarding dialogue than has been possible in the past. Such a dialogue will "discover the creative and redemptive forces in each religion" and "articulate the liberative and unifying potential of each religion."[35]

So as Cardinal Julius Darmaatmadja of Indonesia pointed out to the pope after the synod of Asian bishops, Asians prefer to speak about Jesus not as the "one and only Son of God and Savior" but as the "Teacher of Wisdom, the Healer, the Liberator, the Compassionate Friend of the Poor, the Good Samaritan."[36] These titles point to the specialness of Jesus without necessarily negating the specialness of others and the possibility of both learning from and cooperating with these others.

Further Readings

Amato, A. "The Unique Mediation of Christ as Lord and Saviour." *Pro Dialogo* 85–86 (1994): 15–39.
Carr, Ann. "Merton's East-West Reflections." *Horizons* 21 (1994): 239–52.
Clooney, Francis X. "The Study of Non-Christian Religions in the Post Vatican II Roman Catholic Church." *Journal of Ecumenical Studies* 28 (1991): 482–94.
D'Costa, Gavin. *The Meeting of Religions and the Trinity.* Maryknoll, N.Y.: Orbis Books, 2000, 99–142.
———. "Revelation and Revelations: Discerning God in Other Religions: Beyond a Static Valuation." *Modern Theology* 10 (1994): 165–83.
Dupuis, Jacques. *Toward a Christian Theology of Religious Pluralism.* Maryknoll, N.Y.: Orbis Books, 1997, 170–201. (For post-Vatican II developments.)
———. "'The Truth Will Make You Free': The Theology of Religious Pluralism Revisited." *Louvain Studies* 24 (1999): 211–63.
FABC Theological Advisory Commission of the Federation of Asian Bishops' Conference. "Seven Theses on Interreligious Dialogue: An Essay in Pastoral Theological Reflection." *International Bulletin of Missionary Research* 13 (1989): 108–11.
John Paul II. *Ecclesia in Asia* (apostolic exhortation, 1999).
———. *Redemptoris Missio: An Encyclical Letter on the Permanent Validity of the Church's Missionary Mandate* (1990). Available with commentary in William R. Burrows, ed., *Redemption and Dialogue* (Maryknoll, N.Y.: Orbis Books, 1993), 3–55.
King, Ursula. "Teilhard's Reflections on Eastern Religions Revisited." *Zygon* 30 (1995): 47–72.
Knitter, Paul F. "Catholics and Other Religions: Bridging the Gap between Dialogue and Theology." *Louvain Studies* 24 (1999): 319–54.

---

35. Ibid., 1:315, 300.
36. Darmaatmadja, "A New Way of Being Church in Asia," 889.

Küng, Hans. "Christ, Our Light, and World Religions." *Theology Digest* 42 (1995): 215–19.

————. "No Peace in the World without Peace among Religions." *World Faiths Insight* (February 1989): 3–22.

Lane, Dermot A. "Vatican II, Christology, and the World Religions." *Louvain Studies* 24 (1999): 147–70.

Lefebure, Leo D. "Christianity and Religions of the World." *Chicago Studies* 33 (1994): 258–70.

Painadath, Sebastian. "Theological Perspectives of the FABC on Interreligious Dialogue." *Jeevadhara* 27 (1997): 272–88.

Phan, Peter C. "Are There 'Saviors' for Other Peoples? A Discussion of the Problem of the Universal Significance and Uniqueness of Jesus the Christ." In *Christianity and the Wider Ecumenism*. Ed. Peter C. Phan. New York: Paragon House, 1990, 163–80.

Pontifical Council for Inter-religious Dialogue and the Congregation for the Evangelization of Peoples. *Dialogue and Proclamation: Reflections and Orientations on Interreligious Dialogue and the Proclamation of the Gospel of Jesus Christ* (1991). Available with commentary in William R. Burrows, ed., *Redemption and Dialogue* (Maryknoll, N.Y.: Orbis Books, 1993), 93–118.

Chapter 6

The Fulfillment Model

Insights and Questions

After this review of the Fulfillment Model, we need to step back and try to make some assessments. Though plotted and traveled especially by Roman Catholics, does this path have some road-signs that all Christians would do well to follow? Among the many new directions that the model takes, are there some that could help all Christian churches in responding to the challenge of religious pluralism that we outlined in chapter 1? At the same time, we will ask some critical questions of this model. Does it really lead to the goals that it sets for itself? Does it make for a teeter-totter balanced evenly between the particularity of Jesus' role and the universality of God's love? Does it really follow the new directions it proposes all the way to their logical ends?[1]

Insights

Truth and Grace in the Religions

The only way, or at least the easiest way, for Christians to really mean what they say when they profess that God loves all people is, so it seems, to recognize that there is not only truth in other religions but also grace — not only revelation, as the Replacement Model admits, but also the possibility of salvation, as we have heard from the Fulfillment Model. We have witnessed how slowly, almost fearfully, Catholic theology has struggled its way to the conclusion that the religions can be "ways of salvation, channels of God's saving love." If, as Catholic theologians tell us, there has always been a "development of doctrine" throughout Christian history, this is definitely a new development. And it seems to deserve a permanent, and honored, place in the line-up of Christians beliefs.

For unless Christians recognize that God's Spirit can touch people's lives "outside the church" (for Catholics) and "outside the preached Word" (for Protestants), there does not seem to be any way to "allow" for God's love to embrace all people except through some of the "after-death" options that we heard of

---

1. Having asked all these questions, it is important to remind readers that in the Roman Catholic view of the matter, the teachings of the council and the popes are not merely theological opinions. Instead they represent truth that needs to be explained, not explained away.

earlier — and which may appear to be more the fruit of theological imagination than divine revelation. Furthermore, unless Christians recognize that the Divine Spirit can breathe in other religions, they will not allow the Spirit to be what it showed itself to be in Jesus — an always embodied Spirit. The Spirit touches people through other people, through stories, gestures, music, and dance — and may do so through other religions.

Christians, therefore, will do well to follow the example of the Fulfillment Model and place the Holy Spirit in the center of any Christian theology of religions. This will help balance some of the insights, but also some of the apparent extremes, of the Replacement Model. Yes, we bear a "fallen nature" and evil/selfishness is a reality which, if ignored, is all the more destructive. But within this fallen frame there also breathes the Spirit of God, making our nature, as Rahner put it, a "graced nature" just as much as — no, more than! — it is a fallen nature. To ignore the presence and persistent availability of this Spirit of grace can be even more damaging for humanity's hopes than to ignore the reality of evil. According to the Christian story, if the first Adam dragged us down, the Second Adam lifts us even higher, all of us.

Along these same lines, if the Replacement Model, preserving the spirit of the Reformation, rightly alerts us to the dangers of religion and to the way organized religion tends to organize itself into idolatry, Catholics offer the balancing reminder that other religions and the church are not only necessary evils but wonderful necessities. The Spirit does make use of the externals of religion because, evidently, humans need them. Though the touch of the Spirit occurs in the intimacy and mystery of the heart, it is delivered, as it were, through the community and its words, rituals, and symbols. And as this Spirit touches through the words and sacraments of the Christian community, it may do likewise through the beliefs and rituals of other communities.

It would seem that only if Christians *expect* to encounter the truth and grace of the Spirit in other communities can they see and identify what fruits of the Spirit may be growing in the gardens of other religions. We observed earlier how advocates of the Replacement Model seemed to miss the evident holiness, compassion, and peace glowing in the lives of Hindus or Buddhists or Muslims. To their eyes, such positive qualities were "human works" — examples of humans searching for what could be found only in Jesus. The Fulfillment Model asks whether such eyes are blindfolded by a theology that fails to allow the Spirit to precede Jesus and blow where it will.

Dialogue Essential to Christian Life

We have seen how recent developments in the Catholic Church have brought Catholics to recognize the "duty of dialogue." To be a faithful follower of Jesus in the world of today, Christians must engage in conversation with persons of other faiths — a conversation which, as we heard, is supposed to be a two-way street. Dialogue, Pope John Paul II has said, is an essential part of the mission of the church — that is, part of the way Christians relate to the world. Two evident and urgent reasons suggest why this is a "duty" that all Christians need to take seriously:

- It's what the world needs. Here we refer back to chapter 1 and our description of a world that is racked by forms of violence which are both fomented by religions and which, at the same time, won't really be resolved without the contributions of religious communities. We need to remember Hans Küng's sobering words: "No peace among nations without peace among religions. And no peace among religions without a greater dialogue among them."

- But dialogue is also what Christians need. And they need it in order to carry out the most fundamental law of Christianity — love your neighbor as yourself. Love requires not just that we do "good" to others but that we respect them, affirm them, listen to them, and be ready to learn from them. To truly love others, we have to stand ready to receive from them, at least as much as we hope to give to them. If "doing good" is not accompanied by respect and mutuality, then love becomes patronizing kindness. Which means it is no longer love. Love calls for relationships of mutuality in which there is reciprocal giving and taking, teaching and learning, speaking and listening. And that's what dialogue is all about. "Love thy neighbor" means "Dialogue with thy neighbor."

Nonnegotiables in All Religions

Throughout Part II, we may have grown a little dizzy with the ups and downs of our imagined teeter-totter. Every time theologians or the pope rise to recognize truth and goodness in other religions, they balance it with a reminder that Jesus is the source and standard of it all. Whether that makes for balance or confusion is a question we'll raise in a moment. But the fact that Christians need to balance or check out whatever they say by bringing it back to Jesus seems to indicate something that marks not only Christianity but all religions. Every religion has its own *nonnegotiables*. Here is another important lesson for all Christians as they move into deeper dialogue with others.

There seem to be certain convictions or values or beliefs located in the heart of hearts of all religious persons that they simply are not able to put on the table of dialogue for possible questioning. Even though they might want to, they can't. Even though with their head they might tell themselves that dialogue requires putting everything up for question, in their hearts they know that some things are in a specially protected place and can't be touched. We're talking about convictions or commitments that define the identity of the religious person. To question them is to question who the person is and wants to be. Most of us can't do that, if we're honest about ourselves.

For Christians, these nonnegotiables have to do with Jesus Christ. Trying to describe as broadly as possible how Jesus is nonnegotiable, we can note three Christian convictions about Jesus:

- In Jesus, God has done something very special, something that has not been done, and will not be done, elsewhere.

- Because of this something special, Jesus may have a lot in common with other religious figures, but he will always remain different, irreducibly different. The difference Jesus makes must be preserved.

- The something special that God has done in Jesus is important — very important — not just for Christians but for all people.

Given these nonnegotiable convictions about Jesus, those Christians who follow the Fulfillment Model are open to finding in other religions truths about God and humanity that they have not received in Jesus. Still, they cannot imagine agreeing to anything that would contradict what they have learned in Jesus. The Spirit may have more to say than what was said in Jesus; but the Spirit could never oppose Jesus.

Questions

Does the Fulfillment Model Really Allow Dialogue?

No doubt, we have witnessed in all the theologians and church officials we have met in this part a sincere and genuine desire to dialogue with persons of other religions. But we also might ask whether they can carry through with their sincerity. We heard, and perhaps were surprised by, John Paul II and Vatican officials calling Christians to a dialogue in which they can be "enriched," "challenged," "transformed," perhaps even "converted." D'Costa and especially Dupuis were even more vigorous in their insistence that there must be "mutual fulfillment" in the dialogue. But what they then go on to say about Jesus seems to blunt these high-sounding intentions. Just how deep can enrichment or challenge or conversion go when Christians are convinced that in Jesus they have God's full, final, and fulfilling Word? Even Dupuis's qualifying distinction that Jesus' fullness is only "relative," a "qualitative not quantitative" fullness, sounds like more a matter of words than of reality when he goes on to declare that Jesus is the one-and-only Savior in whom the one salvation intended for all people is constituted and really made known. The "Spirit-centered" approach that Dupuis and others advocate does not, in the final analysis, seem to allow the Spirit to say anything *really* different from what was said in Jesus. We saw how both D'Costa and Dupuis continued to insist that "Christ, not the Spirit, is at the center as the way to God."[2] This means, as we heard, that

---

2. Jacques Dupuis, *Toward a Christian Theology of Religious Pluralism* (Maryknoll, N.Y.: Orbis Books, 1997), 197.

whatever Christians might learn from the Spirit in others will always be essentially only a clarification, a deepening of what they already know in Jesus. Is Dupuis, contrary to his intentions, subordinating the Spirit to the Word in Jesus after all?

It appears to many, therefore, that the effort of Catholic theologians to take one more step beyond the fulfillment perspective of Vatican II doesn't work because it doesn't allow for the level playing field that a two-way dialogue requires. As one critic of the Fulfillment Model put it, in a dialogue in which Christians maintain that they have God's "definitive truth...what we have, in fact, is a dialogue between the elephant and the mouse."[3]

This doesn't mean that Christians, operating out of a Fulfillment Model, necessarily act like elephants or treat persons of other faiths like mice. The desire on the part of most Catholics for a truly mutual exchange that does not use dialogue to set the bait for conversion is sincere. And on the grassroots level of parishes and local communities, Christians *are* experiencing what dialogue can mean. They are learning things that they did not know before. They are being transformed as Christians because they have talked with Buddhists and others. But it seems that a theology of dialogue that operates out of a Fulfillment Model isn't sustained by the theology of religions that they are supposed to endorse. The practice of dialogue is reaching beyond the theology that is taught officially by the magisterium. One might say that Catholics aren't preaching what they practice.

Does Commitment Require Certitude?

We have heard the case that as individuals and as a community of nations, we humans need something like Rahner's "absolute Savior" — one God-given certain norm, one clear assurance, one final word, one ultimate goal so that we can find our way through the maze of problems and paths that make up an individual life and human history. Without one certain truth that brooks no bending to other truths we cannot, they say, really commit ourselves; nor can we take a stand to live by, and die for, what we hold to be true and sacred. One might respond to such assertions with two questions: Are such "absolute norms" or "final truths" really necessary? And are they really possible?

They seem impossible if our so-called postmodern consciousness is correct — that all truth is limited because all truth is historically conditioned or socially constructed. Even contemporary theologians admit this about Jesus. If the Divine truly incarnates itself in the history of one particular human being, this means that the Divine *limits* itself. Incarnation means limitation. St. Paul called it "emptying" (*kenosis*). Dupuis struggled to express this when he admitted that although Jesus delivers the fullness of God's revelation, it is a "relative"

---

3. Henri Maurier, "The Christian Theology of the Non-Christian Religions," *Lumen Vitae* 21 (1976): 59, 66, 69, 70.

fullness. Might claims to need a final or unsurpassable truth be setting up a goal that will ultimately frustrate us when we don't find it or create dangerous illusions when we think we do?

This calls forth the next question. Are absolute or final truths necessary to make absolute or final commitments? Do I have to know that something is the superior and the last truth in order to fully embrace it and in order to die for it? It seems not. If we peer more deeply into our psychological dynamics, it appears that what leads one to commitment is the belief that something is *really* true, not that it's the *only* or the *final* truth. I commit myself to my wife because I feel certain that she is the person she has shown herself to be, not because I am certain that there is no other woman like her or no other woman whom I could possibly marry.

When we judge or feel something to be really right or true, it grabs us. And the grip is not necessarily weakened if we also know that there may be other truths that grab other people in an equally powerful manner — or, even, that there may be other truths that in the future may grab us. We trust that such other truths will not contradict the truth to which we are now committed. Religious commitments require the conviction that God has *truly* called one in Christ, not that this is the *only* call God has issued to humanity.

How Does Jesus Save?

Throughout this review of the Fulfillment Model, we have watched Christians trying to state their convictions while being able to enter into dialogue. The problem, however, seemed to be that the particularity of Jesus tended to outweigh the universality of God's love — giving Christians the last word in any dialogue. The challenge for Christian theology of religions, we see again, is how to understand the particularity of Jesus; or how to understand how Jesus saves, how Jesus transforms lives and fills them with the peace and power of God's presence.

Here we can raise a question that sets the stage for Part III: Have the churches and theologians really followed to its full implications their understanding of Jesus (and the church) as *sacrament*? We saw how Rahner understood Jesus not as the one who fixes what is broken but as the one who reveals what is already given but not yet evident. Jesus in this sense does not build the bridge that enables us to connect with God (or God with us). Rather, he shows us in his message and person that we're already connected. Sacraments make real that which is already there, but which we really cannot see or feel without the sacrament's power to reveal it.

The differences between these two views of how Jesus saves — as bridging what is divided or revealing what is present — make for major differences in a theology of religions. To understand and experience Jesus as he who reveals, symbolizes, and represents the already-given love of God would seem to allow, or even call for, other sacraments. There may be many ways in which God's Spirit could find expression in differing cultures at differing historical periods.

Whether such a sacramental understanding of Jesus is faithful to the New Testament witness and whether it can sustain a Christian life and lead to authentic dialogue are important questions. They will face us again in the coming chapters.

Part III

THE MUTUALITY MODEL
"Many True Religions Called to Dialogue"

Chapter 7

The Philosophical Bridge

"I am convinced that there are millions of mainline Christians in North America for whom the statement that Christianity is *not* the only true religion is 'good news....' We are living in a time when many Christians are beginning to let go of exclusivist [read Replacement Model] and absolutist [read Fulfillment Model] claims."[1] That statement by New Testament scholar Marcus Borg, himself a member and progressive pastor of the mainline Christian community, expresses both the motivation and the direction of what we are calling the Mutuality Model. Christians who resonate with this model also resonate with the questions raised of the previous models. In their Christian bones, they feel that the traditional theological telescopes that show other religions as ultimately having to be either replaced or fulfilled by Christianity aren't really showing what's there, both in the other religions and in the Gospel of Jesus. These established models aren't working for such Christians. And so followers of Jesus are searching for paths that will lead them from what one scholar terms an "absolutist" understanding of Christ and Christianity (in which Christ is the only Savior and final Word) to one that is more "modest" — just what that means is what the Christians and theologians of the Mutuality Model are trying to figure out.[2]

In this part, therefore, we can expect that the up and down of the teeter-totter is going to be different from what we experienced in the previous part. If the Fulfillment Model usually landed more heavily on the side of Jesus' particularity, in this Mutuality Model the greater weight will fall on the side of God's universal love and presence in other religions. Both models seek balance. Which does it better is an ongoing discussion among Christians.

Three Questions

Before we move into our review and analysis of this model, it will be helpful to first have a sense of where we're going. The Mutuality Model wants to answer three questions. And these questions generate both its energy and its direction.

1. *How can Christians engage in a more authentic dialogue with persons of other faiths?* To be completely honest and up-front about this model, we have

---

1. Marcus Borg, "Jesus and Buddhism: A Christian View," *Buddhist-Christian Studies* 19 (1999): 96.

2. Wesley J. Wildman, *Fidelity with Plausibility: Modest Christologies in the Twentieth Century* (Albany: State University of New York Press, 1998).

to recognize that its rock-bottom concern is how to promote genuine dialogue with other religions. For Christians who follow this model, this concern is just as deep and just as foundational as their concern to follow Jesus and remain faithful to his Gospel. Both concerns have to sustain each other. These Christians cannot imagine following Jesus without conversing with other believers — and vice versa. For these Christians, dialogue with other religions is an imperative, an ethical imperative. It is so for many of the reasons we pondered in our first part. But it is also an imperative because for these Christians, dialogue seems to be part and parcel of the imperative to love one's neighbors; as we heard in the previous part, you're not really loving another person unless you are ready to listen to them, respect them, learn from them. That's dialogue.

Therefore, as these Christians look out over the vast field of other religious traditions, what they see is not just diversity but *potential dialogue partners*. What they want to foster is not just the multiplicity and identity of other religions but also and especially a conversation among them. That's why we're calling this the Mutuality Model rather than its frequently given (and misleading) name, the Pluralist Model. For this model, relationship is more important than plurality. And it's got to be a relationship of mutuality — that is, a relationship, a conversation, that really goes both ways, in which both sides are really talking and listening, in which both sides really open themselves to learning and changing. For this model, anything that threatens the mutuality of dialogue is highly suspect, to say the least.

2. *How can we create a level playing field for dialogue?* This question becomes a necessary sequel to the first. Both the noun ("playing field") and the adjective ("level") are crucial for understanding what the question is looking for. "Level" expresses what Vatican II was getting at when it said that for a dialogue to work, it has to be "among equals." If one of the participants enters the field with better equipment than the other, or with a "special relationship" with the umpires or referees, the interchange isn't going to be fair. Therefore, proponents of this model presume what one of them called a "rough parity" among religions.[3] That doesn't mean that all the religions are the same or that they are equal in every respect. But it does mean that they all have "equal rights" to speak and be heard, based on their inherent value. So this model is uncomfortable with, and seeks to avoid, any claims that one religion has a pre-given (especially if it's a God-given) superiority over all the others that makes it "final" or "absolute" or "unsurpassable" over all the others.

But besides "level," we also need a "playing field" on which genuine dialogue can take place. And to make this possible, mutualist Christians, if we may coin that term, want to mix two necessary ingredients that don't seem to mix easily: (*a*) They want to preserve the real *diversity* and *differences* among the religions,

---

3. Langdon Gilkey, "Plurality and Its Theological Implications," in *The Myth of Christian Uniqueness: Toward a Pluralistic Theology of Religions*, ed. John Hick and Paul F. Knitter (Maryknoll, N.Y.: Orbis Books, 1987), 37–50.

for without differences, why talk to each other? The Mutuality Model, therefore, wants to avoid any facile talk about all religions being essentially the same or really talking about the same thing. (*b*) But at the same time — and this "but" is tricky — there's got to be something that the religions have in common that makes the game of dialogue possible in the first place. You might say that they all have to be playing soccer. If one religion, as it were, plays "basketball" and the other "baseball," they're not going to be able to play with each other. The religions have to have something in common that enables them to reach across the apparent chasm of their differences. What this "something" is, we will see, is not easy to determine or describe neatly.

3. *How can we come to a clearer understanding of Jesus' uniqueness that will sustain the dialogue?* Again, this question springs from the previous one. One of the principal reasons why many people, both Christians and followers of other religions, feel that there can never be a level playing field in a dialogue with Christianity has to do with the claims Christians make about Jesus. If Christians enter the game of dialogue insisting that Jesus is the only Savior for all humanity and that God's Word in him is God's final word for everyone, then no matter how much give-and-take goes on during the game, at the final whistle — or at the end of the final (eschatological) play-offs — Christianity has to win. To extend our analogy, the other religions may score some impressive goals, but at the end (of this game or of history), only Christ's team can win. This means that although Christians may learn much from how the other team plays the game, they never are really worried about losing — which means they can never learn anything really important. It seems, in other words, that if God has made only one figure and one religion the funnel for God's love and saving grace for all the others, then a truly *mutual dialogue* of religions, in which each participant stands ready to learn as much as any other, is not possible.

This, then, is how it seems to Christians who choose to experiment with something like a Mutuality Model for understanding other religions. To them, it appears that traditional understandings of Christ and the church throw up *doctrinal* obstacles to the *ethical* obligation to engage in authentic dialogue with others. Something is wrong. Something has to be reexamined and re-visioned. And so they are rereading the Bible in light of their new experience of other religions and are searching for new understandings of Jesus that would enable them to be as open to other religions as they are deeply committed to him. They don't want to water down what makes Jesus unique, but neither do they want to water down the God-given uniqueness of other religious figures and paths. We'll be exploring and weighing various proposals for how this can be done. Once again, another team of theologians is trying to balance the teeter-totter.

We should add here that what the Mutuality Model is saying about the need for, and the obstacles to, a level playing field for dialogue applies not only to Christianity. Other religions who enter the game of dialogue claiming or believing that they are God's chosen team meant to win over all others in the end (some scholars hold that all religions do this in one form or another) will cause similar problems. Whether they recognize such problems, or what they might do about them, is not the business of Christians. The conversation we are trying to foster in this book is for Christians, among Christians.

And the Christian conversation about what we are calling the Mutuality Model is going forward, and heating up. A few decades ago, experts were referring to this model as a minority opinion among the churches and theologians. Toward the end of the previous century, however, a recognized handbook of Catholic theology made the following, for many surprising, assessment: "Pluralist [read mutuality] positions, which are proposed as the most open and adequate theological explanations of the empirical fact of the diversity of religions, ... seem to be replacing inclusivism [read the Fulfillment Model] as the Christian theological position of choice."[4] Not everyone would agree with this assessment — or with this "choice."

Because the Mutuality Model seems to occupy the center of the storm that is disturbing Christians as they grapple with the challenge of religious pluralism, we will spend a little more time in laying out both the content and the criticisms of this model than we have with the others. To negotiate the storm, readers will need as much data as possible.

Three Bridges

A favorite image used by some proponents of the Mutuality Model to describe the implications of their project is "the crossing of the Rubicon"; this model invites Christians to make a move which, like Caesar's, will launch them onto new terrain full of new possibilities as well as new uncertainties. Whether this image describes the facts as well as it expresses theologians' sense of self-importance is open to discussion. Whatever the case may be, although this model may not be calling for something entirely new (which requires Christians to abandon their previous homes), it is exploring something genuinely new (which necessitates some radical remodeling). In order to better distinguish and evaluate the various ways Christians are trying to make this move, we will describe three different, but complementary, bridges which beckon Christians to cross over to a Mutuality Model.

1. The *philosophical-historical bridge.* It rests mainly on two pillars: the historical limitations of all religions and the philosophical possibility (or probability) that there is one Divine Reality behind and within them all.

2. The *religious-mystical bridge.* This bridge is held up by what many religious people would agree on: that the Divine is both more than anything

---

4. Wolfgang Beinert and Francis Schüssler Fiorenza, *Handbook of Catholic Theology* (New York: Crossroad, 1995), 95. Somewhat earlier, and not at all happily, Carl Braaten made a similar assessment when he admitted that a pluralist or mutuality theology of religions "has won hands down within the religious studies departments of universities and divinity schools. It is rapidly making inroads into the liberal and mainstream denominational seminaries" ("The Triune God: The Source and Model of Christian Unity and Mission," *Missiology* 18 [1990]: 419).

experienced by any one religion and yet present in the mystical experience of all of them.

3. The *ethical-practical bridge*. The construction materials for this bridge also seem to be found among most religions: the recognition that the needs and sufferings afflicting humanity and the earth are a common concern for persons of all traditions. Such sufferings are a call issued to all the religious families, which if taken seriously will enable them to realize an even more effective dialogue with each other.

In our walk across each of these bridges, we will generally have one particular theologian as our guide, though we will point out other fellow-travelers. In a sense, this Mutuality Model is more ecumenical than the others: while the main voices of the Replacement Model were Evangelical Protestants and the voices we heard in the Fulfillment Model were especially Catholic, the voices that speak to us in this model make for a polyphony of Christian churches. Remember, too, that these bridges are different ways of trying to get to the same destination. They allow for multiple crossings on different occasions. Depending on the baggage one brings to the trip, or the cultural-personal weather one encounters, one bridge may make for smoother going than another.

The Philosophical-Historical Bridge

Our primary guide across this bridge is one of the first contemporary Christian theologians to have crossed it and to urge others to follow. John Hick is a British theologian — though he spent many years in the United States — whose own spiritual and intellectual journey has plotted a path familiar to many other Christians. Overwhelmed by what he experienced as "the infinite boredom" of much of institutional Christianity in England, Hick sought out other, more dynamic and engaging forms of discipleship. He underwent a "spiritual conversion" that electrified and transformed him into "a Christian of a strongly evangelical and indeed fundamentalist kind." He came to feel personally that Jesus was his "living lord and savior," "God the Son Incarnate," savior of all humanity. Hick was born again and decided to become a minister in the Presbyterian Church. But as he pursued his academic study of religion, as he met and came to work with persons of other faiths especially in his multireligious hometown of Birmingham, Hick was shaken by "the diversity of apparent revelations." His Evangelical moorings were shaken. He underwent another conversion, not in his deep commitment to Jesus but in his theology of Jesus, Christianity, and religion in general. In the early 1970s, Hick sounded his call for what he termed a Copernican revolution in Christianity. That call has been developing and ringing amid the walls of universities and churches ever since.[5] As a philosopher and theologian, Hick raises his call carefully, graciously, but rigorously. He has many critics, many of them his good friends.

5. John Hick, *God Has Many Names* (London: Macmillan, 1980), 1–5.

A New Map of Religions

For Hick, the evidence for the need of a Copernican revolution and for "a new map for the universe of faiths" has been mounting persistently over the past century. But the churches, he feels, have been afraid to realistically confront this evidence. The uneasiness and shifts in the Christian theology of religions that we have reviewed in previous chapters — from Replacement to Fulfillment, from "pagans" to "anonymous Christians," from *no* salvation to *some* salvation outside the church, from utter darkness in the religions to "rays of light" — are for Hick indications that Christians are trying to face the evidence of God's presence in other faiths. But he considers theological efforts to regard other religions as "anonymous Christians" or as "preparations for the Gospel" to be "nice tries." Rahner's argument that other religions are "ways of salvation" leading to fulfillment in Christ is for Hick "a psychological bridge between the no longer acceptable older view and the new view which is emerging." He adds: "sooner or later we have to get off the bridge and on to the other side."[6]

And so in 1973, Hick pushed on to the other side and proposed his Copernican revolution in theology. It reflects Copernicus's model of the universe:

> [It] involves a . . . radical transformation in our conception of the universe of faiths and the place of our own religion within it. . . . [It demands] a paradigm shift from a Christianity-centered or Jesus-centered to a God-centered model of the universe of faiths. One then sees the great world religions as different human responses to the one divine Reality, embodying different perceptions which have been formed in different historical and cultural circumstances.[7]

There we have what Hick thinks is a revolution in Christian attitudes and feelings: the center of the religious universe, at least for human beings on this planet, is no longer the church, no longer Jesus, but God. Later, as Hick's critics helped him hone his revolution, he no longer used the word or symbol "God" to point to the center. Realizing that the image of God all too often bears the "made in Christianity" label, realizing that religions like Buddhism do not even speak of God or *a* Divine Being, he used expressions like "the Real" or the "really Real." He was looking not for a name but for a pointer; he was searching for a term that would indicate not what's at the center but that there is a center, even though humans will never know clearly and fully what it contains.

---

6. John Hick, "Whatever Path Men Choose," in *Christianity and Other Religions*, ed. John Hick and Brian Hebblethwaite (Philadelphia: Fortress Press, 1980), 180–81.

7. John Hick, *God and the Universe of Faiths* (New York: St. Martin's Press, 1973), 131. Hick has since given his pluralist perspective a more elaborate presentation and foundation in *An Interpretation of Religion: Human Responses to the Transcendent* (New Haven: Yale University Press, 1989).

One Real, Many Cultural Expressions

But how can Hick be sure that there is one center or source or goal for all religions? He can't — at least not as a philosopher. That's why he proposed his revolutionary view as a *hypothesis*. It's the best way to make sense of the data of humankind's religious history. According to Hick the philosopher, although one cannot prove the existence of the Divine and the necessity of faith, one can lay out sound arguments why the decision to believe that there is a Divine Reality at the source and heart of the universe makes good sense and contributes to a happy, healthy life. (Such arguments are in his books on the philosophy of religion.)[8] Now, if one makes such a religious choice, then it makes further sense to adopt the hypothesis that the same Divine Reality — remember, we're pointing not naming — forms the heart of all the different religions. Why? First of all, such a hypothesis serves practical purposes of communication and cooperation between the religions. If there is not a common source or goal for the religions, then not only do they speak different languages, but they're going in different directions; or, to resort to an earlier image, they're playing different games. The rules of one don't apply to the other; the concerns of one are totally different from those of others. Communication not only breaks down; it can't even get started. For a creative Intelligence to have come up with such an arrangement would not speak well of either creativity or intelligence.

Besides these practical reasons, Hick also finds internal evidence in his study of religious history. At least since the time of what is called the Axial Period — 800 to 200 B.C.E. — he detects a common agenda, as it were, for most of the religious traditions that began to take shape during that period: in one way or the other, they all are trying to improve on the human condition in this world; and they seek to do so by urging humans to shift or "convert" from a self-centered to an Other-centered, or Reality-centered, way of living. Perhaps that's the reason why, despite the mind-bending differences in beliefs and rituals, those persons who are considered "saints" or "holy people" in each of the religions do look very much alike. They are persons who are profoundly at peace with themselves and trying to live at peace with others. A philosopher might conclude that the very different trees that bear such common ethical fruits most likely have common roots.

Furthermore, Hick finds within all religious traditions a distinction, "both ancient and widespread," that also makes good philosophical sense: they all distinguish "between, on the one hand, the Godhead in all its own infinite depths beyond human experience and comprehension and, on the other hand, the Godhead as finitely experienced by humanity." In other words, all religions seem to recognize that the Godhead or the Real that they are truly experiencing is always

---

8. See John Hick, *The Philosophy of Religion*, 4th ed. (Englewood Cliffs, N.J.: Prentice Hall, 1990), and *An Interpretation of Religion*, 210–30.

more than what they experience. This "more" is what Hick hypothesizes to be the generating energy of all religions.[9]

To try to make clearer sense of the data he finds in religious history, Hick turns to the philosopher Immanuel Kant's understanding of how our mind works when it enables us to "know" something. According to Kant, we never experience anything directly, the way an image is immediately reflected off a mirror. Rather, all the sense data that pour into our mental machinery are accepted, processed, and filtered by the make-up of that machinery. And our machinery is greatly influenced by the time and place, the society and culture, in which we live. As Hick puts it, all experience is therefore "experiencing as." We never get an immediate, accurate take on the object itself (*das Ding an sich* — the thing in itself). Rather, what we claim to know is only an image of the object — an image formed by the way the sense input has been processed and configured by our knowing minds. In philosophical terms, which may or may not be helpful for nonphilosophers, what we know is always the thing's *phenomenon* — the image resulting from the way it presents itself and the way our minds process it. We never really, or never fully, know the *noumenon* — the thing in itself.

Applying all this to his hypothesis of the Real behind all religions, Hick argues that although religious persons really do *experience* the Real, they know it only in the form or shape of their particular historical, social, and psychological categories. They never have a direct, an immediate, take on the Real. They know the Real's "phenomena," but they can never grasp the Real-in-itself, its *noumenon.* Hick states this not on the authority of Kant but because he thinks Kant sheds further light on what he finds all the religions saying — that the Divine is as real as it is mysterious, that what religions know and proclaim about the Divine is true, but the Truth is infinitely more than what is known. The many religions of humanity, therefore, "constitute different ways of *experiencing, conceiving,* and *living* in relation to an ultimate divine Reality which transcends all our varied versions of it."[10]

For Hick, the pieces of the picture that the religions do have are always painted in symbols, myths, and metaphors. Since the subject matter of the picture is the mysterious, ever-more Real, there's no other way by which it can touch us or by which we can try to talk about what has touched us. To claim that we can speak in hard-and-fast concepts and definitions about the Real would be to foolishly think we can climb out of our bodies and set aside our embodied ways of knowing; it would be to claim a direct, immediate, face-to-face encounter with the Divine. Philosophers would say that's impossible (unless you're an angel). The religions would call it blasphemy. And so if all experience of the Divine Real is, like all human experience, a matter of "experiencing as," then symbols and metaphors fill in the blanks behind the "as": We experience the

---

9. John Hick, *Problems of Religious Pluralism* (London: Macmillan, 1985), 28–45; see also Hick, *An Interpretation of Religion,* 343–59.

10. Hick, *An Interpretation of Religion,* 14 and 235–36; emphasis added.

Divine as Father, as Mother, as Spirit, as Fire, as Way, as Force. All these symbols, and the stories and myths in which they usually are nested, *do* tell us, or they *can* tell us, something true about the Divine. But in the end, according to Hick, they really tell us more about ourselves than about the Real — about how we have been caressed by the Divine and how we resolve to live with the Divine, rather than about what the Divine Spirit really is. Again, symbols point to rather than define.

Hick goes on to remind us that if that which is symbolized — the Real — is one, the symbols by which it is perceived and expressed will be many. One divine *noumen,* many religious phenomena. Very many. This is because the Divine Real is so versatile and inexhaustible in its ways of signaling its presence to humans; it is also because the religious symbols, by which those signals are picked up, are fashioned in such a diversity of human cultures. The diversity is such that the many religions and their symbols can be not only different but even contradictory. The Real, for example, is symbolized in both personal and impersonal forms — Father or Mother, Shiva or Krishna — but also as Emptiness or Way or Force. Also, the human being is understood in some religions as an individual self that will live on for all eternity; in other traditions, the person is conceived as a confluence of energies that will find its true being by ultimately losing itself in the ocean of the Real. Hick tells us that we should not necessarily be surprised, or confused, by such head-butting differences. What boggles the human brain as a contradiction may be an invitation to explore more deeply the richness of the Real. Perhaps there are reasons, both in our human nature and in the Real itself, why we can, and should, experience the Real as both loving Father and indescribable Force, or ourselves as both individuals that endure forever and pieces that lose their identity in the bigger picture.

Such contradictions, if we plumb their depths, may well be complementary, or at least non-exclusionary, rather than contradictory. To strengthen this possibility, Hick points out that such differences between religious symbols and beliefs, even when they appear contradictory, usually don't make for much of a difference in the end-product of all religions. Religions appear equally effective, or ineffective, in stirring and guiding their followers to change the direction of their lives from self-centeredness to Other-centeredness whether they use personal or impersonal symbols for the Real or for the ultimate end of humankind. A Christian saint who believes that the Real is Father and a Buddhist holy person who believes that the Real is Emptiness can both achieve similar lives of peace in themselves and compassion for others. Similarities in ethics suggest that differences in doctrine may not be that important.

Avoiding the Slippery Slopes of Relativism

But if there is one Real behind or within the various religious traditions, does this not mean that, despite their evident and distinguishing differences, they are all, deep down, of equal value? Though they use different tools, don't they all get the same job done? Or, in the familiar image: Aren't they all different paths leading to the same mountaintop? No matter what path you choose, won't it eventually get you to the top? Most proponents of the Mutuality Model would answer no. They are aware of the dangers of their model. To expand our image, anyone who holds that there is one mountaintop for all the different religious paths has to take special precautions against sliding down the "slippery slopes of relativism." Relativism is the dark valley in which differences don't matter — or in which one can't see clearly enough to make any value judgments between religious beliefs and practices. A relativist affirms that all religious paths, no matter how strange or weird they appear, are leading *up*. They'll get to the mountaintop, eventually. So whatever path you're on, just keep walking!

But Hick and his fellow-travelers on the philosophical bridge counter: differences do matter — or they can. Not all the religious paths are necessarily leading upward to the mountaintop. This is evident to anyone who has paged through the book of religious history. No one can deny how much damage the religions have done — personally, socially, internationally. In the name of religion, people have been psychologically traumatized; groups have been exploited; wars have been fought. Some of the worst sins of humanity have been carried out because "God wills it" or because "God is on our side" or because "God speaks through me." As one theologian has phrased it, there are many things in the history and present-day practice of religion that are simply intolerable — like the Crusades, or apartheid, or torture, or the burning of widows, or clitoridectomy.[11] Simply put: if there's a lot of good in religion, there's also a lot of bad. And one has to be able to tell the difference. One has to be able to distinguish between religious paths that lead up and those that lead down or get lost in detours.

Hick recognizes this. He maintains that it is "self-evident, at least since the Axial Age, that not all religious persons, practices, and beliefs are of equal value."[12] But then the question immediately pops up: How can you mark the differences in value? What are the criteria for evaluating true and false, good and bad, in the different religions and in the dialogue among them? Hick argues that the religions themselves provide the criteria. If all of them, with their different beliefs and practices, are after the goal of redirecting the energies of the human heart from self to Other/other, from me to us, then the measuring stick for determining a religion's value is quite clear: Does it promote a "self-sacrificing concern for the good of others"? Does it foster "a voluntary renunciation of ego-centeredness and a self-giving to, or self-losing in, the Real" which will generate "acceptance, compassion, love for all humankind, or even for all life"? To weigh the value or truth of a religion, therefore, one must examine whether and how much it promotes "that limitlessly better quality of human existence which comes about in the transition from self-centeredness to Reality-centeredness."[13]

---

11. Gilkey, "Plurality and Its Theological Implications," 44–46.
12. Hick, *An Interpretation of Religion*, 89, 299.
13. Ibid., 325.

For Hick and many theologians who move in this direction, the guide posts that will help us avoid the slippery slopes of relativism and the standards by which we can assess religions are ethical rather than doctrinal or experiential. By their fruits, we will know them.

Yet Hick warns that we will never know them *fully*. With such ethical criteria, we can evaluate particular doctrines or practices or movements within a religion, but we can never really rank "the great world religions as totalities." Why? Because the religions, in the sweep of their belief systems and histories, are much too diverse, complex, and meandering. No one can ever get a full picture or gather all the necessary data to really compare the ethical fruits of, say, Christianity and Buddhism. So while we are still struggling up the mountain sides, while we have not yet attained the view from the top, we cannot say that one path, in its totality, is better than another. We cannot say that Christianity's overall view of the Real and how to live in harmony with it is superior to that of Hinduism or Buddhism. Whether any one religion excels all the others can be known only when the journey is finished, when the top is reached, when history has ground to a close. Hick the philosopher maintains that the debate between atheists and believers will really be settled only "eschatologically" — only at the end of one's life or at the end of history. The same is true for the question of whether one religion surpasses the others. So what can be known only at the end should not distract us during the journey. For now, we should keep trekking — walking together and helping each other along our different paths.

What about Jesus?

The proponents of this historical-philosophical bridge recognize that many of their fellow Christians will feel that such a bridge is closed to them. Why? Because, as we heard in the Replacement and Fulfillment Models, Christians have always believed that Jesus is the only conduit between God and humanity. He's the only Son of God and the only Savior. Hick and his companions want to help such Christians by offering them a picture of Jesus which, based on New Testament scholarship and on concrete Christian experience, will affirm the eminent status of Jesus without lowering that of other religious leaders.

Hick doesn't call Christians to abandon their traditional way of talking about Jesus; he just wants them to understand what kind of language they are using. It's not scientific language that aims to deliver hard facts and clear pictures. Rather, it's poetic language that works with symbols and metaphors. What such language is trying to express is not something you can take a picture of; rather, it's something you sense or intuit, something as real in your feelings as it is beyond description in words. This is the kind of language used for Jesus, in the New Testament and throughout history — Messiah, Savior, Word of God, Son of Man, Good Shepherd, and, especially, Son of God. The early Christians applied all these words and images to Jesus not because they had researched all that he had said and done and so rationally concluded to a definition of who he was;

rather, they were trying to put into words what they had experienced in and through him. They were trying to say how he had affected their lives and what he must be in order to have so affected them. They were talking about matters of the heart, not conclusions of the head. So they used the language of poetry, not the language of philosophy or science.

And they found this language, with its symbols and metaphors and images, in the cultures in which they were nurtured — first Judaism and then the broader world of Greece and Rome. One of the central symbols, though certainly not the earliest, that the first Jesus-followers adopted centered around incarnation: Jesus was the incarnate Word of God, the Son of God. To understand how this came about and what it meant, Hick points out that there is a general consensus among Scripture scholars that Jesus himself never talked this way. He never called himself the Son of God. It was a title that his followers gave him in view of their powerful experiences of him during his lifetime and especially after his death. To try to say who this man must have been — and still is — in order to have so filled their lives with the presence and power of God, they turned to the image of "Son of God," a title often used in Jewish tradition to designate a person who was extraordinarily close to God and used by God. It indicated specialness, not exclusivity.

But as the early community moved deeper into the Greco-Roman world, the image of the Son of God was tightened into the notion of incarnation and unique deification. For Hick, this is entirely understandable: "ideas of divinity embodied in human life [were] ... widespread in the ancient world ... so that there is nothing in the least surprising in the deification of Jesus in that cultural environment."[14] And so we have in John's Gospel the beautiful, but also very Greek, picture of Jesus as the Word of God enfleshed in a human being. John's Gospel, with its image of incarnation, was one of the last books in the New Testament to be written. Yet this metaphor of Jesus as the incarnate Son of God took central stage in subsequent Christian history — and has stayed there ever since. During the early councils of the church, Hick tells us, these poetic images of incarnation and Son of God were set in the stone of Greek philosophy. They became hard and fast definitions, laid out and defended with the philosophical language of "nature" and "person" and "substance." The poetry of the New Testament "hardened into prose and escalated from a metaphorical son of God to a metaphysical God the Son, of the same substance as the Father, within the triune Godhead." And of course, in such philosophical prose, to be son of God meant to be the *only* Son of God.

Hick warns us not to think that such developments were mistakes, as if they led people away from what Jesus was all about. Rather, it was natural that the early Christian community would try to express its experience of Jesus "in the language of absolutes." To understand Jesus as the Son of God consubstantial

---

14. John Hick, "Jesus and the World Religions," in *The Myth of God Incarnate*, ed. John Hick (London: SCM, 1977), 174.

with the Father was for those Greek-Roman Christians "an effective way, within that cultural milieu, of expressing Jesus' significance as the one through whom men and women had transformingly encountered God." But what was effective and unproblematic then, Hick adds, may not be so today. The literal, rational, perhaps naïve way in which incarnation and the title "Son of God" are understood today not only creates insoluble philosophical problems for many people (How can two natures exist in one person, as the Council of Chalcedon in 451 put it?) but also gives rise to the kind of "one-and-only" language about Jesus that blocks dialogue and offends other religious believers.

So Hick's solution is not to do away with belief in incarnation and in Jesus as the Son of God but to take such beliefs for what they are: poetry, symbolism, metaphor. And that means that we understand these central creeds of Christianity *not literally but seriously*. This is another provocative and controversial aspect of Hick's proposed "Copernican revolution" — to move beyond the literalism in Christian beliefs about Jesus, just as the churches have moved beyond the previous literalism in their beliefs about creation. He expects that "Christianity ... will outgrow its theological fundamentalism, its literal interpretations of the idea of the incarnation as it has largely outgrown its biblical fundamentalism."[15] Just as many Christians no longer believe that God literally produced the world in six days, so they will no longer believe that God is literally a Father who literally engenders only one Son.

But if Christians don't take the image of "Son of God" literally as a fact, what does it mean to take it seriously as a symbol? First of all, Hick goes on, it means that the statement "Jesus is the Son of God" is really telling us more about ourselves (or the early Christians) than about Jesus. Symbols and poetry are not meant to give us "empirical, metaphysical" data but, rather, to express or stir attitudes, feelings, convictions, response. So when the early Christians started to call Jesus the Son of God — and when Christians continued to do so through the ages — it was not because they were told by God or by Jesus that this is so but because they had felt God speaking to them, touching them, inspiring them through this man Jesus. To meet Jesus was to meet God, they realized. God had so entered their lives through Jesus that it became difficult to distinguish the two. How to talk about this? How to tell others how Jesus had affected their lives and could do the same for them? The Jews had always talked about sons of God. The Greeks had believed in "divine men." Well, that's what Jesus was, but eminently so. He was divine, the Son of God.

So even though Hick emphasizes that the metaphorical language of "God Incarnate" or "Son of God" tells us more about Christians than about Jesus, it *does* also tell us something very real about Jesus. To try to express what the symbolic language of Jesus as the Son of God means for us today, Hick suggests that Christians make greater use of the Spirit (or inspirational) christology that is also found in the New Testament rather than the Word (or incarnational)

15. Ibid., 183–84.

christology that has dominated the churches since the councils of the fourth and fifth centuries. In a Spirit christology, Jesus is said to be divine not because God literally descended from heaven and literally impregnated Jesus' mother but because Jesus was completely filled with the Spirit that is given to everyone and was so totally responsive to that Spirit. A Spirit christology understands the story of Mary conceiving by the Holy Spirit symbolically; the account tells us that the presence of the Spirit was integral to Jesus from the first moment of his existence.

According to such an understanding of Jesus as Spirit-filled, what is incarnated in him is not the abstract philosophical notion of a divine nature, but the dynamic reality of God's love. In this picture, the Divine is not considered as some kind of substance or stuff that somehow becomes Jesus; rather the Divine is understood as an activity with a purpose — the energy of love embracing all persons and calling them to embrace each other. Because Jesus was fully responsive to this Spirit, he became — one might even say, *literally* became — God's love loving in the world. Hick goes so far as to maintain that there is a "numerical identity" between God's love and Jesus. "Jesus' *agape* [love] is not a representation of God's *agape; it is* that *agape* operating in a finite mode; it is the eternal divine *agape* made flesh."[16] How did Christians know this? Because that's what they experienced in their relationship with Jesus during his life and still after his death — that to meet Jesus along the roads of Palestine or in the pages of the Gospel and to continue meeting him in the breaking of bread is to feel the very love of God enfolding them and urging them to go forth in love for others.

In this view of how Jesus is divine, great things are said about Jesus — without removing the possibility that similarly great things can be said about other religious figures. On the basis of their tradition and their present experience, Christians can say that Jesus *truly* embodies and expresses God's love, but they will be hesitant to say that he does so *solely* or *fully*. Hick the philosopher recognizes that "it is entirely possible that the divine *agape* has been more fully incarnated in this life [Jesus'] than in any other." But he maintains that it is a possibility we would have to establish "only on the basis of historical information" about Jesus and also about other religious figures; such information, however, we would never be able to gather sufficiently to know for sure. Better, therefore, to drop all talk of "only" or "fully" and to speak about what Christians do know: "that God's gracious and demanding love was embodied in Jesus' love in so powerful a way that we ourselves are grasped by it today, some nineteen centuries later."[17]

The bottom line to Hick's understanding of the uniqueness of Jesus can be summarized in a crisply elegant turn of Latin words that lose a bit of their

---

16. Hick, *God and the Universe of Faiths,* 148–58.

17. John Hick, "Evil and Incarnation," in *Incarnation and Myth: The Debate Continued,* ed. Michael Goulder (Grand Rapids, Mich.: Eerdmans, 1979), 83–84.

elegance in translation: before their brothers and sisters in other religions, Christians can and must continue to announce that Jesus is *totus Deus* — wholly God. But they cannot, and should not, claim that he is *totum Dei* — the whole of God. All that he was and all that he did and said were transfused with, and so expressive of, the Divine Spirit. But all that the Divine Spirit is and does cannot be confined to Jesus, or to any human incarnation of the Divine. This is not just a philosophical statement. According to many New Testament experts, it also reflects what Jesus thought of himself: "Contrary to later (and usually heretical) Christologies, Jesus as he is depicted in the Gospels and epistles of the newer Testament, does not wish to be considered (as it were) all the God of God there is."[18] Which leaves open the possibility that other religious leaders and figures might also be *totus Deus,* or "wholly God."[19]

If Hick's philosophical bridge to a Mutuality Model for understanding other religions is too narrow or demanding for Christians of a less rational bent, there are other crossings, as we shall see in the next chapter, that may prove to be broader and smoother.

Further Readings

Apczynski, John V. "John Hick's Theocentrism: Revolutionary or Implicitly Exclusivist?" *Modern Theology* 8 (1992): 39–52.

Cobb, John B., Jr. "Beyond 'Pluralism.'" In *Christian Uniqueness Reconsidered: The Myth of Pluralistic Theology of Religions.* Ed. Gavin D'Costa. Maryknoll, N.Y.: Orbis Books, 1990, 81–95.

D'Costa, Gavin. "The New Missionary: John Hick and Religious Plurality." *International Bulletin of Missionary Research* 15 (1991): 66–70.

———. "Whose Objectivity? Which Neutrality? The Doomed Quest for a Neutral Vantage Point to Judge Religions." *Religious Studies* 29 (1993):·79–96.

Duffy, Stephen J. "The Stranger within Our Gates: Interreligious Dialogue and the Normativeness of Jesus." In *The Myriad Christ: Plurality and the Quest for Unity in Contemporary Christology.* Ed. T. Merrigan and J. Haers. Leuven: Leuven University Press, 2000, 3–30.

Fredericks, James L. *Faith among Faiths: Christian Theology and Non-Christian Religions.* New York: Paulist Press, 1999, 37–54; see also 79–118.

Gilkey, Langdon. "Plurality and Its Theological Implications." In *The Myth of Christian Uniqueness: Toward a Pluralistic Theology of Religions.* Ed. John Hick and Paul F. Knitter. Maryknoll, N.Y.: Orbis Books, 1987, 37–50.

Gillis, Chester. "Radical Christologies? An Analysis of the Christologies of John Hick and Paul Knitter." In *The Myriad Christ: Plurality and the Quest for Unity in Contemporary Christology.* Ed. T. Merrigan and J. Haers. Leuven: Leuven University Press, 2000, 521–34.

Heim, S. Mark. *Salvations: Truth and Difference in Religions.* Maryknoll, N.Y.: Orbis Books, 1995, chapter 1.

---

18. Douglas John Hall, *Why Christian? For Those on the Edge of Faith* (Minneapolis: Fortress/Augsburg, 1998), 33.

19. Hick, *God and the Universe of Faiths,* 159.

Hick, John. *A Christian Theology of Religions: The Rainbow of Faiths*. Louisville: Westminster/John Knox Press, 1995, chapters 4–6.

———. *An Interpretation of Religion: Human Responses to the Transcendent*. New Haven: Yale University Press, 1989, 21–55, 233–51, 299–361.

———. "A Religious Understanding of Religion: A Model of the Relationship between Traditions." In *Inter-religious Models and Criteria*. Ed. J. Kellenberger. New York: St. Martin's Press, 1993, 21–36.

———. "Straightening the Record: Some Responses to Critics." *Modern Theology* 6 (1990): 187–96.

Insole, Christopher J. "Why John Hick Cannot, and Should Not, Stay out of the Jam Pot." *Religious Studies* 36 (2000): 25–33.

Kaufman, Gordon D. "Religious Diversity, Historical Consciousness, and Christian Theology." In *The Myth of Christian Uniqueness: Toward a Pluralistic Theology of Religions*. Ed. John Hick and Paul F. Knitter. Maryknoll, N.Y.: Orbis Books, 1987, 3–15.

Merrigan, Terrence. "The Historical Jesus and the Pluralist Theology of Religions." In *The Myriad Christ: Plurality and the Quest for Unity in Contemporary Christology*. Ed. T. Merrigan and J. Haers. Leuven: Leuven University Press, 2000, 61–82.

———. "Religious Knowledge in the Pluralist Theology of Religions." *Theological Studies* 58 (1997): 686–707.

Min, Anselm K. "Christology and Theology of Religions: John Hick and Karl Rahner." *Louvain Studies* 11 (1986): 3–21.

Netland, Harold A. "Professor Hick on Religious Pluralism." *Religious Studies* 22 (1986): 249–62.

Ogden, Schubert M. "Problems in the Case for a Pluralistic Theology of Religions." *Journal of Religion* 68 (1988): 493–507.

Race, Alan. *Interfaith Encounter: The Twin Tracks of Theology and Dialogue*. London: SCM, 2001, 65–123.

Schillebeeckx, Edward. *The Church: The Human Story of God*. New York: Crossroad, 1990, 1–14, 144–86.

Twiss, Sumner B. "The Philosophy of Religious Pluralism: A Critical Appraisal of Hick and His Critics." *Journal of Religion* 70 (1990): 533–67.

Wildman, Wesley J. "Pinning Down the Crisis in Contemporary Christology." *Dialog* 37 (1998): 15–21.

Chapter 8

The Mystical and
the Prophetic Bridges

The Religious-Mystical Bridge

You might say that the main difference between what we are calling the religious-mystical and the philosophical-historical bridges has to do with where they start. The philosophers-historians begin with the human, arguing that no religion can claim to have the full, final, unsurpassable truth about the Divine because all human knowledge is historically conditioned or socially constructed and therefore limited. The followers of the religious-mystical approach begin with the Divine and lift up what they consider to be evident to all religious persons — that what is found in the heart of every religion is something that infinitely exceeds anything a human being, or community, can feel and express. From this, the same conclusion arises: no religion can deliver the full and final truth. So while the philosophers stress the finiteness of all religious radio receivers, the mystics emphasize the infinity of the Message that is sent.

Yet these variations don't touch the bigger difference between the two bridges. For Christians who walk a religious-mystical bridge, what is really important is not that the Divine is infinite (everyone will admit that) but that the same Divine Mystery or Reality is being experienced within the many different religions. There is a core mystical experience pulsating within the religious traditions that have endured through the ages. And if there is a core mystical experience, there is a core Mystical Reality within them all. Yes, each religious individual and community will hear this Reality through their different "socially constructed" antennae, and, therefore, yes, there are mind-boggling differences — that often look like contradictions — between the religions. In no way do travelers on this bridge want to neglect the startling differences between faith communities. Yet despite these differences, despite the tensions between God as personal and God as suprapersonal or even God as no-thing, those who take the mystical path to understanding religious pluralism affirm that the differences don't dry up the deeper divine current that feeds all the different religious wells.

How do they know this? On what grounds do they make an assertion that seems to fly in the face of contradictory differences? Though they do make use of philosophical arguments and historical evidence that point to astounding similarities within the astounding differences between religions, still the pivotal reason for holding to a mystical center in all religions is mystical experience itself. You know it when you have it. Or as one theologian has put it: "There is certainly a unity [among religions], but this unity can...really be perceived only at the mystical level."[1] That level is down deep. Proponents of this mystical bridge feel that the deeper a person enters into the religious experience that is made possible through her own particular religion, the more aware she will be that what she is experiencing cannot be limited to her own religion — and the more openness and sensitivity she will have to recognizing the same Mystery in other religions. The deeper one descends into one's own religious well, the more one will realize the one underground river that nourishes them all.

Maybe that's why most of the guides who lead us across this bridge are Asian. It's a bridge built for and by mystics — and the flower of mysticism, as the experts admit, has bloomed more abundantly in Asian religious soil than in that of the West. So the Christian theologians who can help us across this bridge live in Asia or have been influenced by their Asian religious cultures — Stanley Samartha, Michael Amaladoss, Sebastian Painadath, Felix Wilfred, Francis D'Sa, Seiichi Yagi; and we can add a well-known Westerner who learned much from the East: Thomas Merton.[2] But for this chapter, our primary guide will be one of the best-known, most-tested, erudite, and challenging pioneers of interreligious dialogue during the past century: Raimon Panikkar.

A Divine-Human-Cosmic Unity

Raimon Panikkar has found his long life's purpose and delight in straddling and connecting vastly different worlds. Born of a Spanish (Catalan) Catholic mother and Indian Hindu father, spending most of his professional academic life commuting between American and Indian universities, he described himself in later years in this way: "I 'left' as a Christian, 'found myself' a Hindu, and 'returned' as a Buddhist, without having ceased to be a Christian." He has always based his interreligious explorations on an amazing breadth of scholarship — he holds doctorates in chemistry, philosophy, and theology; speaks about a dozen lan-

1. Felix Wilfred, "Some Tentative Reflections on the Language of Christian Uniqueness," *Vidyajyoti* 57 (1993): 666.

2. Michael Amaladoss, *Making All Things New: Dialogue, Pluralism, and Evangelization in Asia* (Maryknoll, N.Y.: Orbis Books, 1990); Amaladoss, "The Mystery of Christ and Other Religions: An Indian Perspective," *Vidyajyoti* 63 (1999): 327–38; Francis X. D'Sa, "The Interreligious Dialogue of the Future: Exploration into the Cosmotheandric Nature of Dialogue," *Vidyajyoti* 61 (1997): 693–707; D'Sa, "The Universe of Faith and the Pluriverse of Belief: Are All Religions Talking about the Same Thing?" *Dialogue and Alliance* 11 (1997): 88–116; Sebastian Painadath, "Spiritual Dynamics of Dialogue," *Vidyajyoti* 60 (1996): 813–24; Stanley J. Samartha, *One Christ, Many Religions: Toward a Revised Christology* (Maryknoll, N.Y.: Orbis Books, 1991); Felix Wilfred, "Towards a Better Understanding of Asian Theology," *Vidyajyoti* 62 (1998): 890–915; Seiichi Yagi, "What Can Claim Absoluteness? The Uniqueness of Jesus and the Universality of the Self," *Journal of Asian and Asian American Theology* 1 (1996): 28–42; Yagi, " 'I' in the Words of Jesus," in *The Myth of Christian Uniqueness: Toward a Pluralistic Theology of Religions*, ed. John Hick and Paul F. Knitter (Maryknoll, N.Y.: Orbis Books, 1987), 117–34.

guages and writes in at least six of them; and has published more than thirty books and three hundred essays. Yet the rock-bottom basis of his study of texts and comparison of doctrines is the personal, mystical experience that he pursues in his own practice and that he has identified and learned from in the various religious traditions. An ordained priest and "practicing Catholic," he is also a daily practitioner of yoga and meditation. He sees and speaks not only from erudition but also and mainly from silence.

And what he sees from the vantage point of mystical experience is something that feeds both the prolific variety and the deeper unity of all religions. He has called it "the fundamental religious fact." It's a fact that "does not lie in the realm of doctrine [but] may well be present everywhere and in every religion."[3] It's something that can be known only through experience, but once experienced, it tells us something very real about the world and about ourselves. As an experience, it imbues us with a sense of being at-oned, connected, united, part of. And that with which we are at-oned is not only a divine or transcendent Mystery; it's a Mystery that is also immanent, right here, part of the finite world. It's a Mystery, according to Panikkar, that is experienced as itself being at-oned with human beings and with the material world. So there are three components, as it were, to mystical experience and to what is revealed in such experience: the Divine, the human, and the world. All three are so interrelated that they have their very being in each other; they can't exist without being related to each other. Certainly, the Divine is very different from the human, and the human from the material world; Panikkar is not talking about reducing one to the other. And yet they are as life-givingly related to each other as are fire and the oxygen that feeds it.

In an attempt to find words for something that stretches beyond all verbal description, Panikkar stretches language and speaks of mystical experience as a "cosmotheandric experience" and of all that exists as a "cosmotheandric reality." In Greek, *cosmos* = the world; *theos* = the Divine; *aner* = the human. These three — "the divine, the human, and the earthly — however we may prefer to call them — are the three irreducible dimensions which constitute the real, i.e., any reality inasmuch as it is real."[4] Mystics know — even though they may not use these same words or any words at all — that whatever the Divine is, it breathes within the human and the material. And whatever we humans are, if we aren't aware of the Divine that has its being within us and of the earth that forms us, we don't know who we are. And whatever the earth is, if we can't sense its sacredness and its oneness with us, we will never properly understand or care for it. Also, this interrelatedness between the Divine/human/material is not just a given, static reality. It's alive, and growing, and changing — and dependent

3. Raimon Panikkar, "The Category of Growth in Comparative Religion: A Critical-Self-Examination," *Harvard Theological Review* 66 (1973): 115, 131; Panikkar, *The Intrareligious Dialogue* (New York: Paulist, 1978), 2–23.
4. Raimon Panikkar, *The Cosmotheandric Experience: Emerging Religious Consciousness* (Maryknoll, N.Y.: Orbis Books, 1993), ix.

on how well the human ingredient is aware of and responds to the Divine and the earthly. Focusing on the relationship between the Divine and the human, Panikkar offers some philosophical poetry that teases and tantalizes:

> Man and God are neither two nor one.... There are not two realities: God *and* man/world; but neither is there one: God *or* man/world.... God and man are, so to speak, in close constitutive collaboration for the building up of reality, the unfolding of history, and the continuation of creation.... God, man, and the world are engaged in a unique adventure and this engagement constitutes true reality.... Cosmotheandrism is in a paradoxical fashion (for one can speak in no other way) the infinity of man/world... and the finiteness of God.[5]

So it is this cosmotheandric experience and reality that dwell within and are made available through the various religious streams of the world. They constitute a mystical experience by which persons sense their unity with the Divine and with all fellow creatures, humans and otherwise — an experience that calls one to live out that relationship in ever deeper, life-giving ways, in order, as Panikkar puts it, to foster "the unfolding of history and the continuation of creation." Mystics will have some sense of this, he believes. And because they do, they will know the deeper unity of religions that grounds tremendous diversity. Also, they will be able to value their own religion, and at the same time be free of it: Panikkar affirms that there are "ex-Catholics, ex-Marxists, ex-Buddhists... but I know of no ex-mystics."[6]

One AND Many

But if, for Panikkar, there is the one "religious fact" that grounds the unity of religions, he insists that this unity is just as much many as it is one. Among the mutualist or pluralistic theologians we are getting to know in this part, he stands out as the most resolutely pluralistic. In fact, he thinks that many of his colleagues who want to promote a common dialogue among religions allow themselves to become so concerned about what is common or unifying within the religions that they forget how diverse they are and will, forever, remain. So Panikkar gently chides friends like John Hick for proposing one neat common denominator (like "Reality" or the divine *noumenon*) that will unify all religions. For Panikkar, there isn't such a common denominator to which religious equations can be reduced.[7] Panikkar reminds Hick and others that if they really affirm the pluralism of religions, then, as it were, they're stuck with it. The religions are like the pieces of different puzzles — you're never going to

---

5. Raimon Panikkar, *The Trinity and the Religious Experience of Man* (Maryknoll, N.Y.: Orbis Books, 1973), 74–75.
6. Raimon Panikkar, *The Unknown Christ of Hinduism* (Maryknoll, N.Y.: Orbis Books, 1981), 22.
7. Raimon Panikkar, "God of Life, Idols of Death," *Monastic Studies* 7 (1986): 105.

be able to put them together into a pretty picture or final system. To expand his point, Panikkar turns to the language of postmodernism: "We must accept that some religious traditions are mutually incommensurable."[8] That means you cannot measure one by the other, or all of them by a common yardstick. If there's any unity within the world of religions, it's surrounded and protected by a wall of diversity. You can't find the unity without the diversity. Why is this so?

For Panikkar the "Mystery" within the religions is a reality that doesn't exist "in itself" — that is, without humans and the world. So it has its being within the diversity of humanity and the world. Panikkar gives a jolting but enlightening twist to the familiar image of one mountaintop, a twist that one has to ponder in order to appreciate:

> It is not simply that there are different ways leading to the peak, but that the summit itself would collapse if all the paths disappeared. The peak is in a certain sense the result of the slopes leading to it.... It is not that this reality [the Ultimate Mystery] *has* many names as if there were a reality outside the names. This reality *is* the many names and each name is a new aspect.[9]

In other words, God or the Divine is itself as diverse as are the religions! That's what Panikkar is announcing. The Divine delights in and includes and exists in diversity. The mystics sense this. To think otherwise — to hold that the Divine is one thing — would be to curtail the freedom of the Divine and to box in God: "The living God who speaks through a people, who suffers, who yells or sings or dances is no common denominator. The Christian experience of 'God' through Christ is not the same as the vishnuita [Hindu] experience through Krishna. God is unique — therefore incomparable."[10]

For Panikkar, when it comes to God or to religion, the free-wheeling, unpredictable Spirit will always be one step ahead of Reason or Logos. We're never going to be able to wrap our mind around what the Spirit is up to. Yes, reasonability and clarity and unity are characteristics of God, but Reason, as it were, takes its lead from the Spirit who will always "breathe and move where she will," without a neat script or plan. And this is why, once again, for Panikkar, the diversity of religions will always maintain the upper hand over their unity. Beware, therefore, of "theologies of religion" (like this book?) that are too neat: "Pluralism [that is the diversity of religions or of the Divine] does not allow for a universal system. A pluralistic system would be a contradiction in terms. The incommensurability of ultimate systems is unbridgeable. This incommensurability is not a lesser evil ... but a revelation of the nature of reality."[11] And if

---

8. Ibid., 109.

9. Panikkar, *The Unknown Christ,* 24, 19.

10. Panikkar, "God of Life," 110.

11. Raimon Panikkar, "The Jordan, the Tiber, and the Ganges: Three Kairological Moments of Christic Self-Consciousness," in *The Myth of Christian Uniqueness: Toward a Pluralistic Theology of Religions,* ed. John Hick and Paul F. Knitter (Maryknoll, N.Y.: Orbis Books, 1987), 110.

there's no ultimate system, there's no ultimate religion. All religions must "give up any pretense to monopoly of what religion stands for."[12] Diversity cannot be boiled down to finality. The many will never yield to the one.

Mutual Fecundation

Yet to stop here would not do justice to Panikkar's mystical vision of the religions. If as a mystic he delights in the diversity of the Divine shining through the different religions, his mystical awareness also tells him that the Divine Spirit will not allow the religions, in their splendid diversity, to exist in splendid isolation and ignorance of each other. For this Spirit, though living in diversity, is also one. Within the incommensurable differences of the religions, Panikkar also acknowledges, paradoxically, the one religious fact. What he sees in the world of religions is an almost overwhelming plurality. (For Panikkar, plurality means scattered, unconnected manyness.) But because he trusts that there is the one Spirit who generates and lives within that manyness, he trusts also that there is the possibility and the necessity of connecting, or making relationships among, the many and the varied. Within plurality, therefore, there can be unity. So Panikkar states explicitly that a kind of "peaceful coexistence" between the religions is not enough for them to realize what they really are. Rather, he envisions a "mutual fecundation" amid the different religious communities, an enriching that will enable them to grow more deeply into what they are. By relating to each other, all will discover and expand their own identities.

This is Panikkar's vision of dialogue. He compares it to what Greek theologians of the early centuries called the "dancing together" (*perichoresis*) of the Trinity. Just as the three persons of the triune God receive, maintain, and deepen their differences precisely by dancing in and out of each other, so the religious traditions of the world can dance in dialogue with each other and so grow in both difference and togetherness. Paradoxically, the very incommensurabilities between religious experiences become opportunities to connect with each other and to learn from each other.

Just how this works, Panikkar admits he cannot say. But he does call all religious persons to stir up a *cosmic trust* that such dialogue between utter differences can and does work. The trust is nurtured by their mystical experience, the one religious fact, within them all. Such trust assures religious persons that, ultimately, their differences make not for cacophony but for harmony. Yet it will never be a perfect harmony, one in which all the different notes lose their identity in the sweep of a final symphony. Rather, Panikkar uses the mystical image of "discordant concord" to envision the results of this dialogue. The religions can find ever greater connectedness and deeper unity, yes, but the unity will always remain messy, incomplete. The concord, as beautiful as it might be, will

---

12. Raimon Panikkar, "Have 'Religions' the Monopoly on *Religion?*" *Journal of Ecumenical Studies* 11 (1974): 517.

remain discordant. The dialogue among religions is essentially and happily an unfinished symphony.[13]

To make such a dialogue possible, to feel the One in the many and yet to allow the One always to remain many, the conversation between religious persons must be carried out on the level of experience, of faith, of mystical sharing. Yes, study is essential; learning each other's languages and pondering each other's texts are important; but unless the glow of the mystic's lantern guides all our study and conversation, we will not really see the life and light that connects our differences. So Panikkar is resolutely critical of those scholars who hold that in order to enter the house of another religion, we have to leave our own faith experience at the doorstep. On the contrary: it will be our own religious experience that enables us to recognize and learn from that of our neighbors. In real interreligious dialogue, heart speaks to heart. Only so can persons from differing traditions really "hear" each other. Only so can one's own experience and religious understanding be transformed in the process of dialogue.[14]

What about Jesus?

Like all the bridges to a theology of religions based on mutuality, this mystical-religious approach calls upon Christians to refocus their understanding of Jesus. Such a refocusing is necessary, Panikkar and other Asian theologians suggest, because of the way many Christians, over the centuries and especially during the colonial period, have made Jesus into a "tribal God" — meant to conquer or subdue all the other Gods. This, for Panikkar, is the challenge of the new millennium: "to the third Christian millennium is reserved the task of overcoming a tribal Christology by a Christophany which allows Christians to see the work of Christ everywhere without assuming that they have a better grasp on or a monopoly of that Mystery which has been revealed to them in a unique way."[15] Unpacking and sorting out this statement, we have the essential ingredients of Panikkar's "Christophany" or "authentically universal Christology" — one which allows the Christ to shine forth from all religions (Christo-phany = Christ-appearing) without privileging or giving the monopoly to any one of them. Such an understanding of Christ, theologians like Panikkar and Indian Jesuit Michael Amaladoss believe, will both re-polish and revivify traditional beliefs about Jesus and, at the same time, discard some of the monopolistic accretions.

This re-polished christology hinges on how Panikkar and Amaladoss understand the term "Christ." Essentially, they use Christ as a synonym for the image that goes all the way back to John's Gospel and that was used so extensively and creatively by the Church Fathers: Word, or Logos. Since Christians believe

---

13. Raimon Panikkar, "The Invisible Harmony: A Universal Theory of Religion or a Cosmic Confidence in Reality?" in *Toward a Universal Theology of Religion*, ed. Leonard Swidler (Maryknoll, N.Y.: Orbis Books, 1987), 145.

14. Panikkar, *The Unknown Christ,* 58–61.

15. Panikkar, "The Invisible Harmony," 122.

that the Word or self-communicating urge of God was embodied in Jesus the Christ, Panikkar interchanges "Christ" with "Word." But in doing so, he uses the term "Christ" as the particular Christian way of speaking about the Universal Reality that all mystics know: the marvelous, unspeakable unity between the Divine, the human, and the cosmic. "Christ is . . . a living symbol for the totality of reality: human, divine, cosmic."[16] Or, more accurately, Christ symbolizes the dynamic link, the unifying current, that binds the Divine with the human and cosmic. Whenever humans, in religious-mystical experience, sense something that takes them out of themselves into a Mystery that, at the same time, connects them with other humans and fellow creatures, they are experiencing what the language of Christianity calls "Christ."

But what is the relationship, then, of this universal Christ to the particular Jesus? This, one might say, is the pivotal theological question that challenges every theology of religions. Panikkar struggled to answer it. In the 1964 first edition of *The Unknown Christ of Hinduism*, he stated that "a full Christian faith is required to accept . . . the identity" between Christ and "Jesus the Son of Mary." This makes Christianity "the place where Christ is fully revealed, the end and plenitude of every religion."[17] But in the 1981 edition of the same book and in subsequent writings, he not only changes tone but makes an about-face: "When I call this link between the finite and the infinite by the name of Christ, I am not presupposing its identification with Jesus of Nazareth." This is how Panikkar spells out the implications of that statement: "Though a Christian believes that 'Jesus is the Christ . . .' this sentence is not identical to 'the Christ is Jesus.' "[18] The following is Michael Amaladoss's version of the same claim: "Jesus is the Christ, but Christ is more than Jesus. The mystery of Christ includes all the other manifestations of God in history. . . . We cannot claim any monopoly over Christ. We do not possess Christ."[19] Simply: Christians can and must continue to proclaim that all of Jesus is the Christ; but they cannot tell others, or themselves, that all of Christ is Jesus. This affirms Jesus, but it opens the doors to affirming others as well.

But Panikkar and Asian theologians *do* want to affirm Jesus. To think that they don't would be to misunderstand them profoundly and dangerously. (Orthodoxy is at stake.) On this issue, Panikkar uses words that would gladden the heart of any Evangelical Christian: "nobody for the sake of dialogue has the right to blur the issue [of Jesus' importance] by minimizing Jesus or overlooking the central Christian affirmation of the Lordship of Jesus." He speaks these words not just because he believes that whatever is universal (like the Christ or Logos) can touch us only through some concrete particular person or object (like

---

16. Panikkar, *The Unknown Christ,* 27.

17. Raimon Panikkar, *The Unknown Christ of Hinduism* (London: Darton, Longman and Todd, 1964), 24; *The Trinity,* 55.

18. Panikkar, *The Unknown Christ* (1981), 14, 27; *The Trinity,* 53.

19. Michael Amaladoss, "The Pluralism of Religions and the Significance of Christ," *Vidyajyoti* 53 (1989): 412 [401–20]; Amaladoss, "The Mystery of Christ," 335, 337.

Jesus), but also because he believes, as we have already heard, that the Divine has its being in these particulars. Remember his image of the mountaintop: the paths not only lead up to the mountain but make it what it is. Lose one of the particular paths, and you lose part of the mountain. Water down the particular Jesus, and you've diluted the Divine.[20]

Yet the same can be said about Buddha. Panikkar calls the name "Christ" the "Supername" — what Paul terms "the name above every name" (Phil. 2:9) — because it is a name that can and must assume many names. Panikkar explicitly states that the name of "Christ" can also go by other historical names, such as "Rama, Krishna, Isvara, Purusha, Tathagata." Reject or diminish any one of these names, and one also loses a unique part of the Divine. So in one sentence, Panikkar can attest to the uniqueness of Jesus and at the same time the uniqueness of other religions and religious figures: "Jesus...would be one of the names of the cosmotheandric principle, which has received practically as many names as there are authentic forms of religiousness and which at the same time finds a historically sui-generis (unique) epiphany in Jesus of Nazareth."[21]

But if there are many other names for the Christ — for the Divine's reaching out to all creatures — why does the New Testament almost overwhelm its readers with such an outpouring of exclusive language to speak about Jesus? Why does it insist so persistently that there is *no other name* and that he is the *only* Son of God and Savior? We heard this language repeated throughout previous chapters, especially in the Replacement Model. Other theologians who stand at Panikkar's side offer a response when they ask a simple counterquestion: But what kind of language is this? It is not, they suggest, the kind of language Christians have often thought it to be: it is not a theological or doctrinal way of speaking about Jesus. When the early Christians used this kind of one-and-only language they were not speaking from their heads, trying to give a conceptual, philosophical definition of Jesus. They were, rather, speaking from their hearts, trying to express what they felt about Jesus and what he meant to them. They were using what the experts call "confessional" language. They were confessing what their hearts told them about Jesus. Better, it can be called *love language* — the language someone uses to talk about the person who has transformed one's life and stands at its center: "You are my one-and-only. There is no other like you."

Such language is used in and about a personal relationship. Within that relationship it has its meaning. When a man, for instance, says to his wife in moments of intimacy, "You are the most beautiful woman in the world. There is no other woman in the world for me" he means it; it is, without doubt, true. But if we can imagine that for some reason this man would have to appear the next day in court, and the judge would ask him to put his hand on the Bible and

---

20. Raimon Panikkar, "Christianity and World Religions," in *Christianity* (Patiala, India: Punjabi University Press, 1969), 114.

21. Panikkar, *The Trinity,* 53–54; *The Unknown Christ,* 27, 48; "Christianity and World Religions," 101.

swear that his wife is the most beautiful woman in the world and that there is no other woman that he could have married, he could not so swear. Why? Because before the judge he would be using scientific, or legal, language — another kind of language. What is true as love language is not true as philosophical or doctrinal language. We must understand language, and use it, according to the kind of language it is — in this case, either confessional/love language or theological/scientific language.

The difference between the one-and-only love language of the New Testament and the same language one might use for one's spouse is that the early Christians were speaking as a community, and they were speaking to other communities. They were proclaiming Jesus as he who might touch and transform other communities and become their "one-and-only." Still, Panikkar and other mutualist theologians would suggest that to take up the one-and-only confessional or love language the New Testament uses about Jesus and to use it as scientific language that excludes others or diminishes them is to misuse the New Testament message about Jesus. Proclaiming Jesus as "the only Son of God" was meant to say something positive about Jesus; it was not meant to say something negative about Buddha.[22]

Panikkar, and the theologians who accompany him, recognizes that such a "universal christology" will be new and perhaps jolting for many Christians, especially in the West — though well-known Asian theologian Felix Wilfred thinks it will come naturally to Asian Christians.[23] Whether jolting or refreshing, such an understanding of Jesus, these theologians maintain, is as faithful to traditional, but often neglected, understandings of Christ as it is open to Christianity's new experience of the Spirit in other religions. As we shall see, such a claim has stirred much discussion and controversy.

The Ethical-Practical Bridge

Christians who prefer an ethical-practical crossing to a mutuality theology of religions certainly don't do so because they disagree with those who walk the other two bridges. They, too, would admit the limitations of all historical religions, as well as a mystical center to all religions that constantly overflows with diversity. But they prefer another way of realizing a dialogue of mutuality among religions because, they believe, this other way is both more urgent and more promising. Given the present pain-ridden and crisis-strewn state of the world, the religions have a job to do, a job they all share. Taking up this job together will enable them to get to know each other better. For this bridge, ethical issues and ethical responsibility are the pillars that will sustain a new kind of interfaith exchange. A pivotal term in this approach to pluralism and dialogue, therefore, is *global responsibility:* in being responsible for our endangered globe

22. Paul F. Knitter, *Jesus and the Other Names: Christian Mission and Global Responsibility* (Maryknoll, N.Y.: Orbis Books, 1996), 68–70.
23. Wilfred, "Some Tentative Reflections."

and all its inhabitants, the religions have new opportunities to understand both themselves and each other. In what follows, we will try to summarize what such a globally responsible dialogue means and how it works.

By Their Fruits You Will Know Them

For those who follow this ethical-practical path, a guiding principle, both for assessing past Christian attitudes toward other religions and for formulating new ones, is "by their fruits you will know them." If a particular theology of religions or christology yields the kind of ethical fruits that we would not be proud to collect and bring home to a God of love and justice, then something is wrong with our theology. This means that Christians, in trying to work out their attitudes toward other religions, have to be guided not just by what the Bible says, or by what past councils have declared (as essential as those guidelines are), but also by what kind of particular actions result from particular attitudes toward others. Doctrines or beliefs have to appear in the court of ethics before they can be admitted to the churches and schools of Christianity. What makes a particular belief or theology "orthodox," therefore, is not just that it is based on Scripture and reflects past tradition but also that it enables Christians to carry out what Jesus held up as the law of laws: to love your neighbor. If a theology of other believers does not foster a true love of other believers, then something is deeply dysfunctional with that theology — no matter how biblical it seems to be.

And for Christians seeking a new, mutuality theology of religions, the ethical report card for past theologies is not one they can be proud of. The low grades seem, in general, to result from the way the theologies of replacement or fulfillment have led to, or at least condoned, a degrading or even an exploitation of other "non-Christian" peoples and cultures. The strongest voices — and the hardest graders — are among Christians who live in what were formerly the colonies of Europe and America. These Christians point wounded fingers at the way convictions of cultural superiority and "manifest destiny," or attempts to belittle or demonize religious beliefs, or even justification for economic exploitation have been based upon, or legitimized by, the deeper religious conviction that Christianity was the manifest destiny of all nations because Christ was the one Savior of all peoples. Samuel Rayan, an Indian Jesuit theologian, pointedly poses a question that not only Indians but also Native Americans, Africans, and Filipinos would endorse: "Imperialist missions have projected Christ as a new, religious Julius Caesar, out to conquer.... We [persons of colonized countries] ask about the subterranean connection between the Western conception of Christ's uniqueness and authority on the one hand and the Western project of world domination on the other."[24] Harsh words, but they raise a question that many Christians and theologians feel cannot be casually dismissed.

---

24. Samuel Rayan, "Religions, Salvation, Mission," in *Christian Mission and Interreligious Dialogue*, ed. Paul Mojzes and Leonard Swidler (Maryknoll, N.Y.: Orbis Books, 1990), 134.

Even harsher words, perhaps, are heard by Christians seeking to dialogue with Jews during the second half of the last century, since the horrors of the Holocaust. Jewish brothers and sisters have pointed out what they feel should have been obvious: that the flames of anti-Semitism that burned in Nazi Germany (and throughout European history) were fed, if not caused, by Christian convictions that Jesus was the Messiah meant to bring Jews from the Old Testament into the New Testament. Jews who refused this invitation were guilty in heavenly courts — therefore, also in civil courts. And so Catholic theologian Rosemary Radford Ruether voiced her well-known verdict on Christian theology: "Theologically, anti-Judaism developed as the left hand of christology. Anti-Judaism was the negative side of the Christian affirmation that Jesus was the Christ."[25] If Jesus is understood to be the replacement or fulfillment of Judaism — and of all other religions — then all those who have not yet known him, and certainly all those who turn their backs and adhere to their "old" testaments and ways, are underdeveloped to say the least — or, in the words of the old Good Friday Catholic liturgy, "perfidious."

Even if the exploitation and denigration of other cultures and religions in the name of Christ the only Savior have been based on a misuse and misunderstanding of the name of Christ, still there remains the historical fact that Western Christians have been able to so frequently and so easily misuse this belief. For those who follow an ethical approach to other religions, this means that Christians have not just good reason but an impelling obligation to reexamine the belief that Jesus is the only Savior and Christianity is the religion meant to fulfill all others. This does not mean that these beliefs should simply be thrown out. But it does mean trying to reinterpret them in such a way that their core meaning is preserved while harmful expressions of that meaning are changed. If the bath water is dirty, it can be thrown out without losing the baby! That is what this Mutuality Model, in general, is trying to do.

Common Problems = Common Ground

Like the other bridges we've examined, the ethical-practical bridge is trying to find what the religions of the world might have in common. But instead of looking *within* or *beneath* the various religious traditions for the common experience they all share or the one underground source that feeds them all, these practical theologians look *around* the religions for that which faces them all. The advocates of this bridge urge that there is something that confronts all the religious families of the world, something they cannot deny, something that is much more identifiable and immediate and pressing than Hick's "really Real" or Panikkar's "one religious fact" (without denying the reality of the Real or of

---

25. Rosemary Radford Ruether, *To Change the World: Christology and Cultural Criticism* (New York: Crossroad, 1981), 31.

the one fact). This universal reality impinging on all religions can be pointed to with one word: *suffering.*

There is a tremendous amount of suffering in our world today. If there's not more of it than there ever was, we seem to be more aware of it. Also, it seems to be more threatening or unsettling than ever before. We're talking, first of all, of human suffering. The pains·that afflict millions of people today take on a variety of different but interrelated faces:

- *Poverty.* We hear the statistics every year in the United Nations Development Reports, fluctuating somewhat but continuously pointing to large portions of the human race — one-fourth or one-fifth — who do not have enough of the world's goods to provide their children with the food, shelter, and medical care they need to lead human lives. Poverty dehumanizes, and vast portions of the human race are so dehumanized.

- *Victimization.* This is the pain resulting not just from being poor but from being made and kept poor by other human beings. To be taken advantage of by others, to be excluded by others, to be overpowered by others — this hurts perhaps even more than the gnawing ache of hunger. There need not be so much poverty, experts tell us. Of the earth's bounty, there is "enough to go around." But it doesn't go around because of choices and policies made by those with economic and political and military power.

- *Violence.* Poverty itself is already violence, as is victimization. Understandably, then, they are often the cause or context of the physical violence between spouses, social classes, and ethnic groups. Despite the "new order" after the collapse of Communism, despite the economic growth of the global market, physical and military violence continues to plague our planet. The production and international marketing of arms grow, to the devastation of many and the enrichment of a few. And while there may be numerically fewer nuclear weapons nowadays, their ability to destroy the earth remains and their availability to smaller, so-called rogue nations increases.

- *Patriarchy.* Given the statistics on the feminization of poverty, on domestic violence, on the growing sex trade, on rape as a weapon of war, it appears that women bear a disproportionate burden of humanity's suffering. The reality of patriarchy — of male domination over females — though today seen more clearly and criticized more widely, remains alive and well. Throughout the world, in some countries and cultures more than in others, women are considered — if not defined — to be inferior. And what is inferior is used and abused rather than respected and valued.

Besides the sufferings of humanity, there are also the sufferings of the earth and its creatures. In the way the ever-increasing number of humans are using this earth, especially through the kind of growth and consumption that have become necessary to support the lifestyle of the so-called First World, the human species is wreaking havoc on the life-giving and the life-sustaining capacities of the planet that is home for all species. This is a form of suffering that threatens everyone. Whereas the pain of the poor can be kept at a certain distance on the other side of town or of the world, the hole in the ozone layer or global warming is as great a menace to the inhabitants of Beverly Hills as to the occupants of Chicago's ghettos. And the threat is not just for us but also, and especially, for generations that, we hope, will come and be able to draw life from the earth.

The anguished and anguishing reality of such suffering, in its pain and in its menace, cuts across all religious borders. It surrounds all religious communities. If there are those postmoderns who doubt the reality of a common faith or of a common mystical experience within all the religious traditions of the world, it would be hard to doubt the presence of a common experience of suffering that is available to all religious believers. And this experience constitutes a call and challenge for them all. If a religion denies this experience and refuses this challenge of widespread human suffering, then, according to the advocates of this practical approach to dialogue, such a religion has lost its relevance, if not also its very validity. If a religion has nothing to say about the forms of suffering we have just described, whatever else it says is either uninteresting or distracting.

If human suffering makes up a common experience available to all religions, perhaps even more evidently and impellingly the threatened, endangered earth provides the common ground where they can all stand — and take a common stand. To those postmodern critics who insist that there is no way of bridging the vast differences and "incommensurabilities" of the religions, Christians walking this ethical bridge respond: Oh yes there is! The earth. If there are many, very different religions, there is one beautiful but very threatened earth. As differently as the religions may understand the origins and nature of this earth, they all stand on it and they all can feel it shuddering and failing from the devastation worked upon it. The common ground of a threatened planet provides all the religions with a common agenda. As Thomas Berry, one of the primary proponents of an earth-centered spirituality and dialogue, has put it: "Concern for the well-being of the planet is the one concern that hopefully will bring the nations [and the religions] of the world into an inter-nation [and interreligious] community."[26]

That the different religious communities of the world are being called together to confront a common ethical task is clear from what we heard earlier: the need for a global ethic. As not just philosophers and visionaries, but also political scientists and even political leaders, are beginning to recognize, if humanity is going to be able to find any kind of a solution for the ecological-human sufferings and crises facing all of us, the nations of the world are going to have to act together as never before. But such acting together will require some kind of a common ethical basis on which to deliberate and cooperate. A global ethic, as we heard, would not be a list of unchangeable commandments, but it would embody a consensus of ethical values about the dignity of the individual, the

---

26. Thomas Berry, *The Dream of the Earth* (San Francisco: Sierra Club Books, 1988), 218.

integrity of the earth, the community and responsibility that unite us all, and the need for justice and compassion. But such a consensus of values, such a global ethic, among nations and peoples will be extremely difficult, if not impossible, to realize without the cooperation of religions — not just of each religion but of all of them together. The need for an interreligious dialogue toward an inter-religious formulation of a global ethic was recognized and responded to at the World Parliament of Religions in 1993 and 1999. Construction of an ethical bridge to dialogue is advancing — and traffic is increasing.

The fact that ethical concerns of poverty and justice and ecology are becom-ing more and more the topics of interreligious dialogue throughout the world — both at the parliamentarian and the grassroots levels — is perhaps the best re-sponse to those who worry that such an ethical agenda is an imposition on some religions. Despite the elaborate cases made by some academicians that not all religions are concerned about such "worldly matters" as poverty and ozone depletion, the fact is that there are members of all the world religions (which doesn't mean all the members of each religion) who are indeed concerned about such matters. And that concern is inspired and directed by their religious beliefs and values. Furthermore, the calls they hear from those who are suffering are moving them to talk with members of other traditions who hear the same calls. An interreligious, ethical dialogue is taking place, and gaining speed. It seems to suggest, if not prove, that within all the religions there is a concern to im-prove the lot of human beings in this world, which means improving this world. Whatever "salvation" or "enlightenment" or *moksha* may mean for the interior life of the soul or for life after death, it also is meant to make a difference in life on this earth.[27] At least, so it seems.

Talking after Acting Is Better Talking

So for Christians who walk this practical bridge toward a mutuality theology of religions, the ethical agenda provided by human and ecological suffering is a necessity. But, they say, it is also an opportunity — an opportunity for a deeper, more fruitful religious dialogue among persons of different traditions. A shared *ethical* dialogue, as it were, will open doors and lead the way to a more effective *religious* dialogue. If religious persons first spend time acting together in order to relieve eco-human suffering, they will be able more successfully to talk together about their religious experiences and beliefs. So talking after acting makes for better talking.

Michael Amaladoss, S.J., describes how such a practice-based dialogue can work from his experience of how it has worked in India.[28] He tells of how mem-

---

27. See Paul F. Knitter, *One Earth Many Religions: Multifaith Dialogue and Global Responsibil-ity* (Maryknoll, N.Y.: Orbis Books, 1995), chapter 6.
28. The discussion and quotations in the following paragraphs are from Michael Amaladoss, "Liberation as an Interreligious Project," in *Leave the Temple: Indian Paths to Human Liberation*, ed. Felix Wilfred (Maryknoll, N.Y.: Orbis Books, 1992), 158–74.

bers of different (and in India, often clashing) religious communities — Hindus, Muslims, Christians — find themselves gathered together by a call that comes to all of them from beyond their immediate religious communities: the call of the suffering and the marginalized. As they feel and respond to this call, their sense of togetherness as human and religious persons grows. "The principle of unity is precisely the praxis [practice] of liberation." And as they talk about the problems they are confronting — the situation of the outcasts, interreligious fighting (called in India "communalism"), corrupt governments — they realize that each of them, reacting to the issue or challenge from his/her own spiritual resources, has something to offer. They realize that each of their traditions feels it can provide something of the "inspiration, prophecy, challenge, hope" that are necessary for carrying on the struggle of transforming situations of injustice and greed into ones of caring and equality. In providing such courage and vision and stamina for the struggle, each religion is drawing on its own spiritual depths, on its core religious or mystical experience. Already, there is the sense that such sharing on the level of practice is also a sharing on the deeper level of spirituality.

But, Amaladoss continues, such a practical-ethical dialogue of religious persons requires that, together, they get their hands dirty. The place of dialogue — the physical, socioeconomic setting — and the social class of the participants now assume critical importance. "This means that interreligious dialogue must descend from the level of experts to that of the ordinary people — the poor — who are struggling together for liberation and fulfillment. It will be shown more in symbols and gestures and common activity rather than in abstract discussions. It will be a dialogue of life and struggle." Participants in such an ethical dialogue can no longer be only the scholars and the saints and the religious leaders; the victims themselves — and those who are in the trenches struggling with and for victims or the victimized earth — must also have a voice. And it will be a voice that is necessary not just to analyze the particular problem or form of suffering that is being confronted but also to interpret the teachings or contributions of the religions that are intended to shed light on or solve the problem. The scholars and religious leaders must listen to and learn from the victims.

As such an issue-oriented, ethical encounter and cooperation of religions enter more intimately and personally into the pain and struggles of the victims who have called forth the dialogue, there is a refocusing of what really matters and what is truly at stake. In a dialogue in which suffering calls religious persons together, in which their primary intent is to feed starving children, or to stop the burning of brides who can't pay their dowries, or to make peace between religious groups who are killing each other, or to save a polluted river — in such a dialogue what is most important is not that "our team wins." It no longer is of primary concern to show that my religion is the fulfillment of yours, that my notion of the Divine is superior to yours, that my "Savior" is bigger than yours, or even that my solution for solving the problem at hand is more effective than yours. What matters most is that people actually be helped, fed, educated, and given medicine, that violence and war be avoided, and that the environment be saved and protected. Whatever or whoever's truth or God or Savior can help bring about these ends, let all listen and learn.

And so this ethical approach to an understanding of other religions also has its guard-rails to protect against the slippery slopes of relativism. For Christians participating in a globally responsible religious dialogue, what decides between true or false, good or bad, better or worse among the different beliefs and practices is not whether followers of a religion believe in only one God, or whether they acknowledge Jesus as Savior, or whether they evidence some kind of baptism of desire, but whether a particular religious belief or practice is able to bring about greater peace and justice and unity in the world. As important as the other issues are, here we have the most useable and readily available measuring stick for religious truth and goodness.

Advocates of this kind of dialogue add immediately that the best persons to help apply this measuring stick are the poor and oppressed themselves, ordinary people struggling to make their world better. Again, to decide whether a religious belief or practice is relevant or true, the views of the victims, or of the people in the trenches, carry particular weight and must be heard by the experts and official religious representatives. Indeed, when differences and disagreements arise among the experts about whether a particular religious belief can really transform and liberate the world, those who themselves are in need of and struggling for liberation can serve as arbiters. Let their experience and testimony mediate among the experts. In the language of Christian theology, the voice of the poor and of victims is a "privileged voice" in theological and dialogical matters. These voices can tell religious leaders and professionals things they cannot know by themselves.

But, according to Amaladoss, there is a further step, or level, in such an ethically based or globally responsible dialogue. If this dialogue begins with concrete issues of human or ecological suffering, if it seeks to draw on different religious contributions to analyzing and resolving the cause of the suffering, it doesn't stop there. Religious people who "commit themselves together to promote justice" will also find themselves desiring to "share...perspectives of faith," even to "seek a convergence at the level of faith." The practical dialogue leads, naturally and perhaps necessarily, to an explicitly religious dialogue. Having struggled to protect human rights, to restore land, to stop prostitution, to curtail environmentally damaging industrial practices, persons of differing faith communities will find themselves friends. Having worked together, experienced together the resistance of those in power, suffered together, perhaps gone to jail together, they will feel bonds that connect them on a deeper — yes, a "mystical" — level. They will naturally want to hear from their co-workers and friends in the struggle what it is in their religious faith that inspires, directs, and keeps them going. They might even want to pray together, or sit in silent meditation together, in order to enable that which inspires one to touch the other — or, to allow that which inspires each of them in their differing religions to touch all of them in silence or prayer.

And in this kind of religious sharing among those who have struggled for justice and well-being, people will likely discover that they have "new ears with which to hear" what the friend from another religion is saying. The personal bonds of connectedness — again, we can call them mystical bonds — that are formed in ethical action together become conduits by which the back-and-forth of religious sharing can flow more easily and effectively. More concretely, a Christian who has stood alongside a Buddhist in opposing corrupt governmental practices will be better able to hear and understand her Buddhist friend when he speaks about how enlightenment or the experience of "no-self" calls him to do something about human suffering. And conversely, the Buddhist will be better able to understand the Christian when she explains how Jesus, with his vision of the Reign of God, animates and guides her. This ethical approach to dialogue is suggesting, essentially, that religious believers from vastly different traditions who act together will be better able to pray together and share together.

In such an ethical approach to dialogue, the religions of Asia have begun to form what are being called *basic human communities*. In the way they work and in what they're discovering, they're similar to the basic Christian communities that developed in Latin America during the 1970s and 1980s. These Christian communities experienced a religious renewal by coming together in small groups and studying the Gospels on the basis of their shared struggle to overcome poverty and injustice. By listening to God's Word with the ears of the poor, they heard things they never heard before and came to a new understanding of themselves as religious communities. Similarly, people of different religions in Asia are coming together to form a new kind of religious community — one in which by first acting together to overcome human or ecological suffering, they are able, in the light of this experience, to understand each other's Scriptures and value each other's beliefs as never before. Such BHCs, as they are called, are giving birth not to a new religion but to a new community of religions, one in which shared human concerns and cooperation are the garden in which deeper religious understanding and learning are growing.

Jesus the Liberator

The most critical, and difficult to construct, supporting pillar for all these bridges leading to a Mutuality Model is the one dealing with the role of Jesus: How to affirm traditional Christian convictions about the universal importance of Jesus without diminishing the universal importance of other religious traditions and leaders? We have seen how those who follow the philosophical bridge stress the symbolic nature of all talk of Jesus, with special preference for the symbolism of Jesus as Spirit-filled, while those who choose the mystical bridge understand the particular Jesus as only one expression — though an essential one — of the universal Christ available to all religions. For those who walk the practical-ethical bridge, the approach to Jesus, we might say, is also more practical, down-to-earth, at-hand. Perhaps more than all other versions of the Mutuality Model, this practical-ethical bridge seeks to base its view of Jesus on what contemporary New Testament scholarship tells us about the historical Jesus.

Some might immediately warn that such an approach leads to building on a foundation of sand, for it's not always clear just what "contemporary New Testament scholarship" is telling us. It's true: discussions among specialists on the historical Jesus can be frustratingly divided and controversial. And yet within the fog of differing interpretations, there are a few conclusions about Jesus that command a clear, even a strong, consensus. One of them is that the core of Jesus' message, the "master symbol" of his vision, was the Reign of God. The main theme of Jesus' preaching — and we can presume the burning concern of his heart — was to announce, initiate, and foster the Reign of God. This, first and last of all, was what Jesus was about. As one scholar has put it: "Everything that Jesus says and does is inspired from the beginning to the end by his personal commitment to the coming Reign of God into the world. The controlling horizon of the mission and ministry of Jesus is the Kingdom of God."[29] So in Mark's Gospel, the very first words that Jesus uses to announce his "Good News" are: "The time is fulfilled, and the Kingdom of God is at hand" (Mark 1:15).

But what did he mean by this "master symbol"? Here the views of the experts move in different, but usually complementary, directions. They tell us that because the Kingdom of God is the key metaphor of what Jesus was about, we will never be able to unload its meaning fully; indeed, its power to propel people in the following of Jesus will grow and refocus from age to age. But there is one thing about the Reign of God the experts agree on. It's contained in the prayer that Jesus taught his followers and that is repeated millions of times throughout the world every day: "Thy Kingdom come, thy will be done *on earth,* as it is in heaven." Jesus hoped and expected and spent his life's blood so that God's Reign could take shape on earth, in this world, within society.[30] Certainly, the Reign extends beyond the limits of earthly life, but before it does so, it is meant to affect and transform earthly life. And because it is the Reign — that is, the vision and powerful presence — of a God of compassion and justice, the world of culture and society and politics that takes shape within this Reign will be one in which humans love and do justice to each other and to all of God's creation. Edward Schillebeeckx, one of the most accomplished and venerated Christian theologians of the past century, sums up the picture of the Reign of God that he drew from his extensive studies of the historical Jesus:

The kingdom of God is the saving presence of God, active and encouraging, as it is affirmed and welcomed among men and women. It is a saving

---

29. Dermot Lane, *Christ at the Centre: Selected Issues in Christology* (New York: Paulist, 1991), 11.

30. This runs counter to the earlier prevalent view that Jesus expected the end of the world within, or shortly after, his lifetime. As Marcus J. Borg notes: "the consensus regarding Jesus' expectation of the end of the world has disappeared. The majority of scholars no longer thinks that Jesus expected the end of the world in his generation" (*Jesus: A New Vision* [San Francisco: HarperSanFrancisco, 1987], 14).

presence ... which takes concrete form above all in justice and peaceful relationships among individuals and peoples, in the disappearance of sickness, injustice, and oppression, in the restoration of life of all that was dead and dying.[31]

If the symbol of the Reign of God forms the focus of Jesus' preaching, what does it tell us about who he was? Perhaps the favorite title for Jesus among those who advocate an ethical bridge to dialogue is *liberator* — Jesus is he who brings about the liberation and the transformation of individuals and their social world. But that's a contemporary way of speaking. The biblical version of "liberator" is *prophet.* Jesus took his place in the long line and history of Jewish prophets — individuals who responded to the suffering of victims and who called the Jewish people to move their faith in a God of love and justice from empty words to actual practice. In responding to the pain of the many, prophets usually became a pain for those few who held power — and were often "removed" by those in power. Among the many titles that were subsequently bestowed on Jesus by his followers, one of the oldest and the one that perhaps best captures how Jesus was perceived by people and maybe even how he perceived himself was that of a prophet. It's a thoroughly Jewish title. Jesus, Christians too often forget, was thoroughly Jewish, from birth to death.

But to balance the New Testament picture of Jesus, proponents of an ethics-based theology of religions would want to add an adjectival phrase to this central image of Jesus as prophet: he was a "Spirit-filled" prophet. As a prophet, Jesus was a liberator — you might say, a social activist. But his commitment to liberation and action flowed from his deep religious experience of the Spirit that assured him that God was his, and all people's, Abba or Father/Dad. This is the energy that propelled his prophetic hope and courage. This was the source of personal peace to which he could retreat in the evenings when his energies waned and his hopes were tested. The more his spirit resonated with the Divine Spirit, the more he reached out to the poor and suffering — and vice versa.

This, then, is the Jesus whom, according to this ethical-practical approach to other religions, Christians should bring to the dialogue — Jesus the mystical-prophetic liberator. Certainly, other traditional titles of Jesus will not be denied or set aside — Jesus as Son of God, Messiah, Word of God, Savior. But if the image and implications of Jesus the Spirit-filled liberator do not illuminate and inspire these other images, then something essential to what Jesus was and was about will be missing. If Jesus' divinity is not understood and presented to other believers in terms of his role as social prophet, then the picture of Jesus not only is incomplete but also might be dangerous. There is the danger that he becomes only a deity to be worshiped and extolled over other deities rather than an example to be followed and shared with others.

---

31. Edward Schillebeeckx, *The Church: The Human Story of God* (New York: Crossroad, 1990), 111–12.

Indeed, this ethical-prophetic understanding of Jesus will enable Christians to see other religions more clearly and relate to them more easily. It will equip Christians, as it were, with the same priorities as those that guided Jesus:

- As we heard, for Jesus the Spirit-filled prophet, the focus of his life and relationships was the Reign of God. That meant that he was not — as his followers have often been — *church-centered.* His primary concern was not to increase membership of his own movement or community. Rather, it was to transform people's hearts so as to transform their society.

- Also, he was not self-centered — or *Jesus-centered.* The ultimate end of his preaching was not to bring people to recognize his authority and no one else's, but to follow him in his movement of renewing the way people live with each other.

- In a certain sense, one must also say, according to liberation theologian Jon Sobrino, S.J., of El Salvador, that Jesus was not really *God-centered.* The God that filled and fired Jesus' spirit was the God who willed to establish a Reign, a new society of love and justice in the world. To talk about "God alone" — that is, God without the Reign of God — would have been for Jesus to talk about a false God, an empty and dangerous idol. (And, of course, to talk about the Reign without God would have been for Jesus to determine a goal without the energy to get there.)

- So in the end, the best description of Jesus and his priorities is that he was *Kingdom-centered.* Everything else was oriented toward, and in a sense subordinated to, bringing about this new society, this new ordering of the world in which God's will would be done and all would have life, and have it abundantly. The community and renewal movement that Jesus formed around himself (later to become the church), his call to men and women to believe in and follow him, his announcement that God is indeed an Abba to us all — all of these essential ingredients of his Good News (church, Christ, God) were meant to foster and extend the Reign of God.[32]

So the proponents of this ethical-practical approach to other faiths draw their conclusion: if Jesus was Kingdom-centered, so must a Christian theology of religions be Kingdom-centered. Such a focus will both set the priorities and provide the energy for a Christian encounter with persons of other paths. The first item on the agenda as Christians get together with other believers will not be to soften them up for the right word that will bring them into the Christian community (as in the Replacement Model); nor will the primary concern be to identify in their teachings and practices the "hidden" or "anonymous" Christ that seeks completion in the church (as in the Fulfillment Model); nor will the

---

32. Jon Sobrino, *Spirituality of Liberation: Toward a Political Holiness* (Maryknoll, N.Y.: Orbis Books, 1988), 82–84; Sobrino, *Jesus the Liberator: An Historical-Theological Reading of Jesus of Nazareth* (Maryknoll, N.Y.: Orbis Books, 1994), 69; Sobrino, *Christ the Liberator: A View from the Victims* (Maryknoll, N.Y.: Orbis Books, 2001).

guiding interest be to discover the "Real" or the "mystical source" that runs through all religions (as in the philosophical and mystical bridges to a Mutuality Model). Rather, for Christians who follow Jesus the liberator, the first order of business in a theology and dialogue of religions will be to ask where and how these other religious communities might be trying to bring about what Christians call the Reign of God — where are they seeking to replace a world of human suffering and injustice with a society of compassion and equality.

Wherever and whenever Christians witness such ethical fruits, such "signs of the Reign of God," in other religious communities, they can be assured that they have enough "in common" with these other believers for a fruitful dialogue. Whenever they see other religions responding to the plight of the poor and seeking to promote greater equality and justice and love among people, Christians know that what they mean by "God" or "the Spirit" or "grace" is already alive and active within these other communities. On the ethical-practical bridge to dialogue, Christians can look on other religious persons not as "anonymous Christians" but as "real co-workers" in building the Reign of God in this world.

The Uniqueness of Jesus Rediscovered

This is perhaps one of the distinct achievements and contributions of the ethical-practical bridge to a new theology of religions: it enables Christians not only to discover the riches of other faiths but also to rediscover what is the unique richness of their own. These Christians have a clear and vigorous response to the often-heard criticism of the Mutuality Model — that it dissolves the uniqueness of Jesus into a bland interreligious soup. "On the contrary," claim those Christians who follow Jesus the liberator. If we understand the notion of "uniqueness" as that which both characterizes and distinguishes something or someone, then Christians can tell their brothers and sisters in other religions about a quality of Jesus of Nazareth which both defines what he is about and which also does not seem to be found as clearly or powerfully in most other religions and religious leaders. Aloysius Pieris, a Sri Lankan Jesuit who is perhaps the first proponent and primary architect of this ethical bridge to dialogue, explains as follows.

On the basis of his experience of following Jesus in dialogue with the religions of Asia, Pieris holds up something about Jesus' message and experience of God without which Jesus "hardly can be encountered and much less proclaimed"; but it is also something which in Pieris's view is "conspicuously absent in the Scriptures of other religions," especially those of Asia. This something is found in the way Jesus proclaims and embodies what Pieris calls *"the irrevocable covenant between God and the poor."* Carrying on and intensifying the message of the Jewish prophets and then embodying it in his death on the cross, *"Jesus is the covenant between YHWH [God, the Divine] and the non-persons of the world."*[33] The God that Jesus came to know and feel in his own

---

33. Aloysius Pieris, *Fire and Water: Basic Issues in Asian Buddhism and Christianity* (Maryknoll,

mystical or Spirit-filled experiences is a God who has a particular love and concern for people who have been victimized, exploited, and rendered powerless by other people. It's not that this God does not love other people, including the oppressors, but this God, like a caring parent, reaches out in a special, yes, a preferred, way to those of God's children who are suffering most because they are suffering as victims.

To know and accept the God whom Jesus announces, therefore, one must not only choose to be poor in the sense of being detached from self-seeking greed (this is something all religions call for); one must also opt for and stand with those who have not chosen, but have been forced, to be poor. If people who call themselves religious are not in some way reaching out to the victims of the earth and/or to the victimized earth, something essential is missing in their religious experience. Pieris stresses this point by playing with the old Catholic dictum, "No salvation outside God's covenant with the Poor." He suggests that if we want to use such dramatic language, it might better read: "Outside God's covenant with the poor, there is no salvation."[34]

From this angle, Pieris can identify for Christians what is really unique about the incarnation of God in Jesus. Incarnation in itself — that is, the Divine becoming human — is, Pieris reminds us, nothing unique or surprising. After all, "All that God created was good; the whole creation is God's body. God did not find it demeaning to be human. God could have become a flower without lowering Herself." The real shocker in Jesus is that God, the Almighty and Transcendent, was incarnated as "a slave of human tyrants." In Jesus, God did not just become human; God became poor, a victim, one of the oppressed. There is the real surprise, even scandal. So in Jesus, the Divine identifies itself not just with the good and beautiful in humanity but also — and especially — with that which humans generally tend to discard or ignore. "Humanity is beautiful because it is the finest creation of God, the fruit of love. But slavery is ugly, because it is a creation of human greed, the fruit of sin."[35] Jesus tells us that it is in the ugliness of slavery and oppression that we are to find the Divine and hear its voice calling to new life and commitment.

Therefore, in the dialogue with others, Christians have something distinctive or unique to contribute. Besides all that there is for Christians to learn from others — and there is much — they must also call their dialogue partners to recognize something they might not find that clearly in their own religious treasures: that to experience the Divine, to be enlightened, to be one with the Ultimate is also to be called to a concern for the victims of this world. If Christians are not bringing this particular part of their experience to the interreligious

N.Y.: Orbis Books, 1996), 150–51; see also Pieris, *God's Reign for God's Poor: A Return to the Jesus Formula* (Sri Lanka: Tulana Research Centre, 1998), chapter 4.

34. Aloysius Pieris, "Christ beyond Dogma: Doing Christology in the Context of the Religions and the Poor," *Louvain Studies* 25 (2000): 220.

35. Aloysius Pieris, "Whither New Evangelism?" *Pacifica* 6 (1993): 333.

conversation and collaboration, they are omitting a crucial part of their own identity; they are, one might say, being "unfaithful" to the uniqueness of Jesus.

But, Pieris adds from his own experience, such an announcement, such an insistence on the uniqueness of Jesus, will not come across to other believers in the same way that past Christian insistence that Jesus is unique did. To assert that Jesus is unique because he is the only Savior and only Son of God has sounded to others like haughtiness, and it felt like imperialism. But to locate Jesus' uniqueness in his call to share God's special love and engagement for the victims of the world has been received by Pieris's Buddhist and Hindu friends as "good news." "They have not renounced even an iota of Buddhism to go along with this explanation of the uniqueness of Jesus. Rather, they have been deeply moved by this christology, moved to reflect on our obligation as religious people in contemporary society."[36] Not to have to renounce what one is, but to be "deeply moved" and so changed — this is a wonderful example of what can happen in authentic dialogue.

Further Readings

Aleaz, K. P. "Paul F. Knitter's Proposal for a Relational Uniqueness of Jesus." *Vidyajyoti* 63 (1999): 491–503.

Amaladoss, Michael. "The Mystery of Christ and Other Religions: An Indian Perspective." *Vidyajyoti* 63 (1999): 327–38.

———. "Who Do You Say That I Am? Speaking of Jesus in India Today." *East Asian Pastoral Review* 34 (1997): 211–24.

Forte, Bruno. "Jesus of Nazareth, History of God, God of History: Trinitarian Christology in a Pluralistic Age." In *The Myriad Christ: Plurality and the Quest for Unity in Contemporary Christology.* Ed. T. Merrigan and J. Haers. Leuven: Leuven University Press, 2000, 99–120.

Haight, Roger. *Jesus the Symbol of God.* Maryknoll, N.Y.: Orbis Books, 1999, chapter 14.

Jantzen, Grace M. "Can There Be a Mystical Core of Religion?" *Theology Today* 47 (1990): 59–72.

Jensen, David H. *In the Company of Others: A Dialogical Christology.* Cleveland: Pilgrim Press, 2001, chapters 1, 2, 5.

Karokaram, Anto. "Raymond Panikkar's Theology of Religions: A Critique." *Vidyajyoti* 58 (1994): 663–72.

Molnar, Paul D. "Some Dogmatic Consequences of Paul F. Knitter's Unitarian Theocentrism." *The Thomist* 55 (1991): 449–96.

O'Leary, Joseph S. *Religious Pluralism and Christian Faith.* Edinburgh: University of Edinburgh Press, 1996, chapter 7.

Panikkar, Raimon. "The Crux of Christian Ecumenism: Can Universality and Chosenness Be Held Simultaneously?" *Journal of Ecumenical Studies* 26 (1989): 82–99.

---

36. Aloysius Pieris, personal letter to Philipp Gibbs, SVD. Pieris also admits that he did not bring this understanding of Jesus' uniqueness to the dialogue. It was actually in the dialogue — through the comments of Buddhists and Hindus — that he realized that this was indeed something distinct about Jesus and his message.

————. "The Dialogical Dialogue." In *The World Religious Traditions: Current Perspectives in Religious Studies.* Ed. Frank Whaling. Philadelphia: Westminster Press, 1984, 201–21.

————. "The Jordan, the Tiber, and the Ganges: Three Kairological Moments of Christic Self-Consciousness." In *The Myth of Christian Uniqueness: Toward a Pluralistic Theology of Religions.* Ed. John Hick and Paul F. Knitter. Maryknoll, N.Y.: Orbis Books, 1987, 89–116.

Pieris, Aloysius. "Christ beyond Dogma: Doing Christology in the Context of the Religions and the Poor." *Louvain Studies* 25 (2000): 187–231.

————. "Interreligious Dialogue and Theology of Religions: An Asian Paradigm." *Horizons* 20 (1993): 106–14.

Samartha, Stanley J. "The Cross and the Rainbow: Christ in a Multireligious Culture." In *The Myth of Christian Uniqueness: Toward a Pluralistic Theology of Religions.* Ed. John Hick and Paul F. Knitter. Maryknoll, N.Y.: Orbis Books, 1987, 69–88.

Smith, Wilfred Cantwell. "Idolatry: In Comparative Perspective." In *The Myth of Christian Uniqueness: Toward a Pluralistic Theology of Religions.* Ed. John Hick and Paul F. Knitter. Maryknoll, N.Y.: Orbis Books, 1987, 53–66.

Teasdale, Wayne. "The Interspiritual Age: Practical Mysticism for the Third Millennium." *Journal of Ecumenical Studies* 34 (1997): 74–91.

Wilfred, Felix. "Some Tentative Reflections on the Language of Christian Uniqueness." *Vidyajyoti* 57 (1993): 652–72.

Wolz-Gottwald, Eckard. "Mysticism and Ecumenism: On the Question of Religious Identity in the Religious Dialogue." *Journal of Ecumenical Studies* 32 (1995): 25–34.

Yagi, Seiichi. " 'I' in the Words of Jesus." In *The Myth of Christian Uniqueness: Toward a Pluralistic Theology of Religions.* Ed. John Hick and Paul F. Knitter. Maryknoll, N.Y.: Orbis Books, 1987, 117–34.

Chapter 9

The Mutuality Model

Insights and Questions

Insights

Out of all the new ideas and proposals that the Mutuality Model suggests for a theology of religions, the ones that are most innovative and controversial have to do with its view of Jesus. We saw how each of the bridges we explored in this part ended with an image of the Jesus it was following. Refreshing to some Christians, these images are also disturbing to others. Our insights, therefore, will focus on Jesus and will attempt to summarize the common implications or challenges of the various pictures of Jesus we met in this part. This summary hopes to provide the kind of clarity that will help readers make their own evaluation.

In the way the Mutuality Model understands Jesus, we can signal four key issues or challenges: (1) the need for new answers; (2) Jesus as sacrament rather than satisfaction; (3) a Spirit christology; and (4) what we might call a christology of mutuality.

The Need for New Answers

This is the first, and perhaps most pointed, of the challenges posed by the Mutuality Model. Today, the question which Jesus asked of his disciples and which they are still trying to answer, "Who do you say I am?" (Mark 8:27), is calling for really new answers — answers that will be as boldly creative in confronting new questions as they are resolutely faithful to the Christian community's original vision of Jesus. This need for something really new is felt by Christians in all the models we have reviewed so far. Even so-called conservative Christians in the Replacement Model and mainline Christians in the Fulfillment model sense the tension between, on the one hand, the need they feel to respect, love, and dialogue with other believers and, on the other hand, the traditional Christian claims that Jesus is the one-and-only Son of God and Savior. Something doesn't quite fit. There's a strain between what Christians *experience* in other religions (the clear signs of grace in other faiths) and what they are supposed to *believe* about Jesus (he's the only source of saving grace).

Followers of the Mutuality Model are suggesting to their fellow Christians that these tensions will not be dealt with unless they are willing to revise that which many have thought is utterly unrevisable — the claim that Jesus is the only source of God's salvation and the final word on what God intends for humanity and the world. This is the challenge that God seems to be laying before Christians — a challenge that comes from the very voice of God's Spirit that Christians hear within other religions. One advocate of such revisions dramatically states that this question of whether Jesus is the one-and-only Savior is the issue on which the credibility of Christianity will be decided for many people, both Christian and non-Christian. "It is the fault line in the contemporary crisis of christology; debates over incarnation or Jesus'... self-consciousness are side issues."[1] Other calls for revision are less dramatic but nonetheless clear: "The more we listen to those others [in the religions] on their own terms, the more the claim that God is fully and definitively revealed only in Christ seems in need of revision.... We must go to meet the other religions with the assurance of having a savior, but also with questions about his place on the interreligious horizon."[2]

As radical as such a revision may appear, Christians who are advocating it also maintain that, really, it is nothing new. Throughout the centuries, especially in the early church, there have been marked shifts — some of them seismic — in Christian understandings of Jesus, both his person and his work. To move from an image of Jesus as the final prophet to Jesus as Lord, or from Jesus the new Moses to Jesus the only Son of God, was no small step in the early Christian communities. There have always been "many christologies," many ways of understanding Jesus — different flowers when the same seed of faith is planted in different cultural soils. The earlier New Testament understandings of Jesus (e.g., Mark's view of Jesus as the suffering servant) seem to have been more "modest," while those that came later (e.g., John's image of Jesus as Logos and only Son) were more exclusive. But this doesn't mean that the earlier were supplanted by the later.

This is why some theologians are suggesting that to move forward today toward what they call a more "modest" view of Jesus' role will actually be returning to earlier, original understandings of Jesus in the first Christian communities. It is not true, they tell us, that Christians held to an "absolutist" or "one-and-only" understanding of Jesus' role from the very beginning. "Absolutist Christology was not at first believed almost everywhere, always, and by everyone." In the earliest communities, the question whether Jesus was the one-and-only Savior canceling out all others was "a nonissue, an unthematized matter of taste." An "absolute" or exclusive understanding of Jesus "begins... perhaps in the middle of the second century; it does not culminate probably until the fifth century."[3]

1. Wesley J. Wildman, "Pinning Down the Crisis in Contemporary Christology," *Dialog* 37 (1998): 20.

2. Joseph O'Leary, *Religious Pluralism and Christian Truth* (Edinburgh: University of Edinburgh Press, 1996), 205, 207.

3. Wesley J. Wildman, *Fidelity with Plausibility: Modest Christologies in the Twentieth Century*

Whether Jesus was held up to be the one-and-only from the very start of the Jesus movement or not, many Christians today, as we have seen in this part, are urging not that traditional biblical images of Jesus such as "only Son of God" or "only mediator" be thrown out but that their meaning, especially their implications, be understood differently. As we have seen, some suggest that all talk of "one-and-only" be considered love language whose intent is to affirm the meaning of Jesus, not to deny that of others. Other Christians understand such "one-and-only" language as a pointer to what is special about Jesus — that is, to what God has revealed more powerfully and more provocatively in Jesus than in other figures (for example, God's special concern for victims); such an understanding allows for Buddha to be the one-and-only expression of other universal truths which he discovered more clearly than other mystics did (for example, the interconnectedness of all things). From this perspective, there can be, paradoxically, many "one-and-onlys" — many unique expressions of divine truth, many particular and distinctive revelations in the different religions. All of them would be different from each other, and yet, all of them would be able to speak to each other, enhance, clarify, balance, and, yes, challenge and correct each other. This is the stuff of dialogue — a dialogue of many "one-and-onlys."

Whether these particular ways of reinterpreting the uniqueness of Jesus are valid and acceptable to the Christian community is not, for the moment, the issue. What this first insight or challenge of the Mutuality Model is urging all Christian churches to accept is that *some kind of a reinterpretation* of traditional Christian language about Jesus as the one-and-only or the final Savior and revealer is necessary. And it will have to be an interpretation that provides really new answers to how Christians can continue to announce the uniqueness of Jesus without disparaging, and cutting off possibilities of dialogue with, the uniqueness of Buddha or Krishna or Muhammad. These new answers may not yet be found. But Christians cannot run from the task of continuing to look for them. Otherwise, the fault line may become a fissure in which many lose their faith.

Jesus as Sacrament

There also seems to be a consensus among proponents of the Mutuality Model about the general direction that such a "new answer" might take: followers of Jesus would be better off if they understood (and felt) Jesus more as a *sacrament* of God's love than as a *satisfaction* for God's justice. In the technical language that we've already encountered, the way Jesus "saves" — that is, the way he

---

(Albany: State University of New York Press, 1998), 267, 153–54. Wildman goes on to steel his case: "the Christian tradition itself offers ancient and biblically grounded Christological alternatives to absolutist Christology that are also more conceptually sound, historically responsible, faithful to creedal tradition, and ethically viable." There are many "usually overlooked resources within the classical Christological tradition itself" for an understanding of Jesus that avoids insistence that he is the one-and-only or final Word of God (171).

enters people's lives and connects them with God — can be better understood as a *representative cause* rather than as a *constitutive cause*. More simply: Jesus "saves" people not by fixing something but by showing something. He doesn't have to fix or rebuild the bridge between God and humanity by responding to God's demand for satisfaction for humanity's sinfulness. Rather, his task is to reveal or show humanity that God's love is already there, ready to embrace and empower, no matter how often humans have lost their way in selfishness and narrow-mindedness. In other words, Jesus shows that the "bridge," or the relationship between God and humans, already exists; they just don't know where to find it or are not able to trust that it can be found.

This is how Christians, especially Catholics, have always understood sacraments — how they work and why they are necessary. "Sacraments," which is the Christian word for "symbols," are powerful because they tell us something, and make us feel something, that is already true or already there but perhaps not yet as present and active in our lives as it could be. I give a rose or a ring to my wife not to create (or constitute) my love for her but to show it — and thus to make it really real. My love is already there without the rose, but in a sense it needs the rose to be really there. This is different from the understanding of Jesus as an offering of satisfaction to God, as a way of fixing or building a bridge.[4]

We should not think that this understanding of Jesus the sacrament is a brand new product on the shelf of Christian beliefs. It's always been around, but it's gathered dust because, as it were, it hasn't been advertised sufficiently. Christians have always understood Jesus as a sacrament because they have always felt that Jesus embodies, reveals, and enables them to feel something that transforms their lives. Such a sacramental understanding of how Jesus saves is especially contained in the New Testament writings attributed to John, who stresses that Jesus is the Light of the World and the Word of God who enables us to see and sense who God really is. It is also present in one of the earliest images that the New Testament used for Jesus: he is an expression, even a child, of divine Wisdom — the same Wisdom that is found in all the world, from the very first moments of creation. And we should not forget that besides Anselm's (1109) understanding of Jesus' death as a "satisfaction for the infinite offense of sin" (which became the dominant model in most churches), there was also the view of Abelard (1142), who identified Jesus' saving power in the way he revealed the reality and the persistence of God's love for all, even for sinners. Both these views have been currents in the shifting river of Christian beliefs. Mutualist Christians want to shift back to this early, but neglected, current that understands Jesus the Savior as Jesus the sacrament.

In doing this, Jesus' followers will be able both to hold tight to what he means to them and at the same time to recognize what God may be saying in other traditions. The very different pay-offs for interreligious dialogue of the sacramental-representative and the satisfaction-constitutive views of Jesus are,

---

4. Roger Haight, *Jesus the Symbol of God* (Maryknoll, N.Y.: Orbis Books, 1999), 359, 417.

according to advocates of the Mutuality Model, pretty clear. If we understand Jesus as someone who paid a price that could otherwise not be paid, or fixed a rift that could otherwise not be fixed, we will understand the origin of salvation (that is, of right relations between God and humans) as a *one-time event*. What is once paid does not need repaying; what is fixed does not need refixing. If, on the other hand, we hold that Jesus saves us by powerfully manifesting God's reality and love, we will expect — or at least be open to the possibility — that there are other, even many, manifestations of that love. In order to become real in the many and different cultures of humanity, the universal loving Spirit of God must speak in a variety of revelations. So as a sacramental Savior, Jesus can stand with others; as a satisfactory or constitutive Savior, he must stand alone. True, this understanding of Jesus as sacrament does not, by itself, necessarily imply that other religious figures are on a par with Jesus; but it enables, even requires, Christians to be open to this possibility. That's a big step.

A Spirit Christology

A further challenge inherent in the Mutuality Model's understanding of Jesus flows from this view of him as the sacrament of salvation: the reason why Jesus so powerfully manifests, but does not exhaust, the universally given force of God's love is because he was so Spirit-filled. As we heard from John Hick, advocates of the Mutuality Model urge their fellow Christians to make use of the rich possibilities of a Spirit christology that would help balance, and perhaps correct, the excesses of what is called the dominant Logos christology. In a Logos, or Word, christology, the divinity of Jesus is explained according to the way the Word of God, or second person of the Trinity, is united to the humanity of Jesus. This union is made up of two natures — human and divine — coming together in one person; and the one person is generally understood to be the Word, or second person of the Trinity. Such an understanding of the divinity of Jesus has its roots in John's Gospel, but it came to full and intricate bloom during the early councils of the church when bishops and theologians tried to translate Christian beliefs into the language of Greek culture and philosophy. Despite the precision and richness of this view of Jesus, it remains for many people today both hard to grasp and harder to relate to. Also, it tends to downplay the humanity of Jesus by replacing the human center or person of Jesus with the second divine person; as Karl Rahner used to say, this leads to the view of Jesus as "God walking around in a man-suit." Furthermore, it tends to so place Jesus in a category all by himself that his followers don't really feel able to imitate him (after all, he was divine and we're not), and any other religious figure can't really be compared to him since the incarnation of the Word is a one-time event.

With a Spirit christology, Christians can balance the drawbacks of understanding Jesus only as the incarnation of the Word. If the divinity of Jesus is understood more in terms of empowerment by the Spirit, it would be easier for ordinary Christians to grasp how he was both divine and human, and why they are called to imitate him. The Spirit does not replace the human person of Jesus, it empowers — that is, guides and strengthens and enlightens — the man Jesus. And this is the same Spirit that, according to Christian tradition, is present throughout the world, seeking to empower all men and women. Christians believe that Jesus embodies this Spirit in a unique or distinctive way because he was so fully open and attuned to the Spirit. His vision and his choices were those of the Spirit. He is an ideal, an assurance, for all people.

But it is in regard to other religions that a Spirit christology can provide special help for Christians. Roger Haight, one of the most vocal advocates of this kind of christology, provides us with clarity and precision:

> On the one hand, it [a Spirit christology] accounts for the normativity [the challenge and meaning] of Jesus for humankind generally. For Jesus empowered by God as Spirit offers a salvation that is true, universally relevant, and thus normative. On the other hand, as the Jewish and Christian Scriptures testify, God as Spirit has been present and at work in the world of human salvation from "the beginning," without a causal connection to the historical appearance of Jesus.... A Spirit Christology, by recognizing that the Spirit is operative outside the Christian sphere, is open to other mediations of God. The Spirit is spread abroad, and it is not necessary to think that God as Spirit can be incarnated only once in history.[5]

When Haight states that the Spirit has been, and is, operative throughout the world "without a causal connection to the historical appearance of Jesus," he is not denying an essential relationship between the universal Spirit and the particular Jesus; but he is suggesting that what the Spirit is up to in the world and in other religions has a certain independence of Jesus; the Spirit's agenda cannot contradict that of Jesus, but it can go beyond, or at least be really different from, that of Jesus. Michael Amaladoss, S.J, always speaking from his experience in India, stresses this point even more forcefully than Haight. He warns that to develop a Spirit christology and talk about the universal saving presence of the Spirit in other religions will not get us very far if Christians immediately backtrack and insist that the Spirit can only be the Spirit of Christ (as it seems Gavin D'Costa and Jacques Dupuis do [see chapter 5]). To insist that whatever the Spirit says or does outside of Christianity is already, at least implicitly, contained in what Jesus said or did "tends to subordinate the Spirit to Jesus."[6]

Christians cannot imagine that what the Spirit is up to and making known beyond Jesus would ever blatantly contradict Jesus. But this does not mean that the Spirit cannot go beyond Jesus and have things to say in another religion that are not said in Christianity. So Haight draws a conclusion that encapsulates what Christians of the Mutuality Model are suggesting: if we understand

---

5. Ibid., 456.
6. Michael Amaladoss, S.J., "Listen to the Spirit: 'The Father Is Greater Than I' (John 14:28)," *Vidyajyoti* 63 (1999): 689; Amaladoss, "The Pluralism of Religions and the Significance of Christ," *Vidyajyoti* 53 (1989): 413.

the adjective "normative" to mean a truth that lays claim on us and challenges us, then a Spirit christology enables Christians to proclaim Jesus to the world as "normative," but at the same time it enables them to recognize that "other representations of God can be universally normative, and thus, too, for Christians, even as Jesus Christ is universally normative." Or: "Other mediations of God's salvation [other religions or religious figures] are or can be 'on a par' with Jesus Christ."[7]

A Christology of Mutuality

To experience Jesus as the Spirit-filled sacrament of God's gift of love and call to justice not only will enable Christians to recognize the presence of the Spirit in other believers but will also require them to listen to, learn from, and so engage in dialogue with that Spirit. Which means that the picture of Jesus painted by advocates of this Mutuality Model makes for an authentic christology of mutuality — a Jesus who calls his people to talk to other people. In the stirring statement of John B. Cobb Jr.: "Christ is the Way that is open to other Ways." Douglas John Hall expresses the same conviction more personally: "I can say without any doubt at all that I am far more open to Jews and Muslims and Sikhs and humanists and all kinds of other human beings, including self-declared atheists, *because* of Jesus than I should ever have been *apart* from him."[8] Therefore, if Christians can rightly announce to the world that Jesus is the Word of God, they must also remind themselves that it is a Word that can be understood only in conversation with other Words of God. As the meaning of any word can be really understood only in a sentence — that is, in relation to other words — so the Word of God in Jesus can be understood only within all the sentences that make up the story of God's dealings with humanity.[9]

But this means that even those Christians who believe that God's Word in Jesus is "absolute" or "definitive" have to recognize that, paradoxically, it is an absoluteness or definitiveness that "needs" others and that can be what it is only when it is humbly listening to and learning from others. Therefore, to continue the paradox, if Christians can announce to themselves and others that in Jesus "dwells the fullness of Divinity" (Col. 2:9), it will be a fullness that opens them to the fullness of God possibly found in others. If Christians possess this fullness, they can grasp it, appreciate it, and live it only by relating it to the fullness in others. To sharpen this paradox and make it even more dialogical: yes, Christians *truly* have encountered the fullness of God's saving love and power in Jesus the Christ; but they cannot maintain that this fullness is found *only* in Jesus.

---

7. Haight, *Jesus the Symbol*, 422, 399, 403.

8. John B. Cobb Jr., "Beyond Pluralism," in *Christian Uniqueness Reconsidered: The Myth of a Pluralistic Theology of Religions*, ed. Gavin D'Costa (Maryknoll, N.Y.: Orbis Books, 1990), 91; Douglas John Hall, *Why Christian? For Those on the Edge of Faith* (Minneapolis: Fortress/Augsburg, 1998), 34.

9. O'Leary, *Religious Pluralism*, 244; see also 242, 253.

"Truly" but not "only" — this may serve as a more personal, bottom-line description of the Mutuality Model's view of Jesus. Truly God has spoken with a fullness, finality, and universal challenge in Jesus; but God may not have done this only in Jesus. Therefore, the need to witness, and to be witnessed to. That's the stuff of dialogue.

But, as we shall now see, it's also the stuff of controversy.

Questions

Creeping Imperialism?

The main criticism of this Mutuality Model is that, in the final analysis, it's not very mutual. The central concern to promote *mutuality* often leads its proponents to neglect, or even violate, *diversity*. Christians who follow this approach are so focused on dialogue and on getting along with others that they don't see how different each of the others really is. You might say that mutualist Christians are so intent on nurturing one forest of religions that they miss, or even cut down, some of the individual trees. In other words, these Christians, in seeking to promote dialogue, end up as imperialists who, contrary to their good intentions, take advantage of other religions for their own noble, but self-serving, intents. A creeping imperialism infects this Mutuality Model in two ways: in the way its advocates insist on discovering the common ground they think is necessary for dialogue; and in the way they define and set up the rules of dialogue.

1. Those who endorse this model are so convinced that some kind of common ground is necessary for dialogue that they cannot open their minds even a crack to the possibility that maybe, just maybe, the religions are really so diverse that there is no existing common ground between them. As one critic, William Placher, puts it: "They cannot accept the possibility that there may be just different, even conflicting, religions and no point from which to evaluate them except from within some one tradition or another."[10] In other words, the religions of the world, in what they are seeking and in the ways they seek it, might really be apples and oranges, and not differently colored apples. What the devotees of the Mutuality Model refuse to admit is the simple but immensely consequential possibility that the religions, like so many of the "things" of this world, are really much more diverse than they are similar. Every attempt to bring things together on some kind of common ground or principle of unity will result in damaging the diversity. *E pluribus unum* (out of many one) does just that: the many are lost in the one.

But the critics press their case even more persistently: even if there is a common ground that links the various religions, the theologians we have been studying in this chapter forget that there's no way of getting at it, seeing it, or

---

10. William Placher, *Unapologetic Theology: A Christian Voice in a Pluralistic Conversation* (Louisville: Westminster/John Knox Press, 1989), 144; see also S. Mark Heim, *Salvations: Truth and Difference in Religion* (Maryknoll, N.Y.: Orbis Books, 1995), 103.

evaluating it "except from within some one tradition or another." It's those telescopes again. We all look out onto and try to understand the world around us
and the Divine within us through the cultural-religious telescopes that have been
given to us. There's no such thing as a naked look at the truth. To shift analogies
slightly, we all wear glasses, and the glasses we look through, the critics remind
us, not only enable us to see — they also *determine* what we see. This is where
the analogy, in a certain sense, breaks down, for the cultural lenses through
which we view the world actually become part of what we see. We can't neatly
separate "what we're seeing" from "the cultural lenses through which we see it."

This is what many of the advocates of the Mutuality Model don't seem to
recognize. (Maybe they don't want to recognize it.) After John Hick, for example, admits that all experience is "experiencing as" — that is, is viewed through
our cultural or religious telescopes — he goes on to talk about the "one Reality"
within all religions as if it were no longer something that is "experienced as,"
as if now he were rising above all the different ways of "experiencing as" and
seeing the one thing that everyone experienced — without a telescope. But you
can't "rise above." You can't set aside your telescope. And you can't use more
than one telescope at a time. So if you always have to use a telescope, and you
can use only one at a time, you're always seeing the so-called universal Reality
or common ground through *your* telescope. That means the ground you're claiming to have identified for everyone is much more *yours* than *common*. Every
time you try to locate the universal center of all faiths, you're standing in the
center of one faith. To forget this — to try to talk about the universal center from
the universal center and not from a particular center — is to impose, willy-nilly,
a particular perspective on all the others.

This is the accusation that is raised so often of the mutuality or pluralist perspective: it imposes its own particular viewpoint on all the others in the name of
universality. And this is what transforms Dr. Jekyll into Mr. Hyde — why mutualists become imperialists. Lesslie Newbigin, one of the sharpest critics of this
model, does not mince words: "Every proposal for human unity which does not
specify the center [that is, which does not acknowledge its own specific stand-
point] has the self as its unacknowledged center." S. Mark Heim agrees when
he points out that if those who hold up "God" as the absolute for all religions
do not specify whose God they are talking about, they will make themselves
into God.[11] These critics are asking mutualist theologians to come clean and
to recognize that all religions start from some God-given, or divinely revealed,
absolute position from which they view other religions and make their universal claims. Not to admit, or be aware of, this is to set up your own version of
"absolute truth" and then lay it on others.

2. A second way in which this same kind of imperialism — laying my truth
on yours either naively or with a smile — creeps into the Mutuality Model is in

---

11. Lesslie Newbigin, "Religion for the Marketplace," in *Christian Uniqueness Reconsidered*,
139. S. Mark Heim, *Is Christ the Only Way? Christian Faith in a Pluralistic World* (Valley Forge,
Pa.: Judson, 1985), 144.

the manner in which its proponents set up the field of dialogue. As we heard, they believe that a level playing field requires not just common ground but also common rules. These rules, they think, will be "naturally" affirmed and accepted by all right-minded, authentically religious people. Some Christian dialogical zealots have even developed a "decalogue for dialogue," commandments that are self-evident and acceptable to all: no one is to be excluded; everyone will want to learn as much as they want to teach; all will recognize that there's always more to learn; and therefore no one will lay any absolute or definitive or exclusive claims on the table of dialogue.[12] Here, the critics intervene, the mutualist theologians are at it again — blissfully but harmfully unaware of how much such "rules" or such a "decalogue" is coming out of their own religious or philosophical perspectives. For instance, when the mutualists require that to come to the table of dialogue all exclusive or definitive truth-claims have to be left at the door, they don't seem to be aware how much such requirements offend many religious people. Most religions start with certain truths that they feel have been given them by God; these truths are felt to be superior to all others, or at least they constitute the bar under which all other religious truths must pass. Every religion has its "jealousies" or its "nonnegotiables" that it can never abandon or put up for interreligious debate.[13]

With keen perception, William Placher asks his friends among the theologians mentioned in this chapter to ponder how, by excluding exclusive claims from the dialogue, they themselves become exclusivists. They close themselves to those who close themselves to others. "I announce that I am willing to take your point of view seriously. If you are not willing to do the same, then I am 'open' and you are 'closed,' so it turns out that I do not have to take your point of view seriously." So after the mutualist theologians announce a dialogue that is open to all because none will make exclusive or absolute claims, "it turns out that evangelical Christians, Hasidic Jews, and traditional Muslims, and so on are not really eligible to join that dialogue, because they are unwilling to accept the proposed rules of the game, rules that seem to emerge from a modern, Western, academic tradition."[14]

Those last words point to a deeper aspect of the imperialist agenda that hides behind the benign face of the Mutuality Model. Mutualist Christians certainly don't want to be missionaries whose driving intent is to convert others to Christianity; and yet they are very much missionaries of the Western *cultural* gospel who seek to convert all religions to the "self-evident" truths of the eighteenth-century Enlightenment. When critics of the Mutuality Model examine the foundation stones of all three bridges we have studied in this section,

---

12. Leonard Swidler, *After the Absolute: The Dialogical Future of Religious Reflection* (Minneapolis: Augsburg-Fortress, 1990), 42–46; see also Paul F. Knitter, *No Other Name? A Critical Survey of Christian Attitudes toward the World Religions* (Maryknoll, N.Y.: Orbis Books, 1985), 207–13.

13. J. A. DiNoia, "Pluralist Theology of Religions: Pluralistic or Non-Pluralistic?" in *Christian Uniqueness Reconsidered,* 120ff.

14. Placher, *Unapologetic Theology,* 64, 146.

they find that they are all marked "made in Europe or America." All of them are part of what is called "modernity" — the cultural convictions that were cast when Immanuel Kant and other Enlightenment thinkers subjected all religion to the chisel of "hard reason" and "historical analysis." Most Western theologians (with the exception of the Fundamentalists/Evangelicals) accepted these given convictions of modernity. And now, perhaps without realizing it, they are requiring all other religions to accept them as well, if these religions want to be part of "authentic" dialogue.[15]

What are some of these given truths of Western modernity that mutualist missionaries require all religions to accept? To list some of them is to perhaps shake these "modern thinkers" into realizing that none of these "self-evident truths" can really be proven — and so have to be taken on faith:

- that if there is an Infinite, it is available to all religions, but cannot be grasped fully or finally by any one of them;

- that all religious language is symbolic and mythic;

- that time is linear and history proceeds by evolution;

- that for anything to be really real, it needs to be grounded in history;

- that individual human rights take precedence over all other rights;

- that democracy takes precedence over all other systems;

- that "right action" (orthopraxis) takes precedence over "right belief" (orthodoxy);

- that all religions must promote justice and human/ecological well-being.

The last two truths on this list, which are the foundation stones of the ethical bridge to dialogue, are especially singled out by the critics as a typical move by academicians to herd all religions into a Western corral. Gavin D'Costa, who with S. Mark Heim is one of the strongest voices warning of the dangers of the Mutality Model, is clear: in the new views that call all religions to work toward a global ethic, "A universal ethical imperative is prioritized over metaphysics and religions. . . . All people are subject to this ethical 'ought,' prior to their formation within religious communities, and the value of their formation within such communities is judged by their ability to respond to this ethical imperative."[16] This ethical imperative is usually spelled out in terms of justice. But John Milbank, another British philosopher-theologian who lays bare the dangers of all mutualist or pluralist moves, holds that the notion of justice is so decisively influenced by a Judeo-Christian culture that to use it as the context of interreligious dialogue is to Westernize the entire conversation. This forces us

---

15. Heim, *Salvations,* 103.
16. Gavin D'Costa, *The Meeting of Religions and the Trinity* (Maryknoll, N.Y.: Orbis Books, 2000), 30.

back to the question: *"Whose* justice are we talking about?"[17] What about traditions like Buddhism that don't have a clearly defined notion of, or concern for, justice?

These fears of an imperialism lurking in the heart of the Mutualist Model become downright nightmares when some critics go on to point out that the gospel the mutualists are preaching to other religions belongs not only to the West but to those cultures and nations which, for the most part, are already dominant over most of the world. The danger here is that by preaching the cultural values and visions of the dominant powers of the world, these Christians, who are so sincerely intent on a dialogue among equals, may be unconsciously promoting the status quo of dominance. Such a possibility creeps toward probability when one notes, perhaps to one's horror, how similar the message of the Mutuality Model is to the message coming out of the capitals and boardrooms of the so-called First World nations: all nations, in all their diversity, are called on to embrace one global market, in which all are promised equal opportunities for equal advantages. Or all cultures are beckoned to make use of one global network of communication through ever-more sophisticated media (especially the Worldwide Web), so that all will be able to make their voices heard and their contributions felt. And yet we must ask: Who controls the global market, the communication media — and perhaps most importantly, who controls the military power that is supposed to "protect" the smooth functioning of the global system? Who, in actuality, is reaping the main economic benefits?

There are critics, therefore, who warn that the new calls for a dialogue of true mutuality can easily lead to the "McDonaldization" of dialogue. Kenneth Surin is the most vocal. He compares the new type of dialogue among religions to the "Big Mac." This is a type of food that appeals to something that all cultures of the world have in common, something all can appreciate and enjoy, something that will link them all to each other. "The McDonald's hamburger is the first universal food," Surin admits, but he immediately adds: "but the people — be they from La Paz, Bombay, Cairo, or Brisbane — who eat the McDonald's hamburger also consume the American way of life."[18] In consuming the American way of life, they lose touch with their own and they end up contributing, perhaps unwillingly but nonetheless actually, to the economic and cultural dominance of one nation over others. A universal project — whether it be a global market or a global ethic or a global dialogue — which seeks to bring different participants into a relationship of equality and mutuality but which is based on an unequal distribution of power among the participants will usually end up as a tool in the hands of the powerful to keep things as they are.

This is why people or groups in power love to dialogue. It's usually their dialogue; they can control it:

17. John Milbank, "The End of Dialogue," in *Christian Uniqueness Reconsidered*, 174–91; Alasdair C. MacIntyre, *Whose Justice? Whose Rationality?* (Notre Dame, Ind.: Notre Dame University Press, 1988).

18. Kenneth Surin, "A 'Politics of Speech'," in *Christian Uniqueness Reconsidered*, 201.

A primary means by which privileged groups mask their hegemony is via a language of common contribution and co-operative shaping; to the extent that such groups can convince all partners in public dialogue that each voice contributes equally, to that extent does the conversation deflect attention from the unequal distribution of power underlying it.[19]

Or to make the same point in a traditional proverb: " 'Every man for himself and God for all' said the elephant as he danced among the chickens." As long as some are elephants and others are chickens, calls for a dance of equality under one God or "one Reality" or "social justice" aren't going to work. So these critics, in their bottom line, are warning Christians that all calls for a dialogue of mutuality on a level playing field aren't going to work unless questions of the unequal distribution of power among nations, and among religions, are also (or first) addressed. That most of the Christians calling for dialogue live in nations and cultures that have more power — economic and military — than most others makes this an even more uncomfortable and pressing challenge.

Creeping Relativism?

Among the criticisms of the Mutuality Model, there's a flip-side to the warnings of imperialism: relativism. The Christians who are urging this new form of dialogue not only impose their own Western values and agenda on others but also end up with a dialogue that is bland and boring! It's boring because its advocates are so intent on getting everyone to agree on what they have in common that they lose all possibility of really disagreeing about what makes them different. The common ground that they propose becomes so soft and shifting that it can make room for, or absorb, just about anything — like quicksand. That's the kind of common ground in which relativism grows and thrives. Relativists are people for whom the notion of truth is either so broad, or so diversified, or so distant, that they can never trust themselves to know whether they, or anyone, really have the truth. Relativists live in a kind of twilight world in which all cats are gray.

   In examining more carefully the common ground that each of the three bridges to a theology of mutuality proposes, critics expose how it becomes a kind of quicksand that absorbs whatever steps into it. John Hick's "Real" that hides within all religions is certainly as vague and amorphous as it might be real. It can oblige just about any image of the Divine or of God that the human imagination can come up with. His notion of the "divine *noumenon*" that is beyond the reach of any of the religious phenomena we encounter in history is so far beyond reach that it can adapt to anything that we might ever encounter. After all, Hick himself can make room in his "Real" for both personal and impersonal understandings of the Ultimate or for views that claim that this world

---

19. Raymond Williams, *Marxism and Literature* (New York: Oxford University Press, 1977), 112.

is real and those that say it exists only in our imagination. Is there any image of the Divine or of the world that Hick's Real could not accommodate?

Raimon Panikkar, although he is thoroughly aware of the dangers of imperialism, is judged by the critics to be thoroughly guilty of relativism. In insisting that the many can never be put under the control of the one, in holding that the Mystery discovered in all religions is not only at the top of the mountain but is made up of all the paths leading to the top, in allowing for "the Christ" to have as many names as can be found in the various religious traditions of the world, Panikkar says nothing about how one might tell if a path does not lead to the top or if a religious name might not really fit what the Christ is all about. He is so generous in affirming the validity of all mystics that he seems to lose the ability to discern and wean out the impostors. It seems that Panikkar and those who follow his mystical approach live in an understanding of religious experience that makes all mystics look rather gray.

These dangers of sliding down the slippery slopes of relativism are also noted among those who use the ethical bridge — those who are especially committed to taking strong, nonrelativist stands on issues of justice and eco-human well-being. Again, what this ethical approach forgets is that even such noble concerns as "justice," "well-being," and "global responsibility" are not clear, universal terms. By themselves — that is, before they are understood within some particular system or religion — they can, like the chameleon, take on many different colors and meanings. Even the human reality of suffering will be interpreted and responded to differently according to the different religious glasses one is wearing. So to think that one can use these ideals and concerns as the common ground on which to make common ethical decisions is at best naive. Gavin D'Costa draws his conclusion: "Hence, promoting human welfare is an unhelpful common denominator [for interreligious dialogue] as it specifies nothing in particular until each tradition addresses itself to what is meant by 'human' and the 'welfare' of human beings. . . . [Even] the 'kingdom of God and its justice' is a vacuous phrase if it is not given some normative content, be it Christian, Jungian, or Buddhist."[20]

But all this seems to place mutualist Christians in a dilemma. In order to avoid relativism, they have to give their common ground some specific, *normative* content. Yet as soon as they do that, they take on the role of an imperialist by imposing their normative content on other religions. Is there any way out of this dilemma?

Yes there is. As we shall see in the next section, critics of the Mutuality Model offer a simple reminder, which is also a solution for the dilemma: all participants in interreligious dialogue are always, in a sense, imperialists — and that's good! This solution is rooted in a fundamental fact that is often missed:

---

20. Gavin D'Costa, "The Reign of God and a Trinitarian Ecclesiology: An Analysis of Soteriocentrism," in *Christian Mission and Interreligious Dialogue,* ed. Paul Mojzes and Leonard Swidler (Lewiston, N.Y.: Edwin Mellen Press, 1990), 57, 59.

all practitioners of dialogue are interpreting the others from their own religious experience and beliefs. All of them, therefore, are "imposing" their views on others because all of them are looking at the others through their own religious glasses. Furthermore, the participants in the dialogue have to recognize another fact: that all of them, because they take their religions seriously and base their lives on them, bring to the dialogue certain nonnegotiables, certain convictions which they do believe — explicitly or implicitly — are superior, normative, a firm place to stand. On the basis of these convictions or norms, they can take clear positions and declare that what they do believe is true or false, right or wrong. Such convictions are not at all quicksand; they're solid rock.

So in this understanding of dialogue, everyone comes to the table ready to listen to others but also with two up-front, on-the-table admissions: (*a*) that all participants speak from within their own community, out of their own religious experience and convictions, and under the direction of the God or Truth they have encountered in their own tradition and sacred writings; and (*b*) that all believe that what they have learned from this God will provide the real common ground, the final word, that will bring all religions into a new kind of unity never before experienced or perhaps conceived. In this kind of dialogue, *differences* among the religions turn out to be more important than common ground or a mystical core. For out of the meeting or dialogue of differences — as long as this dialogue is carried out in an open, honest, compassionate, and nonviolent way — we can hope to discover which of the different religions carries the message that might clarify, evaluate, and unify all the others. So, yes, a level playing field for such dialogue is necessary, but not because all the religions are equally good and valid but because the game of interreligious dialogue has to be played in a fair and honest way so that each of the religions can prove what each feels in its heart and history — that it is the winning team.

Such an understanding of dialogue can be readily endorsed, for different reasons, by Christians who follow the Replacement Model as well as by those who choose the Fulfillment Model. In Part IV, we will explore another model that also can embrace this type of dialogue but that seeks to avoid the inadequacies of all the other models.

Is It Really Christian?

The final questions for the Mutuality Model deal with what many Christians consider its most evident and dangerous flaw — its revised image of Jesus Christ. These concerns sift down to three questions: Does the new view of Jesus as "truly but not only" — truly a Savior but not the only Savior — constitute a break with, rather than a renewal of, Christian tradition? Can this view really sustain Christian spirituality? And can it maintain the practice of following Jesus the prophet?

1. *Does this view constitute a break with tradition?* The attempts of mutualist theologians to decipher the "one-and-only" language of the New Testament as

"love language" that is meant to affirm Jesus and not rank him, or their claims that images such as "only Son" or "one mediator" are symbols that are to be taken seriously but not literally, or their urging that Jesus nowadays is better understood as God's prophet rather than God's only Son — all such "reinterpretations" bump up against the wall of what followers of Jesus have always *said* about him and what they *meant* by what they said. In taking their "love language" and their "symbols" about Jesus seriously — in calling him and praying to him as the only Son of God, the one mediator, the only way to the Father, the name above all names — the first Christians were not just expressing their love for Jesus; they were not just stating who he was for them; they were not just signing up co-workers for the Reign of God. They were also giving Jesus a special, a focal, a decisive, a final place in what they believed was the relationship of God to humanity. Yes, they *were* ranking Jesus! And the rank was the highest they could imagine. They were asserting that whatever else God may be up to in history and in other religions, it was related to, grounded in, and had to be evaluated by what God had done in Jesus. This is why there is a constant theme running through the polyphony and variety of New Testament christologies; no matter how different the many images of Jesus were, they all said not only "truly" but "only."[21]

And Christians used such language, with all its implications of "ranking" Jesus, in a world that was teeming with other religions. Mutualist Christians seem to forget this. To suggest that if the early Christians would have had our "awareness" of the many other faiths, they would have, as it were, "watched their language" is way off the historical mark. They did have such awareness, and they did not watch their language. As one critic teases his fellow mutualist Christians: "I find it ironic that people object to the proclamation of the Christian gospel these days because so many other faiths jostle on the doorstep of the global village. What's new? The variety of faiths in antiquity was even greater than it is today. And the early Christians, making as they did ultimate claims for Jesus, met the problem of other faiths head-on from the very outset." Another critic stretches the tease into a taunt: "The exclusive claim of the gospel was from the beginning counter-cultural. It was foolishness to the Greeks, and it remains a scandal of which many contemporary Hellenized Christians have become ashamed."[22] Mutualist ("Hellenized") Christians of today are ashamed of what Christians of the first century boldly and lovingly proclaimed.

What the new mutualist interpretations of Jesus' uniqueness omit or suppress is that the meaning and the contribution of Christianity to the dialogue of religions are found not just in its message but in the *person* who both delivered and

---

21. Hans Küng, *Global Responsibility: In Search of a New World Ethic* (New York: Crossroad, 1991), 99; Claude Geffre, "Christian Uniqueness and Interreligious Dialogue," in *Christian Mission and Interreligious Dialogue*, ed. Paul Mojzes and Leonard Swidler (Lewiston, N.Y.: Edwin Mellen Press, 1990), 67.

22. Michael Green, *Acts for Today: First-Century Christianity for Twentieth-Century Christians* (London: Hodder and Stoughton, 1993), 38; Carl E. Braaten, "Hearing the Other: The Promise and Problem of Pluralism," *Currents in Theology and Mission* 24 (1997): 398.

was that message. "Christians do not simply proclaim a message or a humane way of life of which Jesus is a model. Christians proclaim a *person* as one and the same with God's saving act.... What Christians claim as the ultimate truth is a person not a proposition."[23] This is why the mutualist theologians' suggestions to view Jesus as sacrament rather than satisfaction may be good, but they are also dangerously inadequate. Because of the identification of message and person in Christianity, Jesus does not just symbolize or "represent" the truth of God's love and call to justice; he *is* that truth. He constitutes it. Without his historical reality, it really wouldn't exist and it certainly cannot be known in its full splendor without him. This is why, as we saw in chapter 5, Pope John Paul II warns against separating Christ from Jesus; if Christians can announce that "Jesus is the Christ," they can, and must, also announce that "the Christ is Jesus." Without Jesus, there wouldn't be any Christ. Though the Christ and the Spirit may be active beyond Jesus in other religions, they never lose their point of origin and their point of return in Jesus.

But these concerns, so far, are all theological or historical. More discomforting questions come from pastors and religious educators. If, as all theologians admit, the test of good theology, like the test of good pudding, is in the eating and consumption thereof, Christian leaders fear that these new views of Jesus as one among many will not play very well among ordinary Christians. Simply, such views "go too far." Hans Küng, clearly a theologian who is not afraid to shake and stretch the Christian community, confesses that to "expect Christians themselves to... abandon the conviction of faith in the normative and definitive word of God given with Jesus Christ and called for by the New Testament, in favor of an identification of Jesus Christ with other bearers of revelation and bringers of salvation," would expose any theologian to "the risk of parting company with their own faith-communities."[24] And a theologian who parts company with her faith community cuts off the life-line needed to nurture and guide her job as a theologian.

2. *Can these new views of Jesus sustain Christian spirituality?* In the previous statement by Hans Küng, notice that he described the community's belief that Jesus is God's definitive Word as a "conviction of faith." So the reason why these new views of Jesus will not play in Christianity's Peoria is not just because they seem to contradict what the New Testament and the catechism say, but also — and mainly — because they don't resonate with what Christians feel in their hearts about Jesus. Here we take up the delicate and risky task of examining the emotional hard-drive of a person who has decided to be a follower of Jesus. What are the circuits that are charged, what are the messages that are received, that bring a person to stand up and follow Jesus — and to trust that this following can really make a difference in one's own life and in the world?

---

23. Heim, *Is Christ the Only Way?* 54, 56; Paul Griffiths, "The Uniqueness of Christian Doctrine Defended," in *Christian Uniqueness Reconsidered,* 170.

24. Küng, *Global Responsibility,* 101.

The mutualist theologians we have heard from in this section respond by saying that when a Christian chooses to follow Jesus, she is doing so because she has found that Jesus is *truly* God's Word but not necessarily because she has felt him to be God's *only* Word. That may be true. But the critics of the Mutuality Model want to further unpack that "truly." And when they do, they discover that what Christians feel in their hearts about Jesus is not just that he is truly God's revelation but that he is truly God's decisive and definitive voice in their lives. "Decisive" and "definitive" are abstract terms that are trying to get at clear and compelling feelings. To experience Jesus is to experience a call or a power that *decides* and *defines* one's life; it requires one to act and live in a certain way, a way that will "cut off" (that's the meaning of the Latin *decidere*) and "mark limits" (the meaning of *de-finire*) regarding other attitudes or worldviews. Jesus stands as a turning point, a fork in the road, a source of new beginnings. The New Testament writers called it conversion. So the Word of God in Jesus is experienced in Christian life as decisive: it cuts off many things, but it opens the door to many more.

There's one more ingredient in what Christians feel when they have truly experienced the presence of Jesus in their lives: he is decisive and definitive not just for them but *for all people*. That, too, is an element that one finds when one unpacks the experience of Jesus as truly God's Word and Savior. Whatever is decisive is also naturally felt to be universal. It has meaning and power not just for me, or for the Christian community, but for all human communities. Monika Hellwig offers a succinct description of this experience: to be a follower of Jesus means that one has sensed that he "makes a *definitive difference* in the possibilities for individuals and for human history as a whole" and that wherever "people implement the possibilities he opened up, there is growth toward fuller life, hope, community, and happiness." Jesus gives people hope — the astounding hope that, despite all the evidence to the contrary, this world can really be different from what it presently is. "But Christian hope for the fullness of redemption is directly linked to the definitive difference that Jesus makes in the possibilities of our history." In Jesus, Christians feel that new possibilities are opened up. And they don't seem to find these possibilities anywhere else.[25]

This means that without Jesus, what Christians call the Reign of God cannot really become all that it is meant to be. Yes, many others, many religions, may be working toward this vision; but without Jesus something essential is missing. So Edward Schillebeeckx, who as we have seen wants to affirm the validity of other religions and cure Christians of their disease of imperialism, also agrees with Hellwig: "To believe in Jesus as the Christ means at its deepest to confess . . . that Jesus has an *abiding and constitutive significance* for the approach of the Kingdom of God and thus for the comprehensive healing of

---

25. Monika Hellwig, "Re-emergence of the Human, Critical, Public Jesus," *Theological Studies* 50 (1989): 480; Hellwig, "Christology in the Wider Ecumenism," in *Christian Uniqueness Reconsidered,* 115.

human beings....For Christians, Jesus therefore is the decisive and definitive revelation of God."[26]

So when Christians experience Jesus to be truly God's saving Word, they also experience him to be God's *decisive and definitive* Word. That's something the Mutuality Model doesn't seem to recognize.

3. *With these new views, can Christians follow Jesus the prophet?* This question asks especially those mutualist Christians who hold up Jesus the prophet and liberator whether they really can find the necessary muscle and stamina to follow him. To imitate this Jesus means to take strong, clear stands on practices or attitudes that for Jesus would be intolerable — for example, the existence of poverty in the midst of economic growth, violence against women, the enlisting of children into armies, the destruction of the environment. And such strong stands must be drawn cross-culturally, interreligiously, in the face of other claims that "in our world" such practices can be tolerated. There are evils in this world that are, we might say, absolutely evil — they are so harmful, so unjust, so inhuman that they simply cannot be tolerated. To take the prophetic Gospel of Jesus seriously, Christians have to not only disagree with the evils they find in the world; they have to resist such evils, no matter how much a culture may endorse or allow them, no matter what kind of a religious sanction such practices may have. Such resistance will always be loving and nonviolent, but it will also be clear and unshakable.

So yes, there are what we might call "absolute intolerables" in the world of politics and economics and religions, and these intolerables must be met with absolute stands of resistance. But absolute stands require absolute standing places. And this is where, in the minds of many critics, the Mutuality Model falters. It calls Christians to take firm, resolute positions in the face of evil; but it provides no solid grounding for those positions. If what I hold forth as the truth of God's Reign always stands in possible need of clarification or correction in the light of other truths, how can I be sure that it enables me to pronounce an absolute no to absolute evil?

This is why Gregory Baum, certainly a loud and clear prophetic voice in the Christian community during the past generation, balks at aligning himself with the Mutuality Model. "The liberal view of religious pluralism underestimates this power of evil."[27] Hans Küng and Jürgen Moltmann, veteran proponents for an ethical dialogue among religions, warn followers of the Mutuality Model that it was especially those Christians who insisted on God speaking in many voices who also failed to take a strong prophetic stand against National Socialism and its claims to be the voice of God for the German people. The power of evil is such that if there is no one clear rallying point that provides people — all people — with the certain knowledge and spiritual power that are necessary

---

26. Edward Schillebeeckx, *The Church: The Human Story of God* (New York: Crossroad, 1990), 121; emphasis added.

27. Gregory Baum, introduction to Rosemary Radford Ruether, *Faith and Fratricide: The Theological Roots of Anti-Semitism* (New York: Seabury, 1974), 15.

to stand and resist, the mess that is our world will only grow worse. This is the challenge and task facing all religions. "It is an open question whether any religion will have the requisite toughness for this demanding task unless it at some point makes the claim that it is significantly different and unsurpassably true."[28] Traditionally, Christianity has made this claim. But it is a claim that the mutualists seem to be dismantling.

God's Reign is meant for all, and all can contribute to it. But if there is not a master plan, or a master architect, the builders will often find themselves working at cross purposes. To coherently and consistently proclaim Jesus as prophet and liberator requires one to also hold him up as that master architect.

If we grant that there is validity to all or some of these criticisms of the Mutuality Model, does this mean that to respond to them Christians must return to either the Replacement or the Fulfillment Model? As we will see in the next part, there are Christians who hold that there is still another alternative.

---

28. George Lindbeck, *The Nature of Doctrine: Religion and Theology in a Postliberal Age* (Philadelphia: Westminster Press, 1984), 127.

Part IV

THE ACCEPTANCE MODEL
"Many True Religions:
So Be It"

Chapter 10

Making Peace
with Radical Difference

The model we investigate in this part is, one might say, the youngest of them all. It grew up during the last two decades of the twentieth century both as a "child of its times" and as a reaction to the inadequacies of other models for a Christian theology of religions. So it's an approach to other faiths that feels it can better speak to the way people nowadays understand themselves and their world and at the same time fix those aspects of previous theologies that don't seem to work very well. Regarding the other theologies, this model, once again, makes an attempt at a better balance of the teeter-totter we've been sitting on throughout this book — between universality and particularity. As we noted at the end of the previous chapter, the models for a theology of religions that we have explored so far seem to either so stress the particularity of one religion that the validity of all the others is jeopardized (the Replacement and the Fulfillment Models) or they stress the universal validity of them all in a way that fogs over the real particular differences (the Mutuality Model). What we are calling the Acceptance Model thinks it can do a better job at this balancing act. And as we will see, it does so not by holding up the superiority of any one religion, nor by searching for that common something that makes them all valid, but by accepting the real diversity of all faiths. The religious traditions of the world are really different, and we have to *accept* those differences — that, you might say, is the one-line summary of this model.

It's also a message that reflects the general awareness or attitudes of the times we live in — postmodern times, as they are called. We've heard frequent mention of "postmodernism" or "postmodernity" throughout these pages. For this model, more than for all the others, we have to have a clear picture of just what that means. We can begin, then, by offering a bird's-eye view of postmodernism.

The Context: Our Postmodern World

The first thing to say about a "bird's-eye view" of postmodernism is that, according to postmodernists, it's impossible. There is no such thing as a bird's-eye view of postmodernity because there is no such thing as a bird's-eye view of anything. We can never rise above — or transcend — the location where we are standing in order to see all the other locations. We are always looking at other places from *some place*. Therefore, bird's-eye views are — excuse the pun — for the birds. We are humans. That means we are place-bound.

This is what our "modern" world seems to have forgotten. And the forgetfulness is rooted in the powerful influence that the historical period of the Enlightenment has played on all of Western thought throughout the modern period. That's why postmodernism has the name it does. Though it is frustratingly difficult to give it a tight, positive definition, it is relatively easy to describe it negatively. Postmodernity is a reaction against the high-minded optimism of the Enlightenment — the movement that began in the eighteenth century and that was convinced it was breaking through barriers to untold progress for humanity. The barriers it sought to topple had been built by those who tried to impose external authorities on the human mind — authorities like tradition in general or the church in particular. If we can remove the barriers — or the blinders — of external authority, if we can then give human reason free rein to search for the truth without restrictions and in all honesty, humanity would, so thought Enlightenment liberators, be emancipated and invigorated to make the kind of progress in human understanding and well-being that had never before been realized in the history of our species. So they thought. So they urged. And then came the horrors of two savage world wars, plus an exploitative colonialism that brought the fruits of the Enlightenment to the "primitive" cultures of Africa and Asia.

Postmodernists, to put it tersely, announce that the Enlightenment and the modern world that was born of it aren't working. That's why they describe themselves as *post*moderns. They're the ones, or the movement, who come after modernity. Postmodernists may not be clear about what they are looking for, but they are pretty sure about how *not* to get there. Those aspects of the modern, "enlightened" world that the postmodernists are most wary of and want to avoid might be summarized as follows.

An excessive confidence in the power of reason. Postmodernists warn that reason is not the clear, pure, fail-proof light that will lead us to truth once it is free from the constraints of external authority. Why? Mainly for two reasons: (*a*) reason itself can be contaminated and exploited, and (*b*) reason can mean different things in different cultures.

The primacy and reliability of empirical data. Modern people seem to think that if we can just get the facts and "nothing but the facts," then reason will analyze these facts and lead us to a clarity that all can see and affirm. Postmodernists retort: there's no such thing as "nothing but the facts." Facts always come in different cultural guises.

The exclusion of mythical-mystical views of the world. Since the Enlightenment, science, with its empirical method and hard-headed logic, has been called in as the final arbiter on the way things really are. If in doubt, consult the biologists or physicists or chemists. They practice *hard* science. Postmodernists question this normative authority of science. They suggest that there are other ways of knowing how the world works and what is our place in it, ways that can't be measured or put into formulas — like myths and mystical experience.

The quest for universal truths. Since the Enlightenment, moderns have been trying to move beyond the limits of narrow-minded, local views to get at the big picture of what we really are. They want truths and understandings that will apply to everyone and be recognized by everyone so that everyone will finally be able to agree and live with everyone else. Postmodernists warn that such efforts are not only impossible; they are dangerous. People, and their cultures, are more different than they are alike. *Vive la difference!* If differences flourish, so will humanity.

This last point of difference — that is, that universal truths are dangerous and differences are life-giving — might be tagged as the central pillar of postmodern attitudes. It's certainly the postmodern pillar that sustains the various expressions of the Acceptance Model that we will be examining in this section. This central pillar or claim can be inscribed in one simple phrase: *the dominance of diversity*. Whether you're talking about atoms or molecules or plants or animals or humans — or truths — you can't get away from diversity. "The many" cannot be boiled down to "the one." Yes, different things can be interrelated, connected, and brought into unifying relationships, but never to the point where you lose diversity. Diversity will always, as it were, bounce back, or grow back. It always has the last word — or better, the additional word — over unity. Diversity dominates unity, and we can be happy it does. For otherwise, life and its evolution not only would get dull but would wither away. Remove diversity and you remove vitality.

This, the postmodernist proclaimers tell us, is especially true of truth. Truth is always truths. It always takes different shapes and assumes different identities — to the point that "it" is no longer one, but many. If there is such a thing as "one absolute truth," we'll never know it, at least not in our present human condition. If any one person or culture thinks they have the one unifying truth that will embrace all the others, it will not be a truth that others can see but a truth that will be forced upon them. So truth, too, is dominated by diversity, and this is so for two reasons, which have already come up at various points in this book. Truth is plural not singular because (*a*) all human experience and all human knowledge are filtered, and (*b*) the filters are incredibly diverse. Just as there is no way we can climb out of our skins and still be who we are, so there is no way we can discard the cultural-historical filters by which we see the world and still be the persons we are. This is why Ludwig Boltzmann could make a statement that would stop many people in their mental tracks: "In my opinion we cannot utter a single statement that would be a *pure fact of experience.*" The physicist Niels Bohr explains why: "Any experience...makes its appearance within the frame of our customary points of view."[1] "Customary points of view" = "filters."

The architects of postmodernism offer us what we can call mind-teasers to press their point that every time we think we've got a take on the whole picture,

1. As quoted in William Placher, *Unapologetic Theology: A Christian Voice in a Pluralistic Conversation* (Louisville: Westminster/John Knox Press, 1989), 28.

or a truth that is absolute truth evident to everyone, we can look more carefully to find the filter through which we are seeing or imaging this truth. The
philosopher Willard Van Orman Quine once compared the question "Which sentences in physical theory are definitions?" (that is, What are the foundational,
absolute truths for a particular hard science?) to the sentence "Which places in
Ohio are starting places?" Every "theory," whether it's a philosophical worldview or a scientific system, has one particular starting point rather than another.
And where you start will determine to a great extent the route you follow and
where you end up. Ludwig Wittgenstein, one of the favorite philosophers of
postmodernists, was even more of a tease: "When we find the *foundations*, it
turns out they are being *held up by the rest of the house*." What we think are the
unquestionable, absolute foundations that would support all houses or cultures
turn out to be strong only because they are part of our house and culture.[2] Every
"universal" truth is universal only for its particular filter. That means that the
particularity cancels out the universality.

And the postmodernists insist that the particular filters are not only many;
they are really different. This is the reason for the persistent warnings about
the way modern thinkers extol reason, as if reason were some kind of universal
tool given to all peoples of all times by which they could build their common
house of truth. Because of our cultural filters, the postmoderns remind us, reason
is understood very differently in different cultures. In some cultures, reason is
not the primary tool for understanding our world. Imagination, or feelings, may
rank even higher. The heart may be given the final word over the head — and not
just in personal matters but in those of politics and "science." So we can better
understand why postmodernists are so wary about extolling science as the last
court of appeal. It's not just a question of science itself having its own limited
"starting points" or filters, as Quine reminded us; but also, in some cultures,
the so-called hard-nosed, empirical method of science doesn't weigh in very
heavily when it comes to understanding where the world came from or how we
should live in it. For some cultures, the ancient stories can tell us more about
the universe than the Hubble Telescope can. This is not to say one filter is better
than another. Before we can take up that question, we have to first admit that we
all have our filters (scientific or mythic) and that our filters are really different.

This leads us to another key ingredient of postmodern consciousness that the
theologians of the Acceptance Model will take seriously: the differences between our cultural-religious filters are so great that, for the most part, they are
"incommensurable." That's a heavy-duty word for a heavy-duty claim. Its main
message is that because each of us looks at the world (and the Divine) through
our own cultural-religious glasses, and because, as historians and anthropologists
tell us, these glasses are so very, very different, and because it seems impossible
for anyone to come up with a prescription for a pair of glasses that everyone
would need and could wear, you can't judge one worldview in the light of an-

2. Ibid., 41.

other. You can't measure one according to the measuring system of another. Or, if we might translate what postmodernists mean by incommensurability into a Bible verse: "Do not judge so that you may not be judged" (Matt. 7:1). Here postmodernists might count Jesus on their side, for he realized that no human being can see into the heart of another human being. Only God can. Only God has the "bird's-eye" view. Therefore only God can judge. To try to take over the role of judging other cultures is to try to make oneself into God.

This is why postmodernists are so wary of universal truth-claims. The term they use for "universal truths" is "metanarratives" — that is, a narrative that is above all cultures and applies to all, a supernarrative, you might say. Well, for postmodernists, "metanarrative" is a bad word, or at least a dangerous word. Any narrative — whether it be a religious truth (e.g., God created the world), or an economic system (e.g., capitalism), or a political order (e.g., democracy), or a way of investigating the world (e.g., science) — that is claimed to be "meta," or true for everyone, is dangerous. It's dangerous because it is always the imposition of one culture's filter on another culture, and it usually leads to the exploitation of one culture by the other. Because postmodernists are aware of such dangers and because they are intent on removing them, they have also been called "deconstructionists." In official postmodern jargon: every time a postmodernist meets a metanarrative, he or she will try to deconstruct it. That means, s/he will seek to dissect it and show that the narrative that claims to be universal is really the view of one particular, finite cultural filter. So for postmodernists, narratives or truth-claims should never be universal. Rather, like flowers, they should bloom a thousandfold, each in its own cultural soil.

With this overview of postmodernity in mind (which, we should add, is only "one bird's view"), we can now begin our exploration of the Acceptance Model for a Christian theology of religions. We'll distinguish three different, but very much related, expressions of this model:

1. *Postliberal foundations.* In this section we'll review the ground-breaking and foundation-laying work of a particular theologian, George Lindbeck, who as it were launched this model and soon attracted a wide following of other theologians and ordinary Christian believers.

2. *Many religions = many salvations.* This is a further development of Lindbeck's invitation, which pushes diversity even further than many might imagine. The main pusher in this direction is S. Mark Heim.

3. *Comparative theology.* This expression of the Acceptance Model is not dependent on, but resonates with, the postliberal groundwork of Lindbeck and Heim. It calls Christians and theologians to put their philosophical and theological concerns aside and just plunge into a study and embrace of other religions.

In all of these different versions of what we are calling the Acceptance Model, we will hear frequent echoes of the postmodern perspectives that we've tried to summarize. These theological echoes turn out to be much more positive than all the negative warnings and admonitions about the unavoidability of filters and the dangers of universals. For theologians of the Acceptance Model, the emphasis is on the positive: the beauty and the value and the opportunities of diversity. Diversity doesn't dominate; it invites and exhilarates. The theologians of acceptance whom we will be meeting want to reverence differences. For them, differences are much more interesting, fruitful, and life-giving than similarities.

Postliberal Foundations

One of the first Christian theologians to hear the message of postmodernism and then relay it, clearly and boldly, to theology was George Lindbeck. The little book in which he did this in 1984, *The Nature of Doctrine: Religion and Theology in a Postliberal Age*,[3] shook the foundations of — you might even say, set a fire within — the comfortable houses of many a Christian thinker. A fairly traditional Lutheran theologian teaching at Yale University and interested especially in Christian ecumenism, Lindbeck looked on the postmodern principles that we just reviewed not only as an awakening but as a *rich* awakening for Christians. The "fire" he lit clears the ground for something new. It provides Christians with the opportunity not only to refocus and reaffirm the distinctive identity of Christianity, which had been worn away by the winds of modernity, but also to clarify and value the distinctiveness of other religions. It was an opportunity and stimulus to carry on what Lindbeck's own Christian tradition was all about — *reformation*. He called this reform movement a *postliberal theology*. Like the broader sweep of "postmodernism," it comes after the liberal theology that had held sway in most (non-Fundamentalist) Christian churches since the Enlightenment. Coming after, it hopes to correct the excesses of the liberals. How these distinctions between "liberal" and "postliberal" play out becomes clear when we review how Lindbeck seeks to reform the very notion of religion.

Religion: Words before Experience

Using postmodern awareness, Lindbeck discovered among theologians and philosophers three very different ways of understanding religion. They all have to do with the manner in which one makes the connection between language and religion. All three of these understandings can be found hiding in the different models for a theology of religion that we have reviewed so far.

1. Lindbeck first identifies the *propositional-cognitive* understanding of religion. In this view, religion is primarily a matter of knowing (therefore "cognitive") the truth about God/the Divine through clear and comprehensible statements (therefore "propositional"). The presupposition hiding behind such a perspective is that what is true can be grasped with thoughts and words. This is

---

3. George Lindbeck, *The Nature of Doctrine: Religion and Theology in a Postliberal Age* (Philadelphia: Westminster Press, 1984).

the "nice-fit" understanding of how humans come to know anything. (In philosophical jargon, it's called the "adequation theory of truth.") There's a neat, correct fit between the concept in your head and the thing that you see. Then the concept gets translated into a word — and, voilá, the truth. You might describe this viewpoint as "what you see is what you know." So authentic religion, in this perspective, is getting your words and your doctrines straight. Once you have the truth determined in the right ideas and right words, you can live it out in your life. This is why, for Christians who follow this understanding of religion, God gave us the Bible. It contains the right words. Take them literally, faithfully, and you're on the right track. It is evident that many Christians who follow the Replacement Model of religions would also endorse this propositional-cognitive model of truth.

For Lindbeck, that's a mistake, for this view is oblivious of how much filters determine what we know. It also seems to think that we can capture the infinite wonder and richness of the Divine in human language. That's the same thing as trying to identify God with an idol.

2. The second understanding of religion that Lindbeck identifies is the one that colors the attitudes of believers and the thinking of theologians in most of the mainline, or liberal, Christian churches. He calls it the *experiential-expressive* notion of religion. Those who take this approach may hold to the "nice-fit" theory of understanding when it comes to concrete, finite objects — like rocks and trees and maybe even persons. But when it's a matter of God or the Divine, then we know mainly through what we experience or feel or sense inside of ourselves. First comes the experience, then the expression. First the feeling, then the word. Or: first the internal word, then the external word. For some religious persons, this inner experience comes through the activity of the Divine itself — the Spirit touching us and communicating with us. For others, those who take a more psychological approach (like Jung), the experience may already be implanted in our subconscious, hiding in what some call the archetypes that are common to all human beings. These sleeping archetypes or implanted sensitivities can then be aroused or stirred up by symbols or words. But they're there to begin with.

It is clear that from this experiential-expressive perspective, it is an easy, maybe a necessary, step to conclude that just as the Divine is one, so is the inner experience within all the religions of the world. Languages and expressions may vary, but they all are nourished by and trying to give voice to the same religious experience. We heard versions of such claims in the Fulfillment Model — in those Christians, like Pope John Paul II or Karl Rahner, who affirm a hidden or anonymous presence of Christ within all religions, no matter what words they use. But the claim of one common experience behind all the differing religious languages is even more clearly present in representatives of the Mutuality Model, especially in voices like that of John Hick and his "one Real" or of Raimon Panikkar and his vision of one Mystery made up of all the different religious paths.

For Lindbeck, all such views go astray mainly because they forget, or are not aware of, the central role that language plays in all human experience and knowing. The filter of language does not *follow* experience; it precedes experience. That's why Lindbeck proposes the third view of religion as his own — the postliberal view.

3. He names this third perspective on religion *cultural-linguistic*. Here's a sentence that tries to state succinctly what he means: "A religion can be viewed as a kind of cultural and/or linguistic framework or medium that shapes the entirety of life and thought."[4] Trying to unpack that tight sentence, we can lay out a number of interrelated assertions:

- As strange as it may seem or feel to the way we think ideas are produced, the sequence is not: first the idea and then the articulation in words. Rather, it's the words and images that we are given by our religion that give shape to our religious thoughts and convictions. Really, words enable us to have thoughts in the first place! No one can think nakedly, as it were. Thinking is always dressed in some images and words. Without the dress, no thoughts. Without religious words, we would not have religious feelings. As Lindbeck puts it, we first have to have "external words" given to us by our religion and culture before we can have internal words in our minds and hearts.[5]

- But this means that the religious language we receive from our culture makes and shapes the very religious experience we have. Note: both *makes* and *shapes*. Without language, experience really isn't possible at all. And it is language that gives experience its particular form. In Lindbeck's more technical terms: "communicative symbol systems are a precondition ... for the possibility of experience."[6]

- Therefore, who we are, our very individual identities, is not really *individual* at all. Yes, who we are depends on the genetic inheritance that we received at our physical birth. But also — perhaps even more so — who we are is determined by the communal and religious worldview that we are born into. Our religious identity is not only, not primarily, a matter of our individual choosing and determination; our choices are given to us, specified for us, by the religious family we are part of. In Lindbeck's words: "Like a culture or language, it [religion] is a communal phenomenon that shapes the subjectivities of individuals rather than being primarily a manifestation of those subjectivities."[7]

- This postliberal understanding of religion, therefore, is saying a lot more than what we have been hearing about "filters" throughout this book. Lindbeck and friends inform us not just that we need filters or glasses in order

4. Ibid., 33.
5. Ibid., 34.
6. Ibid.
7. Ibid., 33.

to see and understand the world but that these glasses *determine* what we see. The glasses do not just identify meaning, they *give* meaning to what we see. They do not just mediate, they create. This is why Lindbeck, together with Hans Frei, his former colleague at Yale, speaks about our religious language and stories as *creating* the world we live in. The words of our religion, like the Word of God in Genesis, bring forth our religious world and make it good, comfortable, valuable — a world we can live in.

No Common Ground

Given this understanding of cultural language in general and religious language in particular, it is evident why postliberal Christians are very wary, to put it mildly, of any talk of what all the religions have in common. Really, they are suggesting that there is nothing that can be truly declared "common" to all religions. If our language creates our worlds, and if our languages are different, then our worlds will be different, with no common ground between them. Lindbeck is quite explicit about this when he briskly declares: "Unlike other perspectives, this approach [the cultural-linguistic] proposes no common framework." For those who take language and culture seriously, it's impossible, or at least very difficult, to imagine that there is "a single generic or universal experiential essence" within all the different religions. That would be like claiming that there is a generic language being spoken within all the different languages of the world. "One can ... no more be religious in general than one can speak language in general."[8]

In the following key statement, Lindbeck moves from his negative claim that there is no common experience in all the religions to the positive flip-side that each religion has a different experience. He rejects

an inner experience of God common to all human beings and all religions. There can be no experiential core because ... the experiences that religions evoke or mold are as varied as the interpretive schemes they embody. Adherents of different religions do not diversely thematize the same experience, *rather they have different experiences.* Buddhist compassion, Christian love, and ... French Revolutionary *fraternité* are not diverse modifications of a single fundamental human awareness, emotion, attitude, or sentiment, but are radically (i.e., from the root) distinct ways of experiencing and being oriented toward self, neighbor, and cosmos.[9]

And from the diversity of experiences, Lindbeck takes the next logical postmodern step and concludes to *incommensurability.* You can't really understand one religious language by trying to translate it into another religious language. In fact, that's the word Lindbeck uses to express this unbridgeable gap between religions: they're "untranslatable." If it's possible to translate German into English

---

8. Ibid., 49, 23.
9. Ibid., 40.

with some modicum of accuracy, it's not possible, according to this postliberal viewpoint, to so translate "Buddhist" into "Christian."[10] As Paul Griffiths, a compatriot of Lindbeck, observes: "Bilingualism is possible, but bireligionism is not."[11] So even if the same words come up in various religions — let's say, "love" or "God" — such words will have really different meanings because each has meaning only within the broader system of a different language. The technical term that Lindbeck uses for this claim is "intra-textuality." Religious words and religious experiences can be understood and are "true" only within the given *texts* or language systems of the particular religion. Religious words can be understood only within their own texts. The word "compassion" has its meaning only within the Buddhist texts. In Christian texts, its meaning is vastly different.

So Lindbeck reminds us that to say that all religions speak about "love" or "God" "is a banality as uninteresting as the fact that all languages are spoken."[12] The effort to translate what one religion is "really saying" into another religious language will always result in what Lindbeck calls "babbling" — even though the translators may think they are communicating. He offers another example to make his point: translating a word or concept from one religion into the language of another is like taking a mathematical formula and using it in poetry. The formula will take on a "vastly different function and meaning" in the poem than it had in its original mathematical setting. So "God" in Christian and "God" in Hindu will have vastly different functions and meanings.[13]

Lindbeck offers a further reason why religions are untranslatable from one to another, or immeasurable one by the other. Every religion, he observes, offers a "totally comprehensive framework, a universal perspective" from which the followers of that religion understand *everything* — the world, themselves, the Source of it all. Everything fits into that framework, but the framework cannot, by definition, be fit into any other framework. That's the whole purpose of religion — to give people a point of view, or a story, which, in a sense, explains everything and provides them with ultimate meaning. Well, if every religion offers a perspective that embraces everything and can't be embraced by a more ultimate perspective, then that means no religion will allow itself to be embraced — that is, explained by — another. Conclusion: no religion can be measured by another.

We have to remind ourselves that Lindbeck and other postliberal Christians are insisting on the lack of common ground, and the impossibility of one religion really understanding and judging another, not because they want to build walls between religions but because they want to preserve, honor, and protect the real differences between the faiths. Postliberal theologians might be com-

---

10. George Lindbeck, "The Gospel's Uniqueness: Election and Untranslatability," *Modern Theology* 13 (1997): 423–50.

11. Paul J. Griffiths, "The Properly Christian Response to Religious Plurality," *Anglican Theological Review* 79 (1997): 11.

12. Lindbeck, *The Nature of Doctrine*, 42.

13. Ibid., 49.

pared to security guards who stand at the door of each religion to make sure that its identity and integrity are not violated by another religion.

Dialogue: A Good Neighbor Policy

Still, do such theologians really allow the religions to talk to each other? What do theologians who endorse this Acceptance Model think of interreligious dialogue? Certainly, they are very much for it. But they also want to recognize, realistically, not only its benefits but also its limitations — and its dangers.

To describe just how Lindbeck and the Acceptance Model look at proper relations between religions, we can use the image of "a good neighbor policy." Religions are to be good neighbors to each other. But to do that, each of them needs to recognize that, indeed, "good fences make good neighbors." Each religion has its own backyard. There is no "commons" that all of them share. To be good neighbors, then, let each religion tend to its own backyard, keeping it clean and neat. In talking with one's religious neighbor — and that's what good neighbors do with each other — one is advised to do so over the back fence, without trying to step into the other's yard in order to find what they might have in common with oneself.

Postliberal theologians urge this kind of a good neighbor policy not only because, as we have seen, they know how easy it is violate a neighbor's identity by wanting his backyard to look just like ours. Also, the postliberals realize that to base a dialogue on what we think is common to all our backyards runs the risk of losing our own identity. According to William Placher, who shares Lindbeck's postliberal views, to search for "public criteria" that could apply to all religions or to affirm a "common experience" in all backyards can easily lead to "cutting and trimming the gospel to fit it to the categories and assumptions of a particular philosophical or cultural position." In other words, by trying to adapt the Christian message to what we think is a message common to all our religious neighbors, we can easily lose the distinctiveness of what Christ has to say. And "that inevitably distorts the faith." But it also may be shortchanging the other religions and the broader culture, for what our confused, suffering world may need from Christians (and from each religion) is not a voice that *fits in* but a voice that *disturbs* and offers an alternative vision. Placher exaggerates a bit to make a practical, ethical point: "In a world full of Nazis, one can be forgiven for being a Barthian." In a world full of horrible evil and evildoers, we need people, like the Christian Karl Barth, who stand up and say, absolutely, "That's wrong!"[14]

So in a neighborhood of religions, the first step in being good neighbors will not be to remove the fences and try to build a religious commons, but to try to be who we are as authentically as possible and to let our neighbors see who we are as we talk over our fences. "Christian self-description" — not a search for

---

14. Placher, *Unapologetic Theology,* 169; see also 160, 19–20.

the "anonymous Christ" or the shared mystical center or the one Real in other religions — is the first order of the day. Let our religious neighbors see who we are, whatever they think of us, however they respond to us, whatever may be the similarities they detect — this is the groundwork for being good neighbors. But to do this requires that we really live the Gospel, take it seriously, so that our neighbors can see who we are in our lives, not just in our words.[15]

This approach to other religious neighbors is, Lindbeck holds, the best possible foundation for whatever further dialogue might take place. He admits that this postliberal Acceptance Model does not warm people up for dialogue as much as does the Mutuality Model, with its advertising that all religions have a common core or seek a common end. "The lack of a common foundation is a weakness" that the Acceptance Model brings to the dialogue, "but it is also a strength." Why? Because postliberal Christians do not presume to know what is at the heart of all religions. Therefore, they don't start measuring each religion according to how much each one shows that common heart. Because they don't presume to know what makes each religion tick, they can approach all religions as "simply different and can proceed to explore their agreements and disagreements without necessarily engaging in the invidious comparisons that the assumption of a common experiential core [as in the Mutuality Model] make so tempting." If I start the conversation by first affirming that we are really different, I can more readily take those differences seriously. And so Lindbeck concludes that even though his Acceptance Model does not produce the same "enthusiasm and warm fellow-feelings" for dialogue that the Mutuality Model does, "it does not exclude the development of powerful theological rationales for sober and practically efficacious commitment to interreligious discussion and dialogue."[16]

So if dialogue between religions starts with real fence-like differences between the religions and with each religion laying out as clearly and authentically as possible what it is and what it stands for, what then are the next steps for the conversation? Followers of the Acceptance Model don't really say, because they feel they can't. Each religion will have to say what it thinks is the next step, what it thinks is the reason for talking with other religions. Then, they will have to listen to each other, and maybe a conversation can begin. But there are no predetermined rules for the conversation, no "decalogue for dialogue," no necessary items (like social justice or the environment) that have to be on the agenda for dialogue. The conversation and the relation between religious believers will just happen, if they happen.

William Placher describes dialogue as a "good-natured and liberal muddling through." We do the best we can with the materials we have and with the people in front of us. He compares religious persons in dialogue to the French *bricoleur* — a handy-man or -woman who collects all kinds of tools and materi-

---

15. Ibid., 19.
16. Lindbeck, *The Nature of Doctrine*, 55.

als and is ready to use them differently in different situations; each job is a new job and will be done according to its particular needs and situation.[17] Each dialogue will unwind according to the people involved and the concerns they bring. That's why followers of this model urge that interreligious dialogue should always be ad hoc dialogue, dialogue according "to the concerns of the day"; we talk about what in this particular moment arises or seems to all of us to be important or interesting.[18] One might say that for the Acceptance Model, dialogue is a matter of the religions "swapping stories" about what they feel is important and then seeing what happens. No rules. Just ingenuity and trust.

But in going about dialogue in this laid-back, each-according-to-her-own-viewpoint fashion, real exchange, real learning, and real cooperation can take place. Not that it always will, but it can. And when it does, it will be a genuinely pluralistic conversation, because each will feel that he is speaking out of his own identity and that all are respecting each other's identities and differences. Furthermore, in such a dialogue, I can discover that talking with someone totally different from me has led me to understand my own "identity" differently and to change things in my own backyard. As Wittgenstein himself happily admitted, language-games can overlap; trying to talk to someone who speaks a different religious language can stretch my own language. Or as one author puts it: "although we cannot get outside our own systems, what is outside our systems can nevertheless hit us hard enough to make dents in our systems."[19] In the effort to talk over our fences, we realize that while our fences and our religious systems do define us, they do not totally confine us. But how this takes place, and how deep the dent may be, we can know only in the process of conversation.

Apology for Apologetics

But there are some players on the Acceptance Model team who call for a dialogue-game between religions that is more intensive, you might even say, aggressive. So Paul Griffiths makes his apology for apologetics.[20] He agrees with Lindbeck that every religious viewpoint or claim is, by its very nature and self-definition, *comprehensive,* including or explaining everything else but not able to be included or surpassed by anything else. In addition to being comprehensive, religion for all people (if it's really taken seriously) will also be *central*— that is, the pivot of one's life, that which enables everything else to turn and move forward, the most important possession one has. Well, Griffiths concludes with evident logic, since such comprehensiveness and centrality are felt to apply not only to oneself and one's own group but to all people, then religious

---

17. Placher, *Unapologetic Theology,* 115–17, 67.

18. Ibid., 167–68; William Werpehowski, "Ad Hoc Apologetics," *Journal of Religion* 66 (1986): 282–301.

19. Rolston Holmes III, *Religious Inquiry — Participation and Detachment* (New York: Philosophical Library, 1985), 244.

20. Paul Griffiths, *An Apology for Apologetics: A Study in the Logic of Interreligious Dialogue* (Maryknoll, N.Y.: Orbis Books, 1991).

believers will enter a relationship — or dialogue — with other believers with the necessary claim that their religion surpasses all others. Speaking baldly but honestly, Griffiths points out that every religious believer, in the depths of her heart if not always on the surface of her words, holds that her religion is the best. So when such a believer meets another believer who holds something contrary to her own belief, she will have to say, politely, respectfully, but firmly and clearly, that the other believer is wrong.[21]

This, according to Griffiths, is what makes religion and religious conversations so important, profitable, and, yes, enjoyable. In religious matters, we're dealing with absolute — that is, comprehensive, unsurpassable — claims. "It is just this tendency to absoluteness that makes religious truth-claims of such interest and gives them such power; to ignore it is to eviscerate them, to do them the disservice of making them other than what they take themselves to be."[22] So every interreligious dialogue should also be interreligious apology, but "apology" in the first, dictionary sense of the word: not "an admission of error" (the second meaning) but a "defense" or "formal justification" for the truth that one claims. In other words, in dialogue, each participant seeks to show just why his religious view is more "comprehensive" than all the others. We shouldn't get Griffiths and others wrong. Religious persons engage in such apology not as some kind of a contest, for the pleasure of knocking out the other opponents. Rather, it's a matter of ethical duty, for if I believe that the comprehensive, saving religious truth granted to me is not just for me but can and should transform the lives of all, I want to share it. And that means showing it to be the powerful, wonderful truth that it is — through reasoning, arguing, and contrasting (that is, through apologetics).

Really, if all religious people would engage in such apologetics, if in the dialogue they marked their differences and made their cases why one's own position excels over the others, everyone would find themselves more resolutely and happily on the road to truth. Hegel and Marx were right: this is how the search for truth works — dialectically, through opposing ideas ("thesis" and "antithesis") bumping heads and so leading to clarity or new ideas ("synthesis"). If everyone is overly nice to each other and avoids confrontation, they will all stagnate in their politeness. Indeed, apologetic discussion, Griffiths notes, is the modus operandi in most of the sciences — different hypotheses are proposed, contrasted, argued for; people don't hesitate to say that their colleagues are wrong, always adding why they are wrong. And so science advances. This is not the case, Griffith claims, with the interreligious dialogue he has experienced in academic meetings or in many of the dialogues sponsored by the World Council of Churches or the Vatican. Here the first commandment seems to be that everyone be nice to each other and stress similarities rather than differences, common ground rather than different ground. Such conversations may be socially pleasant

---

21. Griffiths, "The Properly," 19.
22. Griffiths, *An Apology,* 3; also 14–17.

but they are not religiously productive. And so: "Such dialogue is also a practice that ought to cease; it has no discernible benefits, many negative effects, and is based upon a radical misapprehension of the nature and significance of religious commitments."[23] Therefore, Griffiths presses his "apology for apologetics" — his argument for argument.

But we must be careful not to overpaint the argumentative character of dialogue understood as apologetics. If in this dialogue religious persons press their cases resolutely, they also do so religiously; that means, with compassion, sensitivity, and, yes, politeness. Also, Griffiths admits that a Christian, for example, may come to learn something in the conversation with other religious persons that she did not know; such an insight would not contradict Christian belief, but it can add to it. Griffiths also recognizes that an apologetic dialogue does not mean that one never has to change one's mind; it is possible, in the give-and-take of conversation, that a Christian will admit where he is wrong and the other religious believer is right. This is one of the benefits of hard-nosed dialogue. And yet, though there may be some mutual learning and self-correcting in this apologetic form of dialogue, when the final bell sounds, there can be only one winner. And this is what animates the participants. Since each religion claims comprehensiveness — that is, to have the view that excludes or includes all other views — therefore: "There can be any number of claimants . . . but the prize winner stands alone. The notion of a truly comprehensive outlook defines a class of, at most, a single member. . . . Thus of all the religious and professedly nonreligious *Weltanschauungen* which aspire to embrace without being embraced, only one, if that, can be ultimately successful."[24] So let the apologies proceed, let differences thrive and clash — with the trust in the heart of each believer that his/her religious path will be the God-willed winner.

The Place of Christ

As with all the models we have examined so far, we come finally to the question of the role of Jesus. In the case of this Acceptance Model, the answer to that question is pretty clear: "Just read their lips" — that is, just listen to what Christians have always said or written about Jesus. The foundation or starting point for this model, as we have seen, is the more philosophical or anthropological claim that words come first: first the word, then the idea or feeling or experience. Or: beliefs trigger the feelings that must always go along with beliefs. To know what a religion is all about, therefore, one must look to its core beliefs — to the words that have nurtured and guided its experiences through the ages. In the case of Christianity, there is no doubt that among the central and controlling "words" or beliefs, perhaps the most persistent and consistent have been captured in the two Latin words, *solus Christus* — "only Christ." As

---

23. Paul Griffiths, "Why We Need Interreligious Polemics," *First Things* 44 (1994): 32.
24. Lindbeck, "The Gospel's Uniqueness," 430.

we have heard repeatedly throughout these pages, here we have *words* that were part of the Christian vocabulary at the very beginning and throughout the long historical journey of this religion: Jesus Christ is God's only Son, God's only Savior for all humanity.

For the advocates of this Acceptance Model, therefore, the words "only Christ" are a Christian given that they accept without question, not only because they are Christians who want to take seriously what their tradition has passed on to them but also because they are philosophers who know that if you don't take seriously the core words of a religion, you're probably concocting your own view of it. So Lindbeck, always speaking as the scholar, states indirectly but cautiously that one "can authentically speak of the ground of being, the goal of history, and true humanity" only in the "particular language" of Christianity, that is, in the "biblical story" of Jesus Christ. In other words, no salvation without Christ. The Roman Catholic theologian Joseph DiNoia is more direct: "it is a fundamental conviction of the Christian faith that wherever salvation occurs — wherever the true aim of life is attained — it is always through the grace of Jesus Christ." Griffiths, who prefers the forthrightness of apologetics, lays his Christian cards clearly on the table: "humans can learn what they are for and receive the capacity to become what they should be only by attending to Christ. These claims are nonnegotiable features of our account; their abandonment would be like the abandonment of the rules governing noun-verb agreement for a writer of Latin." So if Christians renounce or reduce the "only Christ," they would be speaking to each other in a babble in which nouns no longer fit with verbs.[25]

But as we've seen before in the Fulfillment Model, such an insistence on salvation only through Christ does not mean that Christians have to write off other religions. As Lindbeck puts it tersely, what he wants to do is "to preserve the *Christus solus*, not to deny the possibility of salvation to non-Christians." He and DiNoia recognize that even though Christ is the only channel leading to salvation or full union with God, other religions may be important and surprising tributaries feeding into that channel. They may offer "highly important truths and realities, of which Christianity as yet knows nothing and by which it could be greatly enriched." This means that these other traditions, so different from Christianity, may be "God-willed and God-approved anticipations of aspects of the coming kingdom" and may have "their own particular contributions, which may be quite distinct from the Christian one, to the preparation for the Consummation. . . . The missionary task of Christians [therefore] may at times be to encourage . . . Jews and Muslims to become better Jews and Muslims, and Buddhists to become better Buddhists." In this way, the unique contributions of other faiths to what God has revealed "only in Christ" will shine more brightly.[26]

And these other faiths will shine more brightly *on their own*. In recognizing

---

25. Lindbeck, *The Nature of Doctrine,* 61; Joseph A. DiNoia, *The Diversity of Religions: A Christian Perspective* (Washington, D.C.: The Catholic University Press of America, 1992), 166; Griffiths, "The Properly," 21.

26. See Lindbeck, *The Nature of Doctrine,* 54–56, 61; DiNoia, *Diversity,* 75–82.

that the "only Christ" does not cancel out values in other religions, followers of the Acceptance Model do not want to explain or interpret these values through Christian lenses. They resolutely shy away from any hint of the "anonymous Christian" theory which we met in the Fulfillment Model and which holds that any "ray of truth" in other religions is really part of the Sun that Christians have in Jesus. If other traditions can offer "their own particular contributions" to the salvific music that comes only from Christ, it is because of their own inner genius and merits, not because of some mysterious or hidden presence of Christ within them that makes them Christians without a name. True postmoderns that they are, advocates of this Acceptance Model don't want to impose their own grand theory on others. Metanarratives remain taboo.

But if other religions are, as it were, following their own drummers, how do they, ultimately, march into final salvation? If all salvation is "only through Christ," somehow they have to connect with him and hear his music in order to attain ultimate fulfillment in God. The theologians we have been listening to in this section agree on this. But they all admit that they can't say with certainty just how this happens. DiNoia appeals to Thomas Aquinas and the Roman Catholic tradition that recognize the possibility of God touching and saving us through our moral choices, even when such choices take place within the general framework of a "false religion"; to sincerely follow one's conscience is to respond to God's Spirit. But DiNoia offers what he feels is a cleaner and neater solution to the question of the salvation of non-Christians: the traditional Catholic doctrine of purgatory. If we don't take it literally, it makes satisfying sense: purgatory is the place where those who have died but who are not quite ready to experience the fullness of God's love can experience final preparations and cleansing. Well, we can take this belief and stretch it somewhat to express the possibility that there is a process after death, "which may be thought of as instantaneous and coterminous with death," in which other believers hear of and are connected with the grace won by Christ. Therefore, "The doctrine of purgatory permits Christian theology a wide measure of confidence about the salvation of non-Christians ... without underestimating the distinctive aims they have pursued in life."[27]

Lindbeck suggests a similar eschatological or after-death solution, though, as a good Lutheran, he does not put it in terms of purgatory. "The final die is cast beyond our space and time." We can hope that at the moment of death, "when a person loses his or her rootage in this world and passes into the inexpressible transcendence that surpasses all words, images, and thoughts," all non-Christians will receive an "explicit offer of redemption" in Christ. And since such an offer will be as clear as it is attractive, "We must trust and hope, although we cannot

---

27. DiNoia, *Diversity,* 104–7; DiNoia, "Varieties of Religious Aims: Beyond Exclusivism, Inclusivism, and Pluralism," in *Theology and Dialogue,* ed. B. D. Marshall (Notre Dame, Ind.: Notre Dame University Press, 1990) 264–69.

know, that in this dreadful yet wondrous end and climax of life no one will be lost."[28]

For Paul Griffiths, who mixes hard logic with his hard apologetics, all such theological speculations are just that — speculations. Even more: they all "have a low probability of being true." He prefers the clear language that we do have: salvation comes only through Christ, yet God loves and wishes to save all people. How to put these two core beliefs together is beyond our human comprehension. "In summary, Christians should say of religious aliens first that in so far as they do not attend to Christ they cannot become what God wishes them to be, which is to say they cannot be saved. Second: that knowledge as to the salvation of particular individuals or groups, Christian or otherwise, is in principle inaccessible to us."[29]

So here we have the foundations of the Acceptance Model (perhaps also the first and second floors). It's a theology that insists that the religions of the world are really different and that relationships between them must be built on accepting, cherishing, and, perhaps, learning from these differences. In the next chapter we will see how others are adding further floors to this structure in which there is even greater room for differences.

Further Readings

Bendle, Mervyn Frederick. "The Postmetaphysics of Religious Difference." *Pacifica* 11 (1998): 1–26.

DiNoia, Joseph A. "Christian Universalism: The Nonexclusive Particularity of Salvation in Christ." In *Either/Or: The Gospel or Neopaganism*. Ed. Carl E. Braaten and Robert W. Jenson. Grand Rapids, Mich.: Eerdmans, 1995, 37–48.

———. "The Church and Dialogue with Other Religions: A Plea for the Recognition of Differences." In *A Church for All Peoples: Missionary Issues in a World Church*. Ed. Eugene LaVerdiere. Collegeville, Minn.: Liturgical Press, 1993, 75–88.

———. "Jesus and the World Religions." *First Things* 45 (1995): 24–28.

———. "Varieties of Religious Aims: Beyond Exclusivism, Inclusivism, and Pluralism." In *Theology and Dialogue*. Ed. B. D. Marshall. Notre Dame, Ind.: Notre Dame University Press, 1990, 249–74.

Griffiths, Paul J. *An Apology for Apologetics: A Study in the Logic of Interreligious Dialogue*. Maryknoll, N.Y.: Orbis Books, 1991, chapters 1 and 5.

———. "The Properly Christian Response to Religious Plurality." *Anglican Theological Review* 79 (1997): 3–26.

———. "Why We Need Interreligious Polemics." *First Things* 44 (1994): 31–37.

Lindbeck, George. "The Gospel's Uniqueness: Election and Untranslatability." *Modern Theology* 13 (1997): 423–50.

———. *The Nature of Doctrine: Religion and Theology in a Postliberal Age*. Philadelphia: Westminster Press, 1984, 30–72.

Lints, Richard. "The Postpositivist Choice: Tracy or Lindbeck?" *Journal of the American Academy of Religion* 56 (1993): 655–77.

---

28. Lindbeck, *The Nature of Doctrine*, 58–59.
29. Griffiths, "The Properly," 23–24.

Miller, Ed L., and Stanley J. Grenz. *Fortress Introduction to Contemporary Theologies.* Chapter 13: "Theology in a Postliberal Age: George Lindbeck." Minneapolis: Fortress Press, 1998, 200–216.

Slater, Peter. "Lindbeck, Hick, and the Nature of Religious Truth." *Studies in Religion/ Sciences Religieuses* 24 (1995): 59–76.

Stell, Stephen L. "Hermeneutics in Theology and the Theology of Hermeneutics: Beyond Lindbeck and Tracy." *Journal of the American Academy of Religion* 56 (1993): 679–703.

Tracy, David. "Lindbeck's New Program for Theology: A Reflection." *The Thomist* 49 (1985): 460–72.

Wainwright, Geoffrey, et al. *George Lindbeck's "The Nature of Doctrine."* Entire issue of *Modern Theology* 4, no. 2 (1988).

Werpehowski, William. "Ad Hoc Apologetics." *Journal of Religion* 66 (1986): 282–301.

Chapter 11

Real Differences
Make for Real Dialogue

Many Religions, Many Salvations

S. Mark Heim is a theologian who, one might say, puts his words where his heart is. Nurtured within Evangelical Christianity, he is deeply committed to the Good News of Jesus; but especially because of the time he spent in South Asia, where he not only studied the teachings but also felt the powerful depths of Asian religions, his heart has warmed to the goodness and value of other paths. So in his words and theological explorations, although his personal and primary commitments are to Jesus and the Gospel, Heim seeks to give equal rights and equal respect to both Christ and all other revealers of truth. He has, as it were, sat on both sides of the teeter-totter we have been trying to balance throughout this book. For him, the most promising possibility for achieving (or coming closer) to that balance is the Acceptance Model — but "acceptance" pushed to its limits.

Different Ends, Not Just Different Means

For Mark Heim, the differences between the religions of the world are not just, as it were, skin-deep, or language-deep. They reach right into the soul of religions and, Heim stresses, into their ultimate goals and "fulfillments." If Lindbeck and company argue from language to reality — religions are really different because they have different languages — Heim, as it were, reverses the argument: religions have different languages because they are really different to begin with. In other words, religions not only say they are different; they really, deeply, and forevermore are different. What Heim is getting at is contained in a sentence calculated to stop Christians of the Mutuality Model in their mental tracks: "Nirvana and communion with God are contradictory only if we assume that one or the other must be the sole fate for all human beings."[1] As mutualist thinkers struggle to show that what a Buddhist means by enlightenment in a nonpersonal state of bliss and what a Christian means by union with a loving

---

1. S. Mark Heim, *Salvations: Truth and Difference in Religions* (Maryknoll, N.Y.: Orbis Books, 1995), 149.

God are really the same thing, Heim places a gentle hand on their shoulder and whispers: "Stop. Let it go. Buddhist enlightenment and Christian salvation are different because they are really different." They're two different end-points, two different "fulfillments," and therefore two different realities. This is why Heim used a rather strange word (and one that keeps popping up on any spell-checker) for the title of his ground-breaking book: "salvations." Christian theologians in all the different models we have been reviewing struggle with the slippery question: How can non-Christians who have never heard of the one Savior find salvation? Heim suggests that there's an answer that removes the question: just add an *s* to "salvation." All the different religions of the world are envisioning and attaining salvation*s*, not salvation. They're all moving toward different destinations, and, we can presume, they are arriving. So there is no one "sole *fate* for all human beings." Buddhists arrive at Nirvana, Christians arrive at union with God. And both are happy.

The word "fate" indicates that Heim is dead serious — that is, eschatologically serious — about what he is suggesting. He's not just saying that each religious family holds up and attains different goals in this life. By "goal" he means "final" goal. "There is also good reason to believe that this diversity [of goals] endures in eschatological fulfillments." The diversity of goals in this life will last into an eternal diversity of goals. As it was in the beginning and is now, so shall it be "world without end": the religions shall remain different. And this means that after death people will be "happy" and "fulfilled" in very different ways. Is Heim suggesting what in Christian terms might be called "different heavens"? Not really, for he believes that these different fulfillments can be "explained" and "ordered." And one religion might offer the "best approximate representation" or the closest preview of what fulfillment after death really is and how the differing realizations of it, as it were, line up. Maybe. At the moment, we don't know. So Heim advises: "It is appropriate then for each to argue for and from its own universal view, so long as the diversity and actuality of religious ends are recognized." As long as each religion grants real differences in final goals, let each propose its own perspective of how to understand those differences.[2]

But Heim also recognizes that these real differences in final goals may extend even further — into differences in the Ultimate itself, differences in God. Trying to peer into the inner nature and being of God is, admittedly, both risky and foggy. Where can one stand in order to take a look? Trying to look as a philosopher, Heim logically lays out three possibilities:

1. There is only one Ultimate, which either excludes or includes the ultimates of all the other religions. This reflects the position of what we have called the Replacement and the Fulfillment Models for a theology of religions.

---

2. Ibid., 215.

2. There is only one Ultimate, which is present equally in all the different religious aims and ends. Here we have the foundation for the Mutuality Model.

3. There is a multiplicity of Ultimates. This possibility jolts most Western philosophers and Christians. But what jolts can push open the door to new insights. This view suggests that when we're dealing with what is "ultimate" or "most basic" or "transcendent," we're better off using the *plural* rather than the singular. This last alternative would give even firmer support to the claims of the Acceptance Model.[3]

These philosophical possibilities have to be assessed within the cultural-linguistic framework of each religion. Heim doesn't want to impose any one model of the Ultimate on all the religions. But in a book he wrote after his path-finding *Salvations*, he tries to show his fellow Christians that, contrary to their expectations, Christianity has surprisingly helpful resources with which to understand the manyness of ultimate ends and even the manyness of the Divine Ultimate. Appropriately, he titles that book *The Depth of Riches*.[4]

Differences of Religions Because of Differences in God

Heim admits that to suggest that the final goal — or, heaven — might be different for different people and that there may be more than simply one Divine Being or God sure sounds to most Christians like something that is not only new but downright heretical. This is not what the catechism has told us. Heim confesses: "the perspective I am suggesting does not fit easily into traditional Christian theological frameworks. It requires fresh and imaginative thought." In *The Depth of Riches,* he shows just how freshly and imaginatively — but also carefully and clearly — he can lay out his theological thinking. The recurrent theme of what he proposes is both simple and shattering: Christians really do believe that God is not just one but also many. And the real differences among the religions are both a reflection and a perception of this divine manyness. There's plurality among the religions because there is plurality within God.[5]

It's evident that what Heim is talking about, and building on, is the Christian belief in (and experience of) God as Trinitarian. Through the revelation of Jesus the Christ and in the very experience of Jesus as divine, Christians have felt — and then tried to explain the feeling — that the Divine is not simply and neatly one reality. In some never fully clear, but nonetheless powerful, sense, the Divine is also many — many in the way God relates to the world, but many, also, in the way God relates to God's self.

---

3. Ibid., 153–55.
4. S. Mark Heim, *The Depth of Riches: A Trinitarian Theology of Religious Ends* (Grand Rapids: Eerdmans, 2001).
5. Ibid., Part 3.

To show that he is not simply playing with words or philosophical concepts, Heim goes on to spell out just why Christians have to speak of God both in the singular and in the plural. When Christians announce to themselves and the world that God is plural, they are recognizing that what Jesus taught about "human nature" is also true about "divine nature" (actually, it's true about humanity *because* it's true about God): to be is to be in relationship. One cannot simply exist; one must exist with. And that means that *every-one* needs *an-other one*. And where there are relationships, there are persons. Therefore, stated more philosophically: personhood and relationship define who we are and who God is. In Heim's words: "Being is not prior to personhood in God.... There is no more basic source of divine being than person and communion." "Communion" is another word for relationship. So Heim draws his conclusion that what is true of God is true of the world God created: to affirm that the being of God must be Trinitarian — that is, a community of differences in relationship — is to also affirm that all beings must draw their existence and life from differences that give rise to relationship. "There is no being without difference and communion." I cannot really live unless I'm in relationship; and I can't be in relationship unless there are *others*, many others.[6]

Having painted this Trinitarian picture of the manyness in God, Heim goes on to show how the manyness of religions fits neatly, even necessarily, into it. Just as there is a variety of relations within God, so there is "the possibility of a variety of distinct relations with God." We can expect, in other words, that there will be multiple, really different (just as the divine persons of the Trinity are really different) ways in which creatures will relate to, and find their fulfillment in, God. God wants to relate to creation in really different ways, just as God relates to God's self in really different ways, and we can well expect that those different ways of relating are going to take concrete, living form in the religions of the world.

Heim takes a big step from probability to necessity and suggests that a Christian can't really believe in the Trinity if she does not believe in the real, God-intended differences among the religions: "If Trinity is real, then many of the *specific* religious claims and ends must also be real. If they were all false, then Christianity could not be true." To deny the validity of other religions is to deny the validity of Christianity! Heim has traveled far from the traditional Replacement Model of many of his Evangelical brothers and sisters. In fact, he holds that one of the ingredients that makes Christianity distinct and gives a "universal quality" to its confession is its recognition that there are and must be "permanently co-existing truths" in other religious traditions. "The Trinity is a map that finds room for, indeed requires, concrete truth in other religions."[7]

Notice, again, that he said "*permanently* co-existing truths." Still working with his Trinitarian calculations, Heim continues to hold that the really different

---

6. Heim, *The Depth of Riches,* 175; see also 168–74.
7. Ibid., 167.

ways in which the various religions find salvation or fulfillment continue on
from this world into the next, from earthly experience into heavenly completion.
But from his Trinitarian perspective, he offers a Christian understanding of just
how it is possible to have differing ways of being in the one heaven. He begins
by listing three very general possibilities for what can happen to a human being
after death:

1. On the bottom end of the spectrum, as it were, is the possibility of *being
   lost*. It's the consequence of free choice. But Heim understands it more in
   the sense of annihilation than eternal suffering in hell.

2. On the opposite end, there is the Christian understanding of salvation —
   "true communion with the triune God" — a genuine personal relationship
   with the one-yet-many personal God.

3. And in-between there is what Heim terms "penultimate religious fulfillment." This category encompasses the variety of ways in which pilgrims
   on other religious paths really do arrive at happiness and fulfillment in the
   Divine, but in amazingly different ways from Christian communion with
   the Trinity.[8]

Does the word "penultimate" imply that Heim is, in the end, ranking salvations, marking one "better" than the other? In a sense, yes. Although he speaks
about "parallel perfections" in the different ways of finding fulfillment, he also
talks about a "hierarchy" of these final ends. But this is both unavoidable and
honest, for he is speaking as a Christian. And for Christians, "Communion with
the triune God is thought to encompass dimensions of other fulfillments, to be
better because more consistent with the nature of the ultimate and so more inclusive." And so, yes, "there is a 'hierarchy' between full communion with the
triune God and lesser, restricted participations." But then Heim suggests that
what is "lesser" may be more a matter of the way it *looks* to Christians than it *is*
to God: "But all the types of relation with God are grounded in God, in the co-
existing relations of God's own nature." Furthermore, a form of final happiness
in God that appears to be "lesser" to Christians may not at all be experienced
as such by those who are enjoying it. "There is loss or deficiency in this picture
only when some ends are compared with [Christian] salvation." If there are no
comparisons, if all simply bask in their own fulfillment, "there is no experienced
loss. There is no evil in such plenitude."[9]

This is something that the traditional Christian mind may have trouble getting
a hold of: the other and very different places in heaven may seem inferior to
what Christians have in their experience of God as personal and triune, but that

---

8. See Heim, *Salvations*, 165. In *The Depth of Riches*, Heim adds a fourth category, too complex
to mention here: some people may end up in the afterlife still holding to a "fixation on a created
good" and so spend their eternity in a kind of natural happiness (see 272–73).

9. Heim, *Salvations*, 165; *The Depth of Riches*, 179, 264.

is not at all the way it seems to — and is felt by — others. And, Heim concludes, this may well be the way God (as understood by Christians) wants it. It is the divine way of really taking human freedom seriously. God respects and affirms the diversity of ends that humans choose; and even though those choices may not be the fullness of what God offers, they still turn out to be "full" for the choosers. Heim offers a profound and paradoxical reflection on God's love of freedom and diversity: it is "God's will to make possible what God does not will.... And ... these choices [made by those of other religions] themselves may contain within them true elements of God's intent, including profound relations with God. When humans choose less than all God offers, it does not mean they choose nothing that God desires. This is the extraordinary mystery and wonder of the divine providence."[10] Again, Heim is calling Christians to let loose and embrace the mystery of a God who embraces diversity.

Many Salvations Make for Better Dialogue

Heim takes his case for the real diversity of religions, in this life and the next, a step further. By recognizing that the differences of religions are as indelible as the differences of skin color, we create possibilities for a far richer dialogue than the mutualist theologians could ever imagine. Proponents of the Mutuality Model urged, either subtly or directly, that all religions need to abandon their absolute claims so they can really hear each other. Heim holds that it is precisely such absolute claims that provide the substance and energy of dialogue. This is what the mutualists fail to realize or recognize. For them, according to Heim, there are really only two possibilities every time they sit down for dialogue with a person from a different religious tradition: either mutualists end up disagreeing with the other and therefore declaring him/her to be wrong; or they agree and cooperate with the other because they have discovered how the other really reflects something of the same universal Ultimate that they have known in their own tradition. From the viewpoint of his Acceptance Model, Heim offers a third possibility: other religious persons are so different that you can neither disagree nor agree with them. There may be no easy way to either push them away or welcome them to the ranks. Then — when you are facing someone who is utterly, unimaginably different from you — and only then do you also face another religious truth that is both "real and alternative"; and only then can you open yourself to the possibility of learning something new.[11]

Heim, in other words, is very committed to dialogue. He is well aware of the dangers of the Acceptance Model and of the criticisms it has received: that it leads to a relativism in which what is true in my religious castle might be false in yours, or to a solipsism in which we can never really see anything more than what is in our own castle. So even though he insists that we have to accept an

---

10. Heim, *The Depth of Riches*, 269; see also 256–69.
11. See Heim, *Salvations*, 175–76, 195.

"irreducible plurality of religions" that are incorrigibly different, he also insists that it is possible and necessary that these differing religions talk to each other and learn from each other. But how can *incorrigible* differences also be *dialogical* differences? The framework for such a dialogue of incorrigible differences lies in what Heim calls "orientational pluralism."[12] Such a perspective accepts a fact that the mutualists don't seem to notice: that not only does each religion see the world from its own cultural-linguistic orientation but it also claims, loudly if not always clearly, that its perspective is superior to any other. As we heard from Lindbeck and Griffiths in the previous chapter, to be religious is to be committed to a truth that one feels will either correct or contain any other perspective: "The conviction that one follows the most inclusive true religion, the superior true religion, with a distinctive fulfillment, is not only defensible but inescapable." So every time we meet another religion we are, willy-nilly, inclusivists: "A move 'beyond inclusivism' is impossible and the attempt counterproductive." It's impossible because "we cannot act on two different orientations at once, even if we understand both are defensible." It's counterproductive because "we can only pursue *the* truth by cultivating *our* truth."[13]

All this may sound like a warmed-over version of the Fulfillment Model. It's not — mainly because according to the perspective of orientational pluralism, Heim recognizes not only the *fact* that other religions also make claims of having the "superior" or inclusive truth; he also recognizes the *validity* of such claims. Yes, they are valid within and from another cultural-religious context. But if one accepts the validity of many different cultural orientations, one must also accept the validity of their claims to be superior. Here we dip into paradox: one holds that one's own claim is truly superior yet also accepts the validity of other similar claims. And to *accept* means to take seriously, to open oneself to the possible truth of, such claims. Now we can better grasp what Heim means when he insists that we can be challenged by another religion only when we accept that it is *really* different from our own.

And we can accept the validity of other "superior" claims because all religions, in making their assertions, also do or can recognize that while they believe that their truth is "universal" and "superior," it is also only *"partially grasped."* So even though they are convinced that what they see can include or fulfill other religious viewpoints, they also admit that they see "through a glass darkly." And, therefore, they must be open to the possibility of making that glass a little more transparent by engaging in conversation with others. In fact, for Heim, such conversation with other religious believers seems as important as dedication to one's own religion. He urges a "commitment to learn from as well as differ with those who construe the world differently.... Discussion and argument among the perspectives [i.e., dialogue] are the very lifeblood for each

---

12. Which he draws from the philosopher Nicolas Reshcher in his 1985 book, *The Strife of Systems* (Pittsburgh: University of Pittsburgh Press).

13. Heim, *Salvations,* 137–38, 222, 227.

one."[14] So the lifeblood of every religion comes not only from within but also from without.

Such an interchange will strengthen the two main muscles of dialogue — witnessing and being witnessed to. In the heart of every religious tradition, insofar as it throbs with the conviction of having the superior truth, there is the desire and need not only to tell others about this truth but to convince them that it is superior. All religions, in other words, are in some form or another missionary. They want to go forth and preach their "Good News" to all the world. This reality, Heim insists, need not lead to conflict or religious pride, as long as every missionary religion allows other religions to be missionary as well — and not only allows but accepts these missionaries when they come knocking at one's own door. Heim is clear on this — you can't be a missionary to others yourself unless you allow them to be the same to you: "Witness to others and attentive openness to their witness turn out to be intimately related. The possibility of the first is inextricably bound up with the possibility of the second." He spells out what such openness to the witness of another religion means: it requires a Christian to be "a learner before superior wisdom. This wisdom extends not only to historical knowledge of the other religious tradition and its practices, but to aspects of the divine life, to truths hidden or never expressed to Christianity."[15]

So dialogue can result not just in really new knowledge about other religions but in really new change in oneself. Does this mean that Heim admits the possibility of changing to another religion? He doesn't say so explicitly, but he does use the image of "tacking" between the many different currents flowing within one's own religion. As one grows within one's own tradition, this growth can produce some astounding new shifts or "tacks" through dialogue with other religious believers. One may end up in a place or a view of final salvation and God that would have never been possible if one hadn't taken up the conversation with others. So while each religion has "its own distinctive religious end," it can also include "the means by which people can 'tack' toward the achievement of a substantially different one." One can be "substantially different" through interreligious dialogue, even though one remains within one's own tradition. That's saying much more than what we heard in the Replacement or Fulfillment Models.[16]

Perhaps more importantly than producing "substantial changes" within religious persons, a dialogue based on the Acceptance Model can also produce genuine social and ethical changes within a suffering world. Again, Heim shows why followers of the Acceptance Model can bear greater fruits for the well-being of all creatures than can those advocates of the Mutuality Model who hold up global responsibility as the ethical-practical bridge to dialogue. The reason for

---

14. Ibid., 143, 139.
15. Heim, *The Depth of Riches,* 294–95; *Salvations,* 222.
16. Heim, *Salvations,* 226–29.

this promise of greater fruits is simple and evident: the Acceptance Model allows many more seeds of social and ecological well-being to be planted. The danger in the Mutuality Model is that its proponents are looking for that old chimera of common ground. They want all the religions to get together on some "ethical commons" where everyone starts with a given understanding of global responsibility or justice. There's the problem: a common starting point, or a common understanding of justice. Heim counters with a direct, sobering statement: "To make 'justice' the compulsory subject of dialogue... is unjust."

Why? Because, as we heard in chapter 9, to start with something like "justice" as the common ground is to start with a particular understanding of justice. "I would claim that if we are serious about an inclusive dialogue, we must recognize that 'justice' is already a significantly exclusivistic way of framing the question." But Heim has his own reasons for this warning: if our ultimate goals are really different, so will our understandings of what makes for human happiness on earth be really different. There is, therefore, no one way of understanding justice. There will always be many "justices." So Heim's general advice on how to promote fruitful dialogue also applies in the area of dialogue about ethics or human well-being: each religion holds up its vision of justice or well-being as "the best." But it also recognizes that there are other and valid "best views" in the light of which their own "best" might have to be clarified or modified. No one "justice" because no one "best"![17]

Such an understanding of dialogue as the embrace and the clash of really different "superior" viewpoints will always preserve the character of "competition" or "apologetics" — each religion, while accepting the validity of others, will seek to show that its view is, as it were, more superior. But Heim understands such final superiority not in the sense of the toughest kid on the block who can dominate over all the others but as the most responsive kid who can best show how everyone can get along: "The primary interreligious challenge is to acknowledge authentic human options that are truly distinct and yet seek the most integrated understanding possible of their relations, an understanding that should itself be a frankly particularistic one." Heim is as interested in the future *integration* of religions as he is in their incorrigible *distinctions*. But, he feels, the vision of future integration, if found, will come from one particular viewpoint. On this, the religions can compete: the "inevitable, but possibly fruitful form of 'competition' among the faiths" will consist in "seeing which can most adequately take account of the distinctive testimony of others.... The faith that proves able to do this for the widest possible range of compelling elements from other traditions will not only be enriched itself, but will offer strong warrants for its own truth." If there is to be any final prize in such competition, it will go to the religion that can best call the other religions together.[18]

---

17. Heim, *Salvations,* 195–98, 205–8.
18. Heim, *Salvations,* 209, 176; *The Depth of Riches,* 128.

The Place of Christ

As expected, Heim feels that such a prize will probably go to those religious people who see the world from the particular "orientation" of Jesus Christ. Even though Heim makes use of the Christian belief in the Trinity as the bedrock and blueprint for his theology of religions, he also confesses that his picture of God as triune is "unavoidably Christocentric." So if the Trinity is the foundation, it is Jesus Christ who enables Christians to lay that foundation and then build on it. Heim clarifies that he is Christ-centered for two controlling reasons: first, it is only through Christ that Christians have come to experience and understand God as triune — that is, as inherently and profoundly relational both within God's self and with all creatures; but, second, Christ makes clear (or should make clear) to his followers that precisely because God is so personal and relational, God thrives on *particularity and diversity* in the way God relates. Since God's creatures are so different, God's relationships with them — God's revelations to them — will be really different.[19]

Such a Christocentrism is quite different from the Christ-centeredness we encountered in the Replacement and Fulfillment Models, for it enables Heim to truly affirm both the uniqueness of Jesus and the uniqueness of other religious figures. More practically, it enables Christians to balance that wobbly seesaw between a *full commitment* to Jesus and a *full openness* to other religions. This is because for Heim, Jesus Christ affirms the necessity and validity of particularity: God saves — that is, God touches and transforms lives — not in general, but always in particular. So when Christians lift up Jesus as the universal Savior, they are also affirming the integrity and validity of Buddhist claims that Buddha is a universal Savior. That seems to be what Heim means when he says: "The decisive and universal significance of Christ is for Christians *both* the necessary ground for particularistic witness *and* the basis for recognizing in other religious traditions their own particularistic integrity." So when Christians resolve to follow Christ with their whole mind and heart, they must also keep that same mind and heart open to what God may be up to in Buddha or Muhammad or Krishna. Christ tells them that God loves particularities, lots of them.[20]

From this understanding of Christ as the revealer of diversity, Heim draws a christological conclusion that echoes what we heard in the Mutuality Model: "The Trinity teaches us that Jesus Christ cannot be an exhaustive or exclusive source for knowledge of God nor the exhaustive and exclusive act of God to save us." Neither exhaustive nor exclusive revealer or Savior! Here Heim steps beyond Lindbeck and other colleagues in the Acceptance Model who, as we saw, stress that all salvation is "only through Christ." So when Heim affirms the value of diversity he does so not just as a philosopher who recognizes the fact of many different cultural-linguistic systems; he also does so as a Christian who, because of his belief in the Trinity, believes that God makes use of those other systems

---

19. Heim, *The Depth of Riches,* 134.
20. Heim, *Salvations,* 226.

to reveal and save. Further, Heim is wary of any backdoor attempt to paint these other systems and religions as "anonymous Christians" by claiming that it is really Christ who is saving through them or that they are all inherently pointing to their final destination in Christ. The "ordinary function" of each religion, he reminds us, "is to attain its own religious end, not the Christian one." In the terminology we have encountered in other models, Heim clearly affirms Jesus as the *constitutive cause* of salvation for Christians, but he seems to leave open the possibility of other, very different, mediators or causes for the very different kinds of salvation found in other faiths.[21]

But for Heim and all Christians, Jesus is the clearest and most effective expression of who God is (personal and triune) and what God intends for all creatures (personal communion with and within the Trinity). This, then, will be the claim that Christians make as they converse with other believers — and it will be their hope for what they think will be, or can be, the outcome of the dialogue. Here Heim is cautious but clear: "The fact that this unity [of God's plan] has been manifested to us in Christ...means that Christians will look for such a convergence" — a convergence of all religions in Christ and in communion with the triune God. But Heim immediately adds: "But this in no way requires it." Such full convergence or conversion may not take place either in this life or in the next.[22]

As we saw in Heim's sketch of the afterlife, he recognizes the possibility, if not probability, of many mansions in the heavenly kingdom — many really different ways of finding eternal fulfillment and happiness. To try to specify the place of the Christian mansion, he switches images and speaks of many mountains stretched across the heavenly terrain. Heim is clear that the Christian mountain will not be higher than any of the others, for each will be high enough for those who dwell on it to be fully satisfied on it. But from the lookout on the Christian mountain, one will be able to see and understand just how the diverse peaks of this heavenly skyline give expression to the diversity of divine life and to the diversity of God's relations with God's creatures. So though the other mountains will not be lower than the Christian mountain, "all summits are linked by such ridges to the Christian mountain" insofar as they all reflect and constitute the diversity of the Divine, fully manifested in Christ. Such are Heim's efforts to image, always inadequately, the uniqueness of Christ within the enduring uniqueness of others.[23]

Comparative Theology

Given what we have heard from George Lindbeck and S. Mark Heim, it's clear that the motto of the Acceptance Model might well be, "Vive la difference!" — let differences thrive! If that be so, we should expect to find diversity within the

---

21. Heim, *The Depth of Riches*, 134, 269.
22. Ibid., 269.
23. Ibid., 277–90.

model itself. And we do. In what is called "comparative theology," we hear the same central concern to cherish the distinctiveness of all religions without tarnishing the distinctiveness of Christ and Christianity, but this concern is focused and fostered in an entirely different way than what we have seen in theologians like Lindbeck and Heim.

A Moratorium on Theologies of Religion!

Calls for a comparative theology are coming especially from Roman Catholic theologians who are not just theologians steeped in the study of Christian tradition but also comparativists who have walked many miles exploring the teachings and meeting the believers of other traditions. Primary examples are Francis X. Clooney, S.J., who as part of his long Jesuit training spent years in India and Nepal sampling the fruits of Hinduism and who is recognized today both as a prominent Indologist and as an innovative Christian theologian; or James Fredericks, who after his training to become a priest spent years in Japan training himself in becoming an expert in the teachings and practice of Buddhism. Evidently, it is their two tracked training and experience that stirred questions in them about what it would be like to arrange the tracks differently. What would happen if Christians, in their efforts to develop a theology of religions, would start not with what Christian Scriptures and tradition have to say but with what is heard in the sacred books and teachings of other religions? In other words, might the foundations for a theology of religions be found in *dialogue* rather than *theology*? In talking before assessing? Their own experience urged affirmative answers to such questions.

So comparative theologians like Clooney and Fredericks want to throw the whole process of all the models we have explored into reverse. They want to start where all the other theologians were hoping to finish. The theological architects of all the models we have explored so far (including Lindbeck's and Heim's versions of the Acceptance Model) have started with Christian tradition — the Bible and the teachings of the churches — and from that tradition they have constructed a theology intended to serve as the basis for an authentic encounter, a dialogue, with persons of other traditions. Comparativists want to work backwards. Any Christian theology of religions that they might propose will be the fruit of dialogue with other religions, not a prelude to it. This is the meaning of the name they give themselves: a *Christian* theology of religions must be a *comparative* theology of religions.

The incentives for such bold suggestions are varied. The first might be summarized in the pragmatic admonition: "If something isn't working, stop doing it!" That's the conclusion one might reach after reviewing the current models for a Christian theology (or after reading a book like this one): none of them seems to get to where it wants to go. Or they spend too much time advertising and arguing that their model is the best. So the proponents of a comparative theology urge that "it's time for something entirely different": let's see what happens when Christians forget about (or temporarily put on the shelf) what they think their tradition and theology tell them about other religions and simply go and see what the other religions say about themselves. How often have our presuppositions about strangers — or what others have told us about them — been totally turned upside-down when we actually got to know those strangers? Or worse, how often have we had to admit that it was precisely our presuppositions that were getting in the way of really entering into a relationship with someone we had never met before?

For Clooney and Fredericks, present-day theologians working out their grand theories and theologies of religions might well be compared to arm-chair anthropologists who propose sweeping schemes of how other cultures function without ever having visited them. The data — the construction material — for a theology of religions must come not only, and not initially, from theology but from the religions. It's as simple, but also as revolutionary, as that. Theology is something like the microscope with which Christians examine and try to understand other religions. But it's the actual study of and dialogue with other religions that will gather the material to put under the microscope. Without leaving our comfortable theological armchairs and actually visiting the strange lands and bewildering beliefs of the other religions themselves, our theories and theologies will be spun out of air — or out of our own theological cloth. Or worse, if we start with our own tradition, rather than with the religions themselves, in trying to work out a theology of religions, our own tradition can well become a blinder to really seeing what the other tradition is doing and saying. We protect ourselves, as it were, from having to face the real differences, and the unsettling challenges, that might come from the religious other. We domesticate the other before he/she can open their mouth. This is Fredericks's bottom-line assessment of the models we have studied in the previous chapters: "all three options for a theology of religions [what we have called the Replacement, Fulfillment, and Mutuality Models] inoculate Christians against the power and novelty of other religious traditions."[24]

So advocates of a comparative theology of religions draw their conclusions: because Christians do not yet have enough data, as it were, to put under their theological microscopes and because theology without data can easily become a blinder or an inoculation to what other religious traditions are proposing, let's call a temporary moratorium on all our theologizing about other faiths so that we can allow ourselves to actually talk with and learn from them. The facts seem to be that "a fully systematized theology of non-Christian religions is not possible today." The different models for a Christian theology of religions seem to be stuck; so let's leave them on the side of the road and look for help elsewhere — in the actual study of other faiths. That may be difficult: "Although abandoning

---

24. James L. Fredericks, *Faith among Faiths: Christian Theology and Non-Christian Religions* (New York: Paulist Press, 1999), 167; see also Francis X. Clooney, *Theology after Vedanta: An Experiment in Comparative Theology* (Albany: State University of New York Press, 1993), 193–94.

attempts to erect a systematic theology of religions may be difficult for Christian theologians to accept, honesty to our current situation requires this of us."[25]

Perhaps the word "abandoning" is a little too strong. The comparativists are not asking their fellow Christians to abandon one thing (theology) for another (dialogue). Rather, they want theology to flow from dialogue, not precede it. Or, as Michael Barnes, S.J., phrases it: they want "a theology *of* dialogue," not a "theology *for* dialogue."[26] A comparative theology starts with comparison, but it definitely leads to theologizing.

Understanding Oneself through Comparing with Others

But it would be misleading to present the project and proposals of comparative theology as solely a way of better elaborating a theology of religions. Its proponents also envision it as a way of doing a better job at the overall task of theology — a more effective way of interpreting the entirety of Christian tradition. This, in fact, is the point of Fredericks's working definition of comparative theology: it is "the attempt to understand the meaning of Christian faith by exploring it in the light of the teachings of other religious traditions." Even more clearly: the "real goal of the exercise [of comparative theology] is to gain a better understanding of the meaning of Christianity." Notice: the better understanding of *self* comes through a better understanding of *others.*

With such proposals, comparative theologians are once again flipping over the goals and process of all the models for a Christian theology of religions that we have reviewed, but now in a more drastic, fundamental way. Theologians working within the other models (again, including people like Lindbeck and Heim) have recognized that our new experience of religious pluralism is challenging all Christians to fashion new ways of understanding these other paths. Comparative theologians turn that around: the reality of so many other religions and our new awareness of them are calling and challenging Christians to fashion new ways of understanding Christianity. In fact, the comparativists add, Christian theologians would have greater success (and enjoyment) with their job of theology if they started their work by trying to understand their own tradition in the light of others, rather than the usual procedure of understanding others on the basis of Christian teachings. To reverse the image we used above, for comparative theologians, therefore, the other religions are not just new "data" to be placed under the Christian microscope; they are also materials with which we can build new microscopes. The other religions can become the microscopes with which Christians look at the "data" of Christianity.[27]

This means that comparative theology is not just an "added room" built on

---

25. James L. Fredericks, "A Universal Religious Experience? Comparative Theology as an Alternative to a Theology of Religions," *Horizons* 22 (1995): 83–84.

26. Michael Barnes, "Theology of Religions in a Postmodern World," *The Month* 28 (1994): 270–74, 325–30.

27. Fredericks, *Faith among Faiths*, 139, 169.

to the big house of Christian theology. The comparativists are not suggesting that besides the traditional rooms of biblical, historical, systematic, and ethical theology, we now have this add-on of comparative theology. Rather, "comparison" or "dialogue" with other religious viewpoints is to become a way of living in all the rooms. In a way, the other religious traditions become our roommates as we explore the different levels of the Christian house. We're constantly talking to them as we try to talk to ourselves and to the texts and witnesses of our own tradition. Comparative theology, therefore, takes with demanding seriousness the insights and claims we heard in the first chapter about conversation with others being a necessary stepping stone to truth. To answer the questions Who am I? and Who is my God? we have to ask Who are you? and Who/What is your God? That's precisely what comparative theologians are trying to do. For Clooney, theology *is* a conversation between the texts of his religion and the texts of yours — in his case, the texts of Hinduism.[28]

Both Clooney and Fredericks give startling witness to what can happen to Christian theologians when they take up this comparative or conversational way of doing theology. Clooney confesses that "I have 'learned' to be unable to read anything as I had read it before I encountered the texts of India." He's suggesting that the Bible has, as it were, become a new book after he began reading it alongside the books of Hinduism. Hindu texts have become the glasses with which he discovered treasures and "new meanings" in the biblical texts that he never could "see" before. For him, his understanding of Christianity was not only "extended" through his conversation with Hinduism; it was even "transformed." Fredericks concurs when he admits how much this conversation and comparison with others have sparked changes in *himself* (whatever the changes that might take place in his Buddhist or Hindu conversation partners). Comparative theology seeks first to bring about change in the Christian *before* it thinks about changes in others. And Fredericks declares that these changes can be vivifying: "by using the insights of non-Christian religions as a resource," he has been enabled to embrace his "own cherished beliefs in new ways ... at a deeper level."[29]

Clearly, Clooney, Fredericks, and others are, at this time, proposing and dreaming more than they are describing. If Christian theology is supposed to be comparative theology, then we have to admit that such a theology is only in its infancy. The process has just begun. For this infant to grow up, much will have to change in the structures and methods of theological education in schools, universities, and seminaries. Theologians will have to study at least one other religious tradition as they go about their efforts to learn the Christian tradition. "Other religions" will have to become standard and "required" parts of religious curricula, and not just some "electives" that you might tack on at the

28. Clooney, *Theology after Vedanta*, 201–7.

29. Francis X. Clooney, "Reading the World in Christ," in *Christian Uniqueness Reconsidered: The Myth of a Pluralistic Theology of Religions*, ed. Gavin D'Costa (Maryknoll, N.Y.: Orbis Books, 1990), 66, 70, 72; Fredericks, *Faith among Faiths*, 162, 178.

end of religious or theological education. Admittedly, we're a long way from such a state of affairs. But the dream is taking shape. More importantly, there's a growing number of dreamers among Christians and Christian theologians who have, as it were, been bitten by the bug of comparative theology. They're feeling in their spiritual veins and in their theological minds what an exciting and enriching difference it can make when one "talks" to one's own tradition as one "talks" with another.

How to Do It?

Although the book on "the method of comparative theology" is still being written, theologians like Clooney and Fredericks provide us with enough "notes" to form a general picture of just how they go about such a theology through comparison. First of all, they recommend modesty, or little steps. Rather than fashioning grand, sweeping comparisons between, for example, Hinduism and Christianity as they have developed through the ages, or between broad, abstract themes such as the Ultimate, or human nature, or the purpose of history, comparative theologians prefer to take small steps. They generally try to limit themselves to comparing specific texts, concrete rituals, focused beliefs, particular theologians, limited contexts, or historical periods. They search or sniff out limited areas within the Christian and Hindu teachings that seem to stand out in their apparent similarities or in their enticing contrasts — and then they dig deeply into these particular areas. By limiting the range of their vision, they will increase the depth of their comprehension. By exploring concrete issues of creed, code, or ceremony, they may more readily find themselves touching broader insights into the *Geist* or élan of the two traditions. By limiting the topic of the conversation with the religious other, they are more likely to feel the impact of that conversation on their own spirituality.

But as they explore the terrain of other religions for possible particulars that can be compared with Christianity, comparative theologians also remind themselves that there may be some — or many — areas of another tradition that are so different, or so difficult to bring into focus, that they do not, at least for the moment, admit of any comparisons. Comparative theologians have to be not only modest; they also have to be humble.[30]

And yet where comparative exploring is possible, it is done with dead seriousness and full personal involvement. Much is at stake. Clooney and Fredericks insist that comparative theology is not a form of religious studies. It's theology. And that means that the goal of the undertaking is not just *meaning;* it is also, and primarily, *truth.* Comparative theologians seek not only to clearly and accurately understand what a particular belief means for Muslims or Buddhists; they want to also ask whether this belief is true — that is, whether its meaning is not just interesting but valid, whether it makes claims not just for the Muslim

---

30. Fredericks, "A Universal Religious Experience?" 86.

but also for the Christian. What the comparative theologian learns about another religion will be something not only that s/he can write books about; it may also be something that the theologian has to live and integrate into his/her own life. This means that what is true of all theology (and what makes for the difference between theology and religious studies) is also true of comparative theology: faith is at stake — one's own and that of one's community.

Clooney describes the experience of a comparative theologian (really, we should say "comparative Christian") as an extended and laborious, but also engaging and exciting, process of passing over personally into the world of another religion, exploring that world, letting its symbols and stories seep into one's imagination, and then passing back to one's own religion to see what might happen. It's not an undertaking whose steps one can plan or whose fruits one can know in advance. It will take time; it will also take sweat and patient confidence. One must allow the fruits to mature. As they do mature, Christians begin to feel that the time spent in the world of the other text or the other story has enabled them to return to their own world and see it differently. The Christian returns home with new questions, new awareness, new sensitivities, new insights and so can draw new riches out of old treasures.[31]

But we are also warned not to think that this process of comparative theology will always work smoothly or as naturally as the ripening of an apple on a branch. The branch, perhaps the whole tree, will often shake through the process. There is an unavoidable tension, Clooney and Fredericks tell us, when one returns to one's own Christian house having visited and even felt at home in the Hindu or Buddhist house. This tension is felt in the tug of truths — the exciting truth one has discovered in another religion and the tested truth one has always felt in one's own. How to put these truths together? Are their differences contradictory or complementary? If complementary, how can they be reconciled? How much adjustment or change is required in one's old ways of believing or acting? Again, because we are dealing with theology and not just religious studies, the differences that the comparativist notes are a matter not just of understanding but of commitment. One's life is being touched and possibly transformed.

So for Fredericks, there's generally a bit of a crisis in the process of comparative theology, a crisis between being really open to others and ready to change, on the one hand, and a deep, abiding resting in one's own religious family, on the other. One can feel that one has been "intruded upon" — happily perhaps, but nonetheless uncomfortably. In his words: "The comparative theologian is a believer in a crisis of understanding fomented by the intrusive presence of the Other. This means that the comparative theologian operates within a tension defined by 1) vulnerability to the transformative power of the Other and 2) loyalty to the Christian tradition." Vulnerability and loyalty — there's the life-giving, fruit-bearing tension in comparative theology, both happy and dis-

---

31. Clooney, *Theology after Vedanta*, 4–10, 33–35, 153.

comforting. But for comparative Christians, it's a tension that one has to, or wants to, embrace. For to be *loyal* to Christ, one must be *vulnerable* to others.[32]

One would have to read and feel the descriptions of the fruits that such comparative explorations and tensions are bearing in order to come to a clearer picture of how the process works and how promising are its results. Examples already abound, and they are growing as the ranks and writings of comparative theologians increase. Clooney was one of the earliest with his *Theology after Vedanta*, which both talked and walked his readers through a description and then an example of what comparative theology is. In this book, Clooney first leads his readers step by careful step through a reading of a Hindu text (Advaita Vedanta) and enables them to see and feel the truth that emerges from that text. He then leads his readers back into the world of a particular Christian text — from Thomas Aquinas's *Summa Theologica* — and reveals how with the flashlight of Vedanta, one finds new questions, new insights, yes, new truths in this classic Christian thinker.

In his *Faith among Faiths*, Fredericks follows this same process (in more abbreviated form) as he compares stories of Krishna and the milkmaids with Jesus' parable of the Prodigal Son, or explores the relationship of life and death first from the perspective of particular Zen Buddhist texts and then New Testament passages on the resurrection. In both cases, he reveals how by first allowing our minds and imaginations to be stirred and sharpened by stories outside our religion, we return to our own stories and images with new eyes and ears.[33]

Similar efforts by other theologians to find "new eyes and ears" by first viewing and listening to the world of other religions are growing in North America and Europe but especially in Asia. The team of Christian comparative theologians may still be relatively small, but their voices are being heard.[34]

But one may ask: Is comparative theology really interreligious dialogue? From the explanations and examples we've heard so far, it might appear that all the dialoguing is taking place on only one side. It's only the Christian partners who are listening, who are applying what they heard to their own tradition, who are ready to let the vision of other religious worlds work changes in their own. A bit lopsided, so it seems. Comparativists would admit this. But because they are operating within the general precincts of what we are calling the Acceptance Model, this, they would say, is all they can, or care to, do: they want to *accept* the other religious traditions or persons as they are, without in any way telling them what they have to do. Followers of the Acceptance Model are adamant in their resolve not to fall into the let-me-tell-you-what-you-need approach of the Mutuality Model when mutualist theologians inform all religions that they have to give up their absolute claims if they want to really engage in the game

---

32. Fredericks, "A Universal Religious Experience?" 87; see also his *Faith among Faiths*, 169ff.; Clooney, *Theology after Vedanta*, 5.

33. Fredericks, *Faith among Faiths*, chapter 7.

34. Among Asian theologians, notable are Sebastian Painadath, Aloysius Pieris, Francis Veneeth, Joseph Pathrapankal. Western voices: Leo Lefebure, John Keenan, David Burrell, John Berthrong.

of dialogue. Comparative theologians are Christians talking to Christians, urging their brothers and sisters to take up this new way of understanding their faith. Whether other religious traditions will follow the same recommendations will be determined by these other religions. Still, although comparativists don't want to impose this kind of approach on others, they do want to encourage it — mainly by the power of example. If this method of comparative theology continues to bear rich and evident fruits in renewing and re-energizing Christians, it is only natural that what is good within one religion will be seen as good by others. And to have many religions practicing comparative theology within their own communities is to have many religions practicing dialogue between their communities.

The Importance of Friendship

Fredericks offers a further observation that shows how comparative theology naturally leads to dialogical theology. From his own experience he describes how the process of doing comparative theology leads the Christian not just to a deeper familiarity with the texts of other religions; it leads to deeper friendships with persons of other religions. The comparativists want people to avoid working only with books. It's impossible, they say, to enter into a deep comparison with another tradition without getting to know and appreciate and perhaps love some of the followers of that tradition. Here Fredericks makes a telling distinction that pushes us beyond the limitations of the English language: the love that a comparativist feels for persons of the religions she is talking with and exploring is not that of *agape* but that of *philia*. *Agape* would be the kind of concern and love that, as humans and especially as followers of Jesus, we are to give to all persons, including our enemies. *Philia*, on the other hand, is a preferential love, a love that springs up and fills us because of the particular qualities we have experienced in the other person. It's a love "that treasures the non-Christians not because of Jesus' command to love, but because of the innate goodness and virtue of the friend."[35]

And because of the friendship and love that sprout from the soil of comparative theology, Christians will find themselves embracing their other religious friends not just to learn from them but also to share with and enrich them. As much as these friends want to hear of possible comparisons that *they* might make between their tradition and Christianity, as much as they might want to learn from Jesus and his Gospel, the Christian friends will be there to help with this learning and exchange. Friends do that. But friends are also able to disagree — and to enable their friendships to even be nurtured by such disagreements. In fact, it is only on the basis of friendship that people from different backgrounds cannot only learn from their differences but also live with differences that cannot be learned from. "To be able to differ honestly with another

---

35. Fredericks, *Faith among Faiths,* 173–77.

human being on matters of ultimate importance must be counted an achievement. Friendship makes that achievement all the more impressive. In order to
do theology comparatively, Christians will do well to develop deep and abiding
friendships with their non-Christian neighbors as a useful way to disagree with
honesty and depth." Friends who learn from each other can also disagree with
each other.[36]

The Role of Jesus?

So far we have not said much about the place Jesus occupies in comparative theology. Where do the comparativists stand on the questions that have teased and
taunted us throughout this book? How can Christians understand the traditional
claims that Jesus is the only Son of God and the only Savior in a way that will
enable rather than shut down an honest relationship with persons of other faiths?
We have heard that comparativist Christians recognize and embrace a tension
between their commitment to Jesus and their vulnerability to others. The one
requires the other. But when we dig more deeply into how this tension works
and how far both ingredients might be stretched, we see that the commitment to
Jesus not only is prior to vulnerability but also seems to set the limits of vulnerability. That "seems" is slippery, since comparative theologians themselves
admit that precision on this issue of commitment to Christ and vulnerability to
others not only is difficult but may also be dangerous.

Throughout his writings, Fredericks takes for granted that Christian convictions and claims about Jesus as the unique, real, and historical incarnation of
God in human history are part of the *identity* that Christians bring to the task
of comparative theology and dialogue with others. In fact, he persistently warns
mutualist theologians that by viewing Jesus as one among many saviors or incarnations they so dilute and deform Christian identity that it becomes difficult to
see how they are really carrying out a *Christian* dialogue with other traditions.
And that's not just his opinion, he points out, but the verdict of many Buddhists
and Muslims who have told him that they want to talk with Christians who
speak out of their tradition rather than with those who seek to remove whatever
might be offensive to the dialogue partners. Fredericks is explicit in his admonitions that when theologians like John Hick urge a fundamentally mythological
or symbolic reinterpretation of Jesus' divinity that places Jesus alongside other
symbols or incarnations, they end up with a religion that not only Christians but
Buddhists and Hindus might not be able to recognize as Christian. For Fredericks, therefore, to be committed to Jesus as God's unique Son does not reduce
Christians' vulnerability to other religions or their readiness to be shaken up and
transformed by other texts and symbols.[37]

Clooney tries to sort out why that is so. First of all, he candidly admits that

---

36. Ibid.
37. Ibid., 120–27.

the approach of comparative theology, when lined up with all the models we have explored in this book, bears the greatest resemblance to the "inclusivist" or to what we have called the Fulfillment Model. Why? Because comparative theologians, like fulfillment theologians, "affirm the salvific presence of God in non-Christian religions while still maintaining that Christ is the definitive and authoritative revelation of God."[38] Comparativists, Clooney explains, just like fulfillment theologians, live with the tension and the perplexing and apparently incoherent "double claim" that "God wills to save all people" but "God saves only through Jesus." But Clooney adds that what seems "perplexing" and "incoherent" is for comparative theologians full of "vitality" and even enjoyment. Translated into our familiar image, comparative theologians don't try to balance the teeter-totter of God's universal love and the particularity of Jesus and Christianity; they actually enjoy going up and down on it and draw life from doing so. Why this is so is stated concisely but densely in the following sentence: "The inclusivist [read fulfillment theologian] insists on both salvation in Christ alone and the true universality of salvation, just as the comparative theologian insists on reading back and forth [read up and down on the teeter-totter] from Text to context."[39] We have to unpack that statement to taste its richness.

By "Text," Clooney means the Christian Scriptures and tradition; by "context," he points to the world of many other religious texts and traditions within which, according to comparative theology, the Christian Text must be understood. What he is pointing out here is that just as the fulfillment theologians start with the *doctrinal claim* that Jesus is God's full and final truth, so comparative theologians start with the *practical step* of studying and embracing other texts (what he calls the "context") from the vantage point of their own Text. This means that comparative theologians start with Jesus as their one savior and criterion for all truth not because they have to — not because the pope or the Bible requires this of them — but because this is how any comparative theology works. You're always looking at the other through the lens of your own cultural, religious telescope. You can't help it. Even though what you see in the Other may challenge what you have traditionally believed, you're always going to be seeing and judging the other from the starting point of your own Text or telescope.[40]

Here we can see just how deeply this method of comparative theology is embedded in the foundations of what we are calling in this chapter the Acceptance Model. Clooney and Fredericks resonate with this model's understanding of religion as the "cultural-linguistic" voice which not only expresses but first of all determines our religious experience and worldview. Everyone, as we heard, is religious within and as part of a particular culture and religion. You can't separate "being religious" from "being in a particular religion." You can't look at another religion without looking at it through your own religious glasses; you

---

38. Clooney, "Reading the World in Christ," 73. He is quoting Gavin D'Costa.
39. Ibid., 73.
40. Ibid., 66, 64.

can't take off your own glasses in order to see the other religion "as it is." If you think you can, you're deceiving yourself. Even if what you see in another religion is more than what you saw in your own, it will always be understood through, and integrated into, your own.

This is why Clooney insists that even though the truth or the Divine that the Christian experiences through Christ and the Bible goes beyond Christ and the Bible, it is "nevertheless . . . constitutively shaped by the Bible" and Christ. This is also why he holds that for the Christian there is no "outside" of the biblical view of reality, just as for the Hindu there is no "outside" of the Vedic view of the world. Whatever we meet and try to understand outside of Christ and the Christian texts will always be grasped and evaluated from the inside. This means, further, that even though the Christian comparative theologian will have much to learn from what s/he finds, for example, in Hinduism, still, because of "the world-constructing role of the Bible," it is "quite clear that she or he is not going to adopt a Hindu viewpoint — is not in the final analysis going to see the world as framed by a Hindu text, is not going to make a [Hindu] text . . . central and the Bible peripheral." The Christian won't do this not because "it's not allowed," but because it's impossible — because this is how deeply we are shaped and held and, yes, limited by our own religious culture and language.[41]

But comparative theologians also insist — much more clearly than we heard from Lindbeck — that while our own cultural-religious position always limits us, it does not confine us. There is much to learn from comparing our position with that of others. But then what happens when the Christian conviction that all salvation comes through Christ clashes head-on with similar convictions in another religion? Clooney faces this problem squarely in his own comparing of Christian and Hindu texts. On the Christian side: all salvation comes through the passion, death, and resurrection of Jesus. On the Hindu side: "Knowledge of Brahman is all that is required for salvation." So which is true: salvation through Christ or through knowledge of Brahman? Clooney warns against any quick, facile answer to that question. Why? Because the *truth* contained in both of these assertions cannot, as it were, be lifted out of the text or the language and cultural-religious context in which it is delivered. "Theological truths occur only through their textual forms, and there is no other path of access to them." Shifting images, this means that truth is not delivered naked. It is always dressed in its linguistic attire. Trying to lift the truth of the Christian claim out of its Christian language and then compare or judge it against the truth of the Hindu claim also stripped of its cultural context is like trying to compare two ghosts that you really don't understand because you can't see them.

The truth of what the Christian is saying and the truth of what the Hindu is saying can only be understood and then assessed within their own cultures and systems. And once a theologian realizes that this is the case, once he or she truly feels how inextricably truth is embedded in texts, then, Clooney confesses

---

41. Clooney, "Reading the World in Christ," 74–75.

from his own experience, the differences between the two claims — about Christ and Brahman — which are "seemingly so opposite" will be "diminished, though not eliminated." Though there is still tension, it now appears to the theologian that it is "unlikely [that there is] any direct contradiction between texts about the Passion and theological texts about knowledge of Brahman." As to just how the two claims can be reconciled — that is, whether one is, as it were, "truer" than the other and thus inclusive of the other — Clooney urges Christian theologians to hold off on such questions. Rather, he advocates "the patient deferral of issues of truth." Because we have not sufficiently appreciated and understood how deeply and intricately the truth of the Christian claim about Jesus and the Hindu claim about Brahman are imbedded and bound to their own texts and language, we have to admit that the data for weighing them against each other is "inconclusive."

To those who might judge such a position as fudging the truth or avoiding the clash of truths, Clooney responds that, on the contrary, such a patient deferral that allows for further study and conversation may point to the only path that will lead to truth. He suggests that the longer, more difficult path of further study and further comparing "may also be viewed as a hard-headed acknowledgment of the embodied, textured nature of the claims [i.e., Christian and Hindu], and as a contribution to the necessary foundation for whatever progress one is going to make in evaluating theological truths in a comparative context." Any evaluating of truth-claims will come, if it will come at all, only after a long, patient effort at understanding those claims in their own language and context. And that's precisely what comparative theology is all about.[42]

Further Readings

Barnes, Michael. "Theology of Religions in a Postmodern World." *The Month* 28 (1994): 270–74, 325–30.

Clooney, Francis X. "Comparative Theology: A Review of Recent Books (1989–1995)." *Theological Studies* 56 (1995): 521–50.

———. "Reading the World in Christ." In *Christian Uniqueness Reconsidered: The Myth of a Pluralistic Theology of Religions.* Ed. Gavin D'Costa. Maryknoll, N.Y.: Orbis Books, 1990, 63–80.

———. *Theology after Vedanta: An Experiment in Comparative Theology.* Albany: State University of New York Press, 1993, 1–13, 153–208.

———. "When the Religions Become Context." *Theology Today* 47 (1990): 30–38.

Duffy, Stephen J. "A Theology of Religions and/or a Comparative Theology?" *Horizons* 26 (1999): 105–15.

Fredericks, James. *Faith among Faiths: Christian Theology and Non-Christian Religions.* New York: Paulist Press, 1999, chapters 7 and 8.

———. "A Universal Religious Experience? Comparative Theology as an Alternative to a Theology of Religions." *Horizons* 22 (1995): 67–87.

---

42. Clooney, *Theology after Vedanta,* 187–93.

Heim, S. Mark. *The Depth of Riches: A Trinitarian Theology of Religious Ends*. Grand Rapids, Mich.: Eerdmans, 2001, chapters 2–3, or 4–6, or 7–8.

———. "God's Diversity: A Trinitarian View of Religious Pluralism." *Christian Century*, January 24, 2001, 14–18.

———. "Salvations: A More Pluralistic Hypothesis." *Modern Theology* 10 (1994): 341–60.

———. *Salvations: Truth and Difference in Religions*. Maryknoll, N.Y.: Orbis Books, 1995, 129–57, 211–30.

Renard, John. "Comparative Theology: Definition and Method." *Religious Studies and Theology* 17 (1998): 3–18.

Chapter 12

The Acceptance Model
Insights and Questions

One of the dangers in a book that explores Christian theologies of religions according to models is that one has to line these models up or put them in some kind of order. That means one of them comes last. The danger is that the reader might think that what comes last *is* last. One might presume, in other words, that this Acceptance Model, because it has been placed last, represents the end of our explorations. Such an impression, as we have seen, is strengthened by the way this model has arisen historically as an effort to fix the leaks or redirect the flow of the other models; also, it expresses the feelings and speaks the language of our contemporary postmodern world. So, the reader might conclude, "Since we've come to the end of this book, we're at the end of its search. This is where the author has been trying to lead us."

Not at all! That certainly was not my intent. Although I clearly have my own views, and although those views, I'm sure, have seeped through the cracks of the descriptions and analyses of each of these models, my ideal has been to present each model in as fair and clear a way as possible, so that both its beauty and its blotches would be evident. Always, I've tried to set the stage in a way that the reader could make his/her own decisions as to the merits or demerits of each model. And that applies to the Acceptance Model as well.

So we're not at the end of the road. And if we're approaching the end of the book, it's not the end of the search. In what follows we will, once again, try to line up the insights and the questions that this Acceptance Model stirs up. In doing so, I hope readers will be able to come to their own conclusions. Such conclusions might bring them to regard this acceptance perspective as their model of choice. Or these final assessments might turn readers back to other models for help in formulating their own attitudes toward other believers. For many, however, maybe none of the models makes for a perfect fit. So the exploration — one's own and perhaps that of the Christian churches — will continue.

Insights

We Are All Inclusivists

It would seem that anyone who wants to engage in interreligious dialogue as honestly and openly as possible has to admit one of the central planks of the

Acceptance Model: we are all inclusivists. No matter how much we may try to act differently, we are always — incorrigibly and incurably — going to view, hear, and understand the other religious person from our own religious perspective. That's simply how things work in the way humans go about the process of knowing. We're always standing somewhere when we meet someone. We're always starting at one location when we try to move to another. St. Thomas Aquinas said it neatly and powerfully centuries ago: "Things known are in the knower according to the mode of the knower."[1] As we've heard often enough in these pages, it's simply impossible to step out of what Aquinas calls "the mode of the knower." Or we can't step out of our own cultural, religious skin and, as it were, take on the skin of someone else. So the ideal of "passing over" to another religion, or of walking in the moccasins of another religious person, is just that, an ideal — something we can, and should, strive for, but only with the realization that we can never bring it off completely. One of the moccasins remains our old one. In passing over, part of us stays behind. Or so it seems.

But does this make us inclusivists? "Inclusivism" is the name that is usually tagged on to what earlier we called the Fulfillment Model. This was the approach that affirms the truth and beauty of other religions but assesses that truth/beauty according to its own criteria and then seeks to bring the value of the other religions to an even greater fruition by inviting them to be "included" or "fulfilled" in its own. Proponents of the Acceptance Model inform us that no matter how open-minded or liberal we might be, this is what — at least to some extent — we are always doing. And it seems they are right. This applies also to those who embrace the Mutuality Model. When a mutualist theologian identifies something in another religion as "challenging" or as a "powerfully new insight," what's the basis for reaching such a conclusion? It's because what the theologian finds in the other tradition relates to, or fits into, what she/he already knows and affirms in his/her own religion. Or when this same theologian concludes that certain forms of religion are "inauthentic" or "intolerable," it's because this new perspective or practice can find no footing, no point of connection, with what the theologian already holds as authentic or moral.

So we're always *including* the other in what we hold to be true and valuable, in what we already are. We don't just look at others from where we stand; we also understand them and evaluate them from where we stand. We may not like that, but there's really nothing we can do about it. Not to include others in where we stand would require us to somehow stand in some neutral place that would not so "prejudice" us. But in this case, "neutral" would mean "culture-less," or "nonhistorical," or religion-less. Really, it would mean "beyond this world." It would mean finding that often-mentioned Archimedian standing place, in space, outside of any limiting or biasing cultural viewpoint. Unless you're an angel, such a standing spot just doesn't exist.

---

1. "Cognita sunt in cognoscenti secundum modum cognoscentis" (*Summa Theologica*, II-II, q. 1, a. 2).

So all of us are, always, inclusivists. Is that the bad news? Not really. It's simply reality. The bad news, as any good psychologist would tell us, is not to accept reality or not to be aware of it. And this is where proponents of the Acceptance Model might offer some needed psychological counseling, especially for their fellow Christians who endorse the Mutuality Model: by not realizing how much they are knowing the "other" according to their own "mode of knowing," or by not being aware of how much they are painting their image of the other in their own Christian colors, mutualist Christians end up, contrary to their intent, in not allowing the other to be other. They distort the otherness of other believers. They don't really let that otherness reveal itself to them because they have already *included* the other in their own world of seeing and understanding. By not being aware of how much we are all, always, *inclusivists*, we become, unavoidably, *imperialists*. Maybe those words are too strong, but they do make an important point, or sound an important warning, for whenever Christians forget that they are always inclusivists in their approach to other believers, they do harm to both sides of the encounter. As just stated, they hurt the other religious person by not allowing her/him to really be other. But such Christians also hurt themselves by denying themselves the opportunity to really hear and be challenged by someone or something that is so different, so "other," that it is for Christians literally inconceivable — that is, something utterly beyond all Christian categories and ways of viewing God and the world. By always *including* the others in our own viewpoint, we distort who they are and keep ourselves locked in who we are.

But what can be done about this unavoidable, inextricable inclusivism in the way we encounter other believers? How can we break through our inclusivist conditioning and really see and hear and be challenged by the other? Proponents of the Acceptance Model don't offer any clear-cut, sure-fire directions. Here we're at the sensitive and complicated heart of what interreligious dialogue is all about. Their main piece of advice would be: if we're ever going to see beyond our inclusivism, we first have to be aware of it and confess it. And then, simply open ourselves to the other — and wait to see what happens. Yes, wait, be patient, step back, lose control of what is happening in the dialogue. In letting the other be the inconceivable, totally other, in admitting our inclusivist defenses, in simply being with the other in the desire to respect and learn from them — maybe, just maybe, what is totally different and beyond us can become for us a new possibility, a new insight, a new challenge to our own "mode of knowing." Only by admitting that we are caught in inclusivism, only by accepting it, is there any possibility of getting beyond it.

This means that if there might be any possibility of "common ground" between two different religions — any possibility of the two utterly different others connecting with each other — such common ground can only be discovered *in* and *through* the dialogue itself. Or maybe instead of "discovered," we should say "created." It's impossible before the dialogue to know what two starkly divergent religious traditions might have in common. The reason for that is simply because before the dialogue we're always identifying "the common" from our own "mode of knowing." Only after we've been hit in the face, as it were, with the utterly other mode of knowing of our dialogue partner, only after we've patiently waited and allowed the totally different mode of knowing to possibly seep into and affect our own mode of knowing — only then can we say, together with our partner, that we have something in common. Common ground can never be predetermined before the dialogue. Whatever might be common ground among differing religions will be created out of the differences among these different religions.

And it will have to be created more than once! This, too, is an insight and lesson that all Christians might learn from the Acceptance Model. Whatever common ground might be established or created from within the dialogue, it will be, as one author has put it, *shaky* common ground.[2] It will shift as new differences from other religions are discovered or as limitations of the Christian perspective become evident. Furthermore, what is common ground today might not be so common tomorrow, for there are always new situations and questions that religions have to face, and there is always something even more different and surprising in the utterly other religious partner who is engaging us in dialogue. If common ground among the religions is possible, it will never be a "one-and-only" common ground.

So since we are all inclusivists, we can learn from each other and can determine whether we might have anything in common only by first recognizing that we are all inclusivists and then by allowing ourselves to be included by the inclusivism of our partners. Inclusivists including inclusivists — that, perhaps, is another way of describing dialogue.

The Value of Differences

At the beginning of this part, we used a one-liner to describe the Acceptance Model: "The religious traditions of the world are *really* different, and we have to *accept* those differences." Here we have, one can say, not only the most striking, but also the most mind-bending difference between the Acceptance Model and all the other models we have been exploring. The Acceptance Model differs from the others in the way it regards differences. For the other models, differences are something they want to get beyond; for the Acceptance Model, differences are not only something it can live with temporarily but something it wants to live with permanently. The Replacement Model seeks to respect the differences it encounters in other religions, but its goal is to remove and replace these differences and so usher the followers of these other religions into the new-found unity of the Christian family. For the Fulfillment and Mutuality Models, the differences Christians meet in other religions are to be valued and respected

---

2. Mark Kline Taylor, "In Praise of Shaky Ground: The Liminal Christ and Cultural Pluralism," *Theology Today* 43 (1986): 36–51.

and learned from; but more important for these models are the similarities that Christians can find between themselves and followers of other religious paths. These similarities — whether in the notion of God or of the self or in a concern for the poor — then become the basis for dialogue and for a greater unity between Christians and other believers. The stress is on finding similarities and overcoming differences.

For the Acceptance Model, it's the other way around. Differences are just as valuable as similarities. In fact, one can say that for most of the advocates of the Acceptance Model whom we have met in this chapter, differences are *more valuable*. Differences are going to be more life-giving and more God-revealing than similarities. Christians are going to be better Christians and learn more about the Divine not just by recognizing the differences in other religions but by affirming them and letting them be. The goal of interreligious dialogue, the Acceptance Model tells us, is not to attain a greater unity among the religions but to maintain their diversity and learn from it. This is certainly a difficult message for most Christians.

In so much of Christians' beliefs and practices, unity holds center stage or constitutes the main goal. There is only *one God,* so for Christians it is only natural that all peoples are both embraced by this one God and called to come together in unity under this one Divine. This conclusion follows even more tightly and demandingly from the Christian belief in Jesus as the *one Savior;* the whole purpose of Jesus' coming is to bring all peoples into the unity of life in and through him. And that's why there is *one* holy, apostolic *church* which, though it may take different denominational forms, is really the final destination for all peoples (if not on earth, then at least in heaven!). The momentum of Christian belief is to start with diversity and bring it to unity. Diversity among religions is wonderful, challenging, surprising — but for most Christians its fundamental purpose is to serve as the clay, as it were, out of which greater unity can be shaped. And the "ever-greater unity" is meant to lead to a final unity.

Advocates of the Acceptance Model — all of them also speaking as Christians — warn their fellow believers that this drive toward unity, or this finalizing of oneness over manyness, may be dangerous. It may threaten, if not contradict, other basic Christian convictions and beliefs. One of the most fundamental ingredients in Christian experience and doctrine is that God, as close to us and as loving of us as God is, always remains *other*. The Divine can never be reduced to, contained by, identified with the human. Even in Jesus, where there is a "hypostatic" union between the divine and the human, the real difference between humanity and divinity is not erased. No matter how close God comes to us, no matter how sure we are that we have been grasped by and therefore know this God — God remains and must remain other. Well, proponents of the Acceptance Model suggest to their fellow Christians, it is precisely in the otherness of other religions that the otherness of God is expressed and preserved. The other religions serve, one might say, as the spokespersons and defenders of the God who is always other. As one theologian puts it, "God's shattering otherness" and "the neighbor's irreducible otherness" are very much related. Just as the Divine can never be captured in our doctrines or definitions, so the other religions can never be reduced to "the consoling communality of 'religion.' "[3]

In the other religions (but not only in them), God keeps reminding us of the divine otherness, of the divine "more" that is always more than we can ever know, even more than we can ever imagine or expect. So it is precisely in the finite other that the Transcendent Other of God keeps entering our lives, keeps showing itself to us in the very act in which it evades us. This is what is going on, for the Acceptance Model, in the dialogue with other religions. God is being other in the otherness of the religions. Therefore, to reduce the otherness — that means the real diversity — of the religions to some kind of higher or final unity is to reduce the otherness of God to what we can know and possess. But that's another word for idolatry.[4]

So on the basis of God as other, advocates of the Acceptance Model challenge their fellow Christians to accept the otherness and diversity of religions. But we also saw how S. Mark Heim makes the same challenge on the basis of the even more distinctive Christian belief in God as triune. Just as the "threeness" or manyness of God, for Christians, can never be absorbed into unity or oneness, so the diversity and plurality of religions can never be reduced to a final unity and similarity. Religion, we heard from Heim, will always come in the plural. So will the salvations they preach and strive for. This is the reality "now and forevermore." Whatever one may think of Heim's theological interpretation of the Trinity, Christians, it would seem, have to genuinely open themselves to the possibility of what he is proposing. Heim and other followers of the Acceptance Model are urging their fellow Christians to admit the possibility, if not the necessity, that the salvations, or the final goals, of the various religions can never, and will never, be reconciled. Both in interreligious dialogue now, and in whatever is waiting for us in eternity, differences will have the final word. They will never be resolved or sorted out into a higher unity. In a popular cliché, we have to agree to disagree — and then learn from our disagreements. If we don't accept the possibility of incorrigible, but life-giving, disagreements, we run a twofold peril: we will be exposed to the temptation to push for a forced agreement (which will always be on our terms), and we will cut ourselves off from the possibility of meeting the true otherness of God that is revealing itself to us in the "disagreeing" face of the religious other. The mysterious otherness of God is revealed more clearly, perhaps, in what is unclear and disagreeable than in what we can understand and affirm.

---

3. David Tracy, "Theology and the Many Faces of Postmodernity," *Theology Today* 51 (1994): 108.

4. The insight into the religious other as the mediator of the Divine Other draws much from the thought of E. Levinas. For a clear review of Levinas's thought and its implications for Christian theology of religions, see Mervyn Frederick Bendle, "The Postmetaphysics of Religious Difference," *Pacifica* 11 (1998): 1–26.

Dialogue Has the Right-of-Way to Theology

It is especially in order to truly open themselves to the startling, maybe disagreeable, otherness of other religions that Christians need to follow the admonitions of the comparative theologians — to give dialogue with other religions the right-of-way over a theology of religions. The comparativists seem to be right: by trying to have all our theological pieces in place before we Christians approach other religions, by trying to figure out whether the fundamental relationship of Christians with other believers is one of "replacement," or "fulfillment," or "mutuality" before we actually study the sacred books of other traditions or talk with those who follow other paths — by so "theologizing" before dialoguing, we Christians run the real risk, as Fredericks warns, of *inoculating* ourselves against "the power and novelty of other religious traditions."[5] This danger of theorizing before acting, or of mapping the territory before exploring the territory, also applies to the advocates of the Mutuality Model who want to set up the rules or the common ground for dialogue before actually stepping into the dialogue. If the map is not the territory, we may miss much of the territory if our map is too detailed! That's especially the case when the territory is so new, so strange, so utterly other as are the religious communities of the world. Better to explore before mapping. Better to observe before assessing.

So, the comparativists conclude, all efforts to work out a theology of religions must begin with a dialogue with these religions. More pointedly: any Christian theologian who proposes a theology of religions but who doesn't know much about any other religion than her/his own should be regarded as highly suspicious, if not dangerous.

Also, the general directives that the comparative theologians offer for how one should go about a dialogue with other believers make good sense. Instead of taking up broad, often complex, issues like "the Christian and Buddhist notion of Ultimate Reality" or "the Self in Hinduism and Christianity," comparativists suggest that we zoom in and focus on particular texts or movements or images. In other words, limit the territory and explore it carefully. What one finds by way of similarities or differences in one small plot of dialogue will be road signs for further paths of conversation and exploration. In so urging us to, as it were, "take baby steps" on the path of dialogue, comparative theologians are being faithful to a general conviction of the Acceptance Model: the truth (not the devil) lies in details. We will come to know the religious other not through broad generalities ("Hinduism believes in reincarnation," or "Buddhism does not believe in God") but through concrete particularities — an individual text, a precise historical movement, a concrete devotional practice. This is a method of dialogue that starts with particulars and that discovers what it's doing by doing it. For such a form of encounter with other religions, the comparativists add,

---

5. James L. Fredericks, *Faith among Faiths: Christian Theology and Non-Christian Religions* (New York: Paulist Press, 1999), 167.

one will have to have much patience and trust. Such dialogue moves slowly, at its own pace. And one has to trust the process, especially when its movement slows to a crawl.

A further piece of advice from the comparative theologians is equally important for this process of finding one's way in a totally new religious territory: make friends who will guide you along the way. The counsel that James Fredericks offers — which came out of his own experience — should be heard and embraced by any Christian who feels both the need and the difficulties of entering into a new religious world: we can learn more from a Buddhist friend than we can ever learn from a Buddhist text. Or more accurately, the friend will enable us to see and hear what is in the text more clearly and engagingly than can ever happen if the text is only something that sits on our desk. This is because a friend enables us not only to understand but to feel Buddhism; a friend is not just someone we're impressed by but someone we are touched by, someone we simply and genuinely like. It's not just the friend's knowledge, it is also her virtue, her goodness, and the quality of her life that stir our caring for that person, perhaps even our love for her. Such a person-as-friend will tell us more about the other religion than we can ever comprehend if we are only studying that religion.

With real friends in other religions — Hindus, Buddhists, Muslims, Jews with whom we like to talk, eat, see a movie — we will also be able to accomplish another requirement of interreligious dialogue as understood in the Acceptance Model. As we heard earlier, there may be times in the conversation when we have to agree to disagree — and then, possibly and hopefully, to learn from such disagreements. This isn't easy. When we really encounter in another religion a belief or practice that out-and-out seems to contradict what we hold to be true and urgent, it is practically impossible to really let it be, to accept it as the truth for them, even though it is untruth for us. On the intellectual, maybe even the ethical, level, it seems impossible to do so. But when such a "contradiction" is embodied in a friend, in someone we respect and care about, then somehow it becomes easier to accept and to live with. As baffling as it seems to our understanding, we see it as part of that which nurtures and gives life to our friend. And we are more disposed to walk patiently with our friend, to see and learn more of how what is "false" to us is true to him — and how, possibly, his "falseness" may add to, or correct, our "truth." Friendship can teach us things that can be taught in no other way.

There is a further important lesson that Christians might learn from comparative theology's urging that dialogue has the right-of-way over theology. It has to do with perhaps the most fragile, or explosive, question that has surfaced in each chapter of this book: How are we to understand the unique role of Jesus in a world of so many other religions? Francis Clooney hit that problem head-on when he felt the tension — no, the contradiction — between Christian convictions that all salvation is through Jesus and Hindu convictions that knowledge of Brahman is what saves us. His solution? "A patient deferral of issues of truth!"[6] The question that has taunted and teased us throughout this book, comparative theologians are announcing, cannot be solved *theologically;* it can only be solved *dialogically.* We're not going to be able to figure it out through further intellectual distinctions (e.g., between "truly" and not "only"), or through further historical study into the language of the New Testament (it's "love language," not philosophical language). Rather, we know, thanks to the insistence of the Acceptance Model, that just as a flower can be appreciated and understood only in the soil in which it grows, so truth-claims such as "Jesus saves" or "knowledge of Brahman saves" can be valued and understood only within their own cultural-linguistic soil. Therefore, we will continue our efforts to enter into, and move back and forth between, these two very different worlds. We will compare; we will continue to dialogue. And through our continued study, conversation, and friendships we might come to realize how the two contradicting claims between the uniqueness of Jesus and the uniqueness of knowledge of Brahman might be resolved. Or, maybe, we will realize that they don't need to be resolved. For Christians and theologians who have been frustrated and battered by the question of the uniqueness of Jesus, this might sound like very good news.

Questions

Is Language a Prism or a Prison?

If "diversity" is the word that has sounded most frequently throughout these chapters on the Acceptance Model, it is because of another word that comes in a close second: "language." Because there are different languages/cultures, there are different religions. This is the postmodern realization that the Acceptance Model takes with courageous seriousness: we don't first have experience and then look for words; it's the other way around — the words we have been given by our culture and community determine the experience we have. This message has resounded throughout these last three chapters. Its implications follow clearly, even if (for some) painfully: because the differences between our languages and cultures are so stark and irreducible, so too will be the differences between our religions.

But we may ask: If followers of the Acceptance Model have rightly recognized that religion, like all language, is a *prism* for all we see and do, have they also made it into a *prison*? It's one thing to identify language as that which influences and colors all that we see and know; it's quite another to describe language as that which *determines* all that we see and know and prevents us from seeing it differently. It's one thing to see religion as the perspective from which we always view everything else; it's quite another to announce that we are stuck in that perspective or that the perspective can never change, let alone change

---

6. Francis X. Clooney, *Theology after Vedanta: An Experiment in Comparative Theology* (Albany: State University of New York Press, 1993), 187–93.

profoundly. This possibility of getting stuck in a religion can be identified in three dangers that critics of the Acceptance Model warn of:

1. *Isolationism.* If we take seriously the "untranslatability" of one religious text into another, if we hold to the impossibility of learning to speak another religious language, if we insist on "incommensurability," then it seems that, indeed, every religious person is confined only to his/her own text or language or religious community. That looks like a prison. What Lindbeck calls *intratextuality* — the insistence that we can see the world and live our lives only within one particular text or viewpoint — seems to lock us into that world. It becomes impossible to truly talk with and understand another person from another language or tradition, for one can see only what appears on one's own religious radar screen. Each screen can take in only so much. What is beyond its technical powers is beyond its understanding and consideration. That means that whatever appears on one screen is the truth for that screen, and it can't be questioned by another screen for the simple fact that it doesn't register on that screen. This leads to the second danger.

2. *Relativism.* We've heard this warning before. It was leveled against the proponents of the Mutuality Model because of their inclination to recognize divine presence and truth everywhere. The same danger of relativism results from the Acceptance Model's determination to keep divine truth, as it were, packaged tightly in multiple traditions. The truth of each religion is self-contained in the language and texts of its own tradition. Everything makes sense within the language and worldview of each religion; and nothing makes sense outside of them. That's the meaning of incommensurability and untranslatability. Well, that seems to imply that each religion is isolated and therefore protected from the criticisms of the other. You can't tell me what's wrong with my world because you're always looking at me from your world. That seems to imply, further, that whatever is declared to be true in my world is true because it was so declared. It can't be criticized from the outside. Truth is whatever truth is for the individual culture or religion (and perhaps even for the individual individual!). This sounds like relativism, where "anything goes" as long as it goes within my world, my tradition, my experience.

3. *Fideism.* All this also sounds like what theologians call "fideism." This technical term describes situations in which religious people are, as it were, speechless to explain, both to others and to themselves, *why* they hold certain things to be true or revealed by God. The reason why they can't give an explanation to others is because they will always do so in their own religious language — which others cannot speak or understand. And when they ask themselves why their own religious language is telling them the truth, the only reason they can give is that it is their own religious language! If they are pressed further to answer why this language is

their own language, it seems that only two responses are possible. First, they might admit that this is the language they have always had, the religious world they were born into and grew up in. But that would make their religious identity either fortuitous or fatalistic — the result of chance or fate. So the other response makes more sense: their religious identity is the result not simply of fate but of their own decision. And yet, when asked for the reason for such a decision, all they can provide are reasons from within their own religious language. In other words, they choose this religion because it is this religion. That sounds like what some people might call "blind faith." One's religious choice is a matter of just "leaping" or "diving" into the cold water and then finding that one can swim and get used to the temperature. But why one dives into one pool rather than another, that cannot be explained.[7]

Lindbeck himself recognizes such dangers. He explicitly admits that "intratextuality seems wholly relativistic," turning "religions . . . into self-enclosed and incommensurable intellectual ghettoes." He also confesses to "the fideistic dilemma: it appears that choice between religions becomes purely arbitrary, a matter of blind faith."[8] To avoid such pitfalls, Lindbeck admits that there have to be some "universal norms of reasonableness" — something by which people in different religious communities can connect with each other and not be caught in their own prisons. But Lindbeck's problem is how to get at these norms of reasonableness. Reason, he tell us, won't work. Neither will a common language. He suggests that efforts to bridge the religions are more a matter of "aesthetics" than logic, a job more for artists than theologians.[9] Good. But he might say more about where such religious artists can start, what they have to work with, how they can begin communicating their images and values. Art can be very different from culture to culture. What is beautiful and stirring in one culture may be unintelligible or even repulsive in another.

Perhaps this is where some of the Christians in the Mutuality Model might enter into a dialogue with the Acceptance Model and provide some help. If, as Lindbeck and company insist, the link or common ground between the religions cannot be a matter of doctrine or words, perhaps the common ground or the "universal norms of reasonableness" can be found in the *ethical* area, in the very real problems of violence, starvation, and environmental degradation that face all peoples of the entire earth. Perhaps here is where the religious artists whom Lindbeck calls on can start sharing their images and responses and create a means of communication that all can share in. Perhaps.

But more fundamentally, if any such efforts to bridge gaps between religions are going to work, if religions are going to be recognized as prisms without mak-

---

7. Many of these concerns about the dangers of the Acceptance Model are laid out in the review symposium on Lindbeck's *The Nature of Doctrine* in *The Thomist* 49 (1985): 392–472.

8. George Lindbeck, *The Nature of Doctrine: Religion and Theology in a Postliberal Age* (Philadelphia: Westminster Press, 1984), 128.

9. Ibid., 130–31.

ing them into prisons, then it seems that the followers of the Acceptance Model are going to have to qualify their understanding of language. The Acceptance Model has indeed done a great service to Christian theology of religions by reminding us of how much language affects experience. But it seems they have not sufficiently recognized that experience affects language. There is a two-way street between language and experience — even though the traffic starts to flow on language's side of the road. So yes, Lindbeck and others are certainly correct in insisting that all our experience begins with, is made possible by, and is always expressed in language. But they don't sufficiently perceive that the experience that language has made possible can start moving in the opposite direction and have effects on the very language that got it started. The experience that language originates and facilitates can go beyond language. To shift our image: the telescopes that we always have to use in order to look into the universe of truth can also bring us to the awareness that there is more to the universe than what *our* telescopes can detect. In seeing what we see, we know there is more to see. This is especially the case when dealing with religious "telescopes" and religious language and experience.

And so we can ask the advocates of the Acceptance Model whether they have made a too neat, or too sharp, distinction between language and experience. In technical terms, they seem to have created a *dualism* between the two, as if you first have language and then experience, as if one is always the cause and the other the effect. Rather, the relationship between language and experience is similar to that between matter and spirit in human beings (or in all living beings): the two need each other to be what they are — matter is always "en-spirited," and spirit is always "en-fleshed." So as one commentator on Lindbeck has pointed out, while Lindbeck rightly stresses that all experience is "languaged," he forgets that all language is "experienced."[10] So just as language has a formative influence on what we experience, so too what we experience can bounce back and have a formative influence on our language. If language is always the parent of experience, then experience, as the child of language, can grow up and, as it were, "talk back" to its parent.

So especially when we're dealing with religion, there's always a surplus in the experience that language makes possible — something that, though made possible by language, goes beyond it. Although language may define our experience, it does not confine our experience. And here we have the basis for understanding other religious languages — that is, for not only being able to, but even needing to, learn other languages. Because our own religious experience, always mediated in our own language, tells us that there is so much left unsaid in our own language, we will want to learn other languages. The desire to learn another language will come out of what we have realized in speaking our own. But further — and here we are stretching the analogy of language —

---

10. Stephen L. Stell, "Hermeneutics in Theology and the Theology of Hermeneutics: Beyond Lindbeck and Tracy," *Journal of the American Academy of Religion* 56 (1993): 679–703.

that surplus, or something more, that we have sensed through our own language will be the guide, the teacher, the motivator as we study a "foreign" religious language. Therefore, we have to question — carefully but resolutely — the insistence of some advocates of the Acceptance Model that it is impossible to be religiously bilingual.

The example of someone like Thomas Merton might help: the more he increased his proficiency in his own Christian language, the more he realized that there were things to say about the Divine that could only be said in other religious languages. What he learned in his own Christian language enabled him to be a "fast learner" of other languages; but what he learned from others also enriched his own Christian vocabulary.[11] Nowadays, the number of religious bilinguists who follow Merton's example seems to be growing. There is much discussion about what is called "dual-belonging" or "multiple-belonging" — living within or between more than one religious practice. To the insistence that you can't speak two different religious languages, many people are responding: "But I think I'm doing it. And it seems to work."

If it is working, then another contention of the Acceptance Model must be questioned: that all religious language by its very nature is, and must be, "totally *comprehensive,*" that is, "including or explaining everything but not able to be included or surpassed by anything else."[12] Every religion, we have been told by this model, makes absolute claims. And to request, or require, that the religions give up such claims (as the Mutuality Model has urged) is to ask them to do something they simply can't do; such a requirement is an imperialistic imposition. But this is precisely what we are now asking: Is it really? Certainly, throughout the course of religious history, religions have made absolute claims. But we must ask whether such convictions about having the "only" or the "final" or the "full" truth have come from the heart of their religious experience.

If what we are suggesting is valid — that religious experience originates in religious language but always goes beyond it — then all religions have to be very careful about making claims that their language says it all. And they have to be careful, not because some outsider is telling them to do so, but because of what their own language makes known to them. Here we might remind advocates of the Acceptance Model that within all the religious traditions, we find not only absolute claims but also clear recognition that God, or the Divine, or Nirvana is beyond anything that humans can comprehend or express. And if there is always a surplus, a "something more," to what our religious language tells us, then no language can really be "totally comprehensive."

Are we at a stage in the religious history of humankind in which all religions can admit this? In which all religions can make universal claims without making absolute claims? In which, yes, there will be need of *apologetics* (that is, dis-

---

11. See *The Asian Journal of Thomas Merton* (New York: New Directions, 1975), especially 305–19; also Thomas Merton, *Thoughts on the East* (New York: New Directions Books, 1995).

12. Paul J. Griffiths, "The Properly Christian Response to Religious Plurality," *Anglican Theological Review* 79 (1997): 19.

agreement, efforts to convince and persuade each other); but there will also be room — much greater room — for *dialogics* (that is, expanding or clarifying or correcting one's own grasp of truth through dialogue with others)?

Can Many Salvations Save Our World?

In the previous chapter we saw that S. Mark Heim's was the strongest and clearest voice among advocates of the Acceptance Model in stressing the real and abiding differences of the religions. With his notion of many salvations, not only in this world but in the next, Heim, in a sense, absolutized diversity. Diversity dominates. The *many* will always have the last word on the *one*. But he insists that it is precisely out of such a whirl of diversity that real dialogue can take shape.

Certainly, we must take seriously the warnings of Heim and others that Christians in the Mutuality Model too easily trim off real differences among the religions in order to plant them all into some kind of predetermined common ground. But further questions arise: Does this insistence on diversity — this "preferential option for differences" — really allow for the give-and-take of authentic dialogue? Does it facilitate the kind of exchange in which people coming from one world are able to enter into another world not only to understand it but also to learn from and perhaps challenge it? Even more so, does the Acceptance Model encourage or allow for the kind of ethical cooperation that a world racked by human and ecological suffering seems to require of all religions?

Clearly and importantly, the main message of this model is urgent: the religions of the world have to *accept* each other. What a different world we would have if that much could be accomplished — if the many religious wars that are presently spilling blood throughout the world would cease and religious communities would accept, tolerate, and let each other be. This definitely is the first step in the encounter of religions — tolerance, acceptance. But if we want to realize a dialogue among religions, acceptance and tolerance aren't enough. They prepare the ground and clear the weeds, but if there is going to be a meeting of religions that also becomes a *relationship* between them, something more has to happen. If there is going to be not just respectful listening to each other but also an understanding of what the other is saying, an understanding that enables everyone both to learn something new from the other as well as to disagree with the other, then there have to be deeper lines of communication than just acceptance. Communication goes further than acceptance, but in order to "go further" there has to be, so it seems, some kind of a path, or shared direction, along which religious persons can take these next steps.

Such difficulties loom larger when theologians like Heim go even further in solidifying religious differences by claiming that the religions of the world are really going in different, even opposite, directions. With his notion of *salvations* — salvation in the plural — Heim told us that religions differ not only in the means they use but in the ends they pursue. But if two people have different goals, if the momentum and motivation and hopes of their lives are moving in different directions, how will they ever be able to understand each other, help each other in reaching their goal, or perhaps confront each other about the value of what they are seeking? Heim pointed out that it is only on the basis of accepting such total differences not only in means but also in ends that we have the possibility of learning something new. But if the "something new" is found in a goal that is of no interest to me because I'm going somewhere else, what is there to learn? As Joseph DiNoia, when confronted with Buddhist claims, honestly admits: "I do not want to attain Nirvana."[13] The Christian goal is the Reign of God, not Nirvana — two different goals. When the religious communities of the world are on journeys that have divergent final destinations, then all they can do is wave at each other as they pass; to join each other on their journeys just doesn't seem possible.

So we're once again wrestling with an issue that has nagged us throughout this book: besides the real differences between religions — or better, because of the real differences — there also has to be something that the religions have in common if there is going to be real dialogue between them. There's got to be something that will help establish lines of communication between such real, apparently overwhelming, differences. In calling all Christians to take seriously and accept the differences between the religions, proponents of the Acceptance Model, as we have seen, have also recognized the need for dialogue between the religions. But if they really take this need for dialogue seriously, then they have to say more about how to link or make connections between these differences. It seems, however, that they so insist that these differences are "incommensurable" or are going in different directions that they lose the possibility of making connections. We heard earlier that according to the Acceptance Model, if there's any hope of common ground between religions, it has to be created *in the dialogue.* But it seems that it would have to be a "creation out of nothing." There doesn't seem to be anything within the religions out of which we can envision or fashion what they might have in common. When you're traveling in different directions, what do you share?

This leads to another question for the Acceptance Model: In so insisting on the differences between the religions, even differences in final destinations, are these theologians perhaps missing, maybe suppressing, something that *is* common to all the religions? We're talking about something that we seem to hear in most if not all religious traditions: they make *universal claims.* What they proclaim to be true is true not just for themselves but for all people. And that means that it is, or can be, common to all people. In every religion, so it appears, there is the belief or the hope that there is Something — deeper, higher, within, ahead, hidden, potential — that can make for the well-being of *all* people. "God," "Allah," "Brahman," "Nirvana" — as different as they are — are understood by the

---

13. Joseph DiNoia, "Christian Universalism: The Nonexclusive Particularity of Salvation in Christ," in *Either/Or: The Gospel or Neopaganism,* ed. Carl E. Braaten and Robert W. Jenson (Grand Rapids, Mich.: Eerdmans, 1993), 46.

religions to embody the goal not just of one's own community but of all persons. In other words, it seems to be part of the experience and convictions of each religion that there is Something that can be meaningful for persons in all religions — Something, in other words, that can ground connections and the possible relationship between the religions (whether that relationship be understood as replacement, fulfillment, or mutuality).

Therefore, just as the followers of the Mutuality Model can be accused of imperialism when they impose their claim that all religions are really intending the same goal, so might the Acceptance Model be slipping into a similar imperialism when it insists that the goals of all religions are totally different. Most religions would agree with each other that there is only one goal for all humanity, even though they may disagree on how to get there. To ask the religions to accept that there are multiple salvations, multiple and very different ultimate goals, for humans and their religions would be, for most religions, a strange if not heretical belief.

This is certainly true of Christianity. When Heim confesses that there are tensions between his proposal for many different salvations and traditional Christian belief, he may, as is said, be "putting it mildly." Christians have always taken for granted, and still do, that because there is one God, there is one final destination. Heim's efforts to draw out the possibility of many salvations from the Christian doctrine of the Trinity go only half-circle. Yes, Christian belief in three divine persons does mean that diversity is alive and well and a permanent part of the very nature of God; and this could well mean, as Heim concludes, that it is alive and well and enduring among the religions. But that's only the first half of the circle of Christian belief in God as triune; the other half swings back to oneness: the three divine persons, Christians also affirm, have something in common that enables them to relate to each other, enhance each other, achieve ever greater unity among themselves. Heim does not seem to apply this part of the Trinitarian circle to the world of religions: as diverse as they are, as incommensurable as their differences may seem, they also, like the persons of the Trinity, have something in common that enables them to transcend their differences without doing away with them. Belief in the Trinity, therefore, would seem to call Christians to affirm not only, as Heim urges, real diversity among the religions, but also the real possibility of common ground — a common ground that recognizes different paths, but not different final goals.

If, however, all the religions trust that there is some — at least potential — common ground between them, we still have to ask: Where do we find it? Or, how might the religions bring it forth, together? The answer we are suggesting is a further question for the followers of the Acceptance Model: To discover, or create, what the religious families of the world might have in common *among* themselves, might it be helpful for them to look *beyond* themselves? We're talking about the real world that surrounds all the religions, a world full of injustice, violence, and ecological devastation — realities that pose threats and crises for all humanity, all nations, all religious traditions. If the religions do not have any given common ground, don't they have common problems? And all of these problems are focused or fed, one might say, in one reality: *suffering*. There is a tremendous, horrible, menacing amount of suffering in the world today, both human and ecological, that cries out and can be heard by — is being heard by — persons in *all* the religions.

Can suffering, therefore, be the material, as it were, out of which the different religions can fashion or find the common ground where they can stand and act with each other and talk to each other? To be sure, the common problems and the common questions that arise out of suffering don't automatically lead to common answers. But they do provide a common starting place where common answers might be worked out — or better, where differing answers can be coordinated and shared. We're talking about something we encountered on "the ethical bridge" of the Mutuality Model: a globally responsible dialogue that tries to work out a global ethic. Such an ethical dialogue, for many, has to be more than an ad hoc or provisional opportunity, a possibility that we *might* consider. Rather, it bears the urgency of an ethical imperative. If proponents of the Acceptance Model would recognize this urgency, perhaps they might see that the religions have more in common than meets the academic eye.

Many Absolutes = No Absolute?

There's another way in which the Acceptance Model might be setting up roadblocks to the very dialogue it wants to further. We saw that representatives of the Acceptance Model were juggling two balls, both of which they tried to keep up in the air simultaneously: the real diversity of all religions and the claim of each religion that it holds the final, the fullest, truth. There are two reasons why this model insists that the diversity of religions must include the claim of each religion to hold the absolute truth. First, religiously, this is what all religions have always done — claim to be the best; so we must respect such claims. Second, philosophically, it's unavoidable; we naturally think that our religious perspective is the best because that's the only perspective we have; it's the one from which we view, and that means evaluate, all the others.

But we can ask: Must this be? The question that we posed earlier in this chapter finds an echo here: yes, it is true that most of the religions of the world have made claims to have the absolute or final or highest form of truth. But in the world as we experience it, a world direly in need of not just acceptance but cooperation and dialogue, must each religion continue to insist on being "the best" or having the "final word"? If I take up a conversation with someone else with the conviction that "I have the final word," can the conversation really become a dialogue, an exchange in which all parties are ready and able to learn? How can a person really be open to listening and learning if s/he believes that God has given him/her the revelation meant to supersede (the Replacement Model), or complete (the Fulfillment Model), or better understand (Heim and the Acceptance Model) all others? So we face the hard question — hard for Christians certainly but also for many other religions as well: Is it possible for religious traditions to give up, or modify, the absolute claims they may have made in the past?

To give up what we are calling *absolute* claims to truth would not mean abandoning both the particular and the universal claims to truth that are inherent in both religious experience and the teachings of most religions. Every religion, so it seems, believes and asserts that in a particular person or event — Jesus, Buddha, Muhammad, the Exodus — God or the Ultimate has done, or been revealed as, something unique: that is, distinctive, special, unrepeatable. Further, religions maintain that the value or meaning or power of this particular event or person is universally meaningful; it is meant to extend to and help ("save" or "enlighten") all people of all times. Such particular and universal claims are not at all denied when religions are asked to pull in the reins of their absolute claims. Each religion continues to announce that what it contains is really true and important for all people. But in abandoning their absolute claims, each religion would also be open to the possibility (if not probability) that other religious figures or events may also bear truths — very different perhaps — that are also really and universally important.

Though such questions and suggestions sound like the Mutuality Model, we might ask whether they could just as well come from the Acceptance Model, especially in Heim's version of it. Heim took up the general concern of the Acceptance Model that we should respect and preserve diversity and pushed it even further when he argued that the diversity of the religions is a matter not just of means but also of ends. Not just many religions, he urged, but many salvations! Well, one might ask, why not go a step further: Not just many salvations but also many *absolutes*? By "many absolutes" we mean that there are many unique and universally powerful revelations of truth or the Divine; that's what we mean by absolute. "Absolute" indicates a particular truth that is universally meaningful. But none of these absolutes would have the final say or constitute the ultimate goal for all the others; that's because there are *many* absolutes. None of them, in other words, would be "more absolute" than any other. Heim, in a sense, was moving in this direction when he urged Christians to accept and open themselves to the "absolute" truth-claims that one finds in other religions; he went on, even more boldly, to make his case that these different absolutes, or different salvations, will remain so throughout all eternity. But he also added that one of these absolute truths — that is, Christian revelation — will, in the end, prove more absolute than all the others, for it will be only on the Christian mountain that we can understand the Trinitarian nature of God and see how all the other religions can be understood and ranked.

But we are asking why this must be so — both philosophically and theologically. Philosophically, yes, the Acceptance Model is right, we always view other truth-claims from our own; and we are convinced that our truth is really so and really important for others. But that doesn't rule out the possibility — which we can recognize right from the start of our dialogue with other truths — that what we encounter in other religions might expand or clarify or even correct the truth that we started with. Theologically, why must there be among the religions one *absolute* expression of absolute truth? As we suggested earlier, since all the religions, in making their truth-claims, also admit that the Divine is more than anything a human can know or articulate, all religions can also recognize that the absolute can never be absolutely known. That means that if a religion wants to make absolute claims, it has to be open to other such absolute claims.

This seems to be consistent with the way Heim uses the Trinity to ground his theology of religions: just as none of the three divine persons are "better" or "fuller" or "more absolute" than any other, so none of the diverse religions can be said to be "more absolute" than any other. In the early church, they called any effort to make one of the divine persons of the Trinity more important than the others the heresy of "subordinationism." The early Christians insisted that "the three divine persons," though very different, were all equal. Neither Father (Parent), nor Son (Child), nor Spirit can speak a "final word" for the others. Each, as it were, is "absolute." Can't Heim, and other Christians with him, say the same of the religions?

But we have to clarify what we are asking or suggesting. First of all, to suggest that *many* religions can be considered to be absolute in that they deliver a saving message for all people is not to say that *all* religions do so. As we have already heard, "many" does not mean "any." Discernment, evaluation, and looking carefully remain important, for as history indubitably shows, much mischief and self-seeking hides under the cloak of religion.

Also, and perhaps more importantly, we have to try to clear up the fuzziness and limitations of the language we're using. To talk about "many absolutes," of course, is a contradiction in terms. "Absolutes" don't come off an assembly line. An absolute is a one-time production. Therefore, to suggest that there are many absolute expressions of truth is to imply that there are no absolute expressions of truth. We have been playing with a paradox here: "many absolutes" equals "no one absolute." That's the purpose and value of using such teasing, paradoxical language. It invites us to ponder how there *are* many absolute expressions of divine truth — religious persons do indeed enter the dialogue convinced of what they believe, eager to share it, even ready to die for it. But at the same time, none of these absolute expressions of truth is absolute because each religious person in the dialogue must not only respect the absolute claims of the others but also be ready to learn from them, maybe even be changed by them. So maybe, instead of concluding that "many absolutes" equal "no absolutes," it would be better to say that the "many absolutes" among the religions of the world are in need of each other and have to connect in dialogue with each other. There is — or there might be — a *complementarity of absolutes.*

If that makes sense, then perhaps the Mutuality and the Acceptance Models are not that far apart from each other. Maybe a fruitful dialogue (even a merger?) between them is possible. Mutuality Christians can learn from the acceptance perspective that the religions of the world are really different — much more different than most of the proponents of the Mutuality Model seem to realize — and that these differences will never be able to be reduced to one common experience or end or ground. But Christians who endorse the Acceptance Model can also learn from the Mutuality Model that amid the vast variety of religions, none of them necessarily has to stand out, or end up, as the final, clearest, or absolute expression of divine truth and revelation. Perhaps religions might be compared to the galaxies of the universe: while the universe (the Divine) can be considered absolute, none of the galaxies occupies its center. Or, there are many centers.

Can Comparative Theology Be "Theology-Free"?

Certainly, as we pointed out in the "Insights" section of this chapter, there is much in comparative theology from which Christians can, and need to, learn. The primary lesson has to do with the danger of trying to work out a theology of religions before we actually engage in a dialogue with them. We first have to talk with a stranger before we can really understand her. But while this is no doubt true, a kind of boomerang question may hit us as we try to carry on a conversation with strangers: Aren't there also certain dangers in trying to engage in a dialogue with religions *before* we think about our theology of religions? Don't we always bring certain attitudes, perspectives, and convictions to any conversation with someone we haven't met before? And don't these general predispositions influence the way we carry on the conversation?

What we are asking the advocates of comparative theology, therefore, is not to abandon their insistence that dialogue with other religions must provide the materials out of which a theology of religions is constructed; rather, our question invites the comparativists to balance their program and recognize that one's theology is already present in the way one gathers those materials, or in the way one takes up the dialogue. So another image for the relationship might be more appropriate. Instead of dialogue and theology meeting at an intersection where dialogue always has the right-of-way, we can imagine a traffic light at the intersection: sometimes dialogue has the green light and sometimes theology. In other words, the relationship between theory and practice — between a theology of religions and a dialogue with them — is not "first this, then that," first the practice of dialogue, then the theory of theology. Rather, it's *both-and*. To really engage in a comparative theology we need to sometimes drive forward into an engagement with other religions in which we're not sure of where we are going. But at other times, we also have to look at how our own religious tradition and our own personal convictions are guiding and influencing us as we try to explore the new road. Theology guides dialogue; but dialogue will also guide, even transform, theology. As one critic of comparative theology puts it, the two movements — the data of theology and the data of dialogue — "are two essential and interrelated moments of a single undertaking."[14]

---

14. Stephen J. Duffy, "A Theology of Religions and/or a Comparative Theology?" *Horizons* 26 (1999): 106.

The importance of sometimes starting with theology before we step into the dialogue is grounded in what we have heard throughout this section on the Acceptance Model: we're always looking at the others from our own perspective, through our own glasses. If, as we have heard, there's no such thing as a *pure fact,* but only interpreted facts, that means that there is no such thing as a "pure dialogue" — that is, a dialogue that is "theology-free," a dialogue in which we set aside our own religious glasses and look at the other religion as it "really is." And if we're always seeing it through our own glasses, it is very important to be aware of that and to ask ourselves how our glasses may be influencing, perhaps skewing, what we are seeing. True, what we see in the other religion may prompt us to, as it were, get a new prescription for our own glasses. But we always begin with our own glasses.

So in a sense, the call from some comparative theologians to proclaim a moratorium on the theology of religions is a call for the impossible. That's because we cannot entirely abandon our own given perspectives or take off our theological glasses. But that doesn't mean we should not move forward when dialogue has the green light and drive into territory for which our theological maps provide no clear guidance. This is what the comparativists are urging and what Christians need to hear: plunge into the dialogue without knowing for sure what's going to happen. Trust your friends in other religions and let them lead you to understandings or feelings that are going to illumine or maybe threaten your own Christian, theological perspectives. While we have to be aware that we bring our theological baggage to the journey of dialogue, that doesn't mean that during the journey we may not have to rearrange, or even dispose of, some of that baggage.

In a sense, this is what has actually happened with Christians who are using the Fulfillment and the Mutuality Models. It's not that they are trying to work out their theology of religions before encountering persons of other faiths, as it appears to comparative theologians. For many Christians, it's precisely because they have already engaged in dialogue, because they have been shaken up by their friends in other religions, that they are trying to rearrange their theological baggage and work out new models for understanding other religions. What the comparativists are calling for has been taking place. Christians have followed the green light for dialogue; and because of what they have discovered, they're waiting, as it were, at the next intersection for the green light for theology. What they've seen in the dialogue doesn't quite fit what their theology has been telling them. Before they can explore further in the dialogue, they have to readjust their theological maps.

And maybe such readjustment will have to extend further than comparative theologians think it can. Or maybe there are certain theological preunderstandings (perhaps unconscious) that prevent comparative theologians from hearing, and being challenged by, what other religions are really saying. This is a final question for comparative theologians. It comes as no surprise that this question has to do with their understanding of Jesus. As we saw, the two spokespersons for comparative theology whom we listened to in this part — James Fredericks and Francis Clooney — hold firm to their given understanding of Jesus as the only source of salvation for all humanity. When Clooney felt the clash and contradiction between his own belief in Jesus as the only Savior and the Hindu belief in the experience of Brahman as bearer of salvation, all he could do was "patiently defer" the complexity of this contradiction. It's a question that can't be solved now, if it can ever be resolved.

Still, we can ask: Can the question of Jesus' role as sole Savior really be avoided? Or has the deferral run its course? The reason for asking this question comes from comparative theology itself: this theology calls Christians to plunge into dialogue with other religions and to engage in it with fully open minds and hearts. But is this really possible when Christians, consciously or unconsciously, approach other believers with the presupposition that all salvation and the fullness of revelation are found only in the life, death, and resurrection of Jesus? We've felt the press of this question often throughout these pages. One feels it again as one accompanies Fredericks and Clooney on their journeys into other religions.

Fredericks offers beautiful insights into what Christians can learn from Hindus' love of Krishna or from the Zen understanding of the nonduality of life and death. But in the end, Krishna offers Christians the opportunity "for opening up the familiar story of the Prodigal Son for Christians to read in new ways." And Zen urges Christians to "explore the full meaning of the resurrection."[15] It seems that this dialogue is providing Christians only with new ways to come to a deeper understanding of what they already have and implicitly know. But is there the possibility for Christians to learn something they really did not know before, something that was not contained in Jesus' revelation? Yet how could that be possible if Christian revelation is full and final?

Perhaps this is why Fredericks staunchly rejects any consideration that Krishna and Jesus might be carrying out similar and equally important roles in incarnating a saving presence of the Divine in history. Or better, such similarity or equality doesn't seem to register on his horizon of possibility. The same seems to be true of Clooney. He doesn't appear to entertain the possibility that salvation might be provided *both* by Jesus and by the experience of Brahman, in equally satisfying and "final" ways for both Christians and Hindus (as S. Mark Heim would urge). It seems that the type of daring, open-minded dialogue that comparative theologians are urging their fellow Christians to embrace is also urging these same theologians to look more closely and daringly at the question of Jesus' uniqueness.

---

15. Fredericks, *Faith among Faiths,* 160.

An Inconclusive Conclusion

In a sense, this book ends where it began — with pluralism. In the introduction, we started with the bewildering reality of *religious* pluralism — the multiplicity and variety of religions. And in this conclusion, we look back over the bewildering reality of *Christian* pluralism — the multiplicity and variety of theologies of religions. In that introduction, we laid out the challenge that the manyness of religions places at the Christian doorstep — how to make sense of these other religious paths and how to make sense of Christianity itself in light of these many Ways. But having explored how Christians are trying to respond to that challenge, we end up with a manyness of Christian viewpoints and models that for some may be even more bewildering than the manyness of religions.

In this conclusion, I want to raise, and try to answer, this question: Can we say the same thing of the pluralism of Christian theologies that we said of the pluralism of religions — that it is *a problem which is also a promise*? Is the variety of Christian models that we have reviewed in these pages just as much a blessing as it is an embarrassment? Might the manyness of Christian approaches to other religions be as fruitful for the churches as it is frustrating? Might Christian pluralism be, as we said of religious pluralism, not just a "matter of fact" (resulting from human decisions and so, we hope, temporary) but a "matter of principle" (resulting from God's will and so the way things are supposed to be)?

These are not easy questions. And there are no clear, certain answers. That's why I've called this an *inconclusive* conclusion. The answers I offer are only suggestions. They'll have to be tried before the court of community and theological discussion. But I do want to lay out the reasons why I believe — or better, why I hope — that the differing, often disagreeing, models for a Christian theology of religions that we have explored can be just as much a promise as they are a problem. The different recipes for a Christian theology of religions can be opportunities, if really tasted, to enhance each other. But for this to happen, for the problem to become also a promise, I suggest and urge all of us Christians to do two things: to *talk* to each other and to *cooperate* with other religious believers.

The Need for Inter-Christian Dialogue

Trying to lay out a conclusion for this book has helped me clarify what I really wanted to do in the book from the start. Yes, my intent, like that of so many other theologians, was to call my fellow Christians to a more serious, a more

238

fruitful dialogue with persons of other religions. But to do that, I have been trying in these pages to help Christians engage in a more serious and fruitful dialogue with each other. That's what I really had in mind, at least implicitly, in the way I have tried to present each of the models for a theology of religions. Throughout, I have tried mightily to keep my own views and preferences off-stage — though one can never succeed perfectly in such an effort. I didn't want the flow of the book to build up to my own preferred model. So I tried to describe the ingredients, the motivations, the ideals of each of these approaches as carefully but also as persuasively as possible. I wanted to not just describe but also to advocate. I wanted you, the reader, not just to understand each of these theological models but also to feel and be attracted by their insights and power. I wanted the names I've given them to be both reflective of what the model is about but also as neutral, or nonjudgmental, as possible. Again, since names are always so contextually and subjectively loaded, I suspect that the nomenclature didn't succeed as well as I hoped. (Perhaps I should have followed the advice of a friend and called my models *A, B, C,* and *D* instead of Replacement, Fulfillment, Mutuality, and Acceptance.)

In any case, my hopes were that the descriptions of each of these models would offer you sufficient and provocative data so that you would feel inspired and enabled to navigate your own way through these various possibilities and so come to your own conclusions — maybe to your own "model of choice." In the way we have walked through these different models, I hope that the questions and concerns have become your own and that you have searched for your own answers, talked about them with others, tried to figure out where you stand. If now, having walked and talked your way through this book, you have a clearer picture of where you stand in relation to other religions (or at least where you don't stand), I guess the book has worked.

But wherever it is that you might be standing, I hope the book has also convinced you that you'd better not build a fence around your standing place. To be honest with you, in trying to write the book the way I did, this is what I have come to conclude for myself. In seeking to paint each model as correctly, persuasively, and critically as I could, I came to see, more clearly and uncomfortably than I have in the past, both the advantages of other perspectives and the inadequacies and dangers of my own. Yes, I still have my own model of choice, and having written this book I feel as committed to it as I have been; but I am also more convinced than ever that if I am going to avoid the excesses imbedded in my own theological approach to other religions, I have to be listening to the voices and insights of Christians who have chosen other perspectives. The image that seems to convey what I hope you will see for yourself is that of a network of checks and balances. The different models we have identified within the Christian churches can serve as a dynamic interplay of checks and balances for each other. Each directs the spotlight on particular ingredients or convictions that are essential to any Christian approach to other religions. But in concentrating the spotlight on a particular piece of the Gospel, each model runs the risk of leaving others in the background. Thus the need for the different models to shine for each other and check and balance each other.

Here at the end of our journey, let me look back and try to focus on the particular Gospel gems that shine at the center of each of the models we have studied.

1. *The Replacement Model.* This model vibrates with the experience and conviction that when the message of Jesus is really understood and accepted, *it upsets*. It changes things, or at least it moves things around. The state of affairs in one's life, or in one's religion, after meeting Jesus is not the same as it was before. Things — at least some of them — are going to have to be replaced. This is the natural result of something about the Gospel of Jesus that all Christians recognize: Jesus wants to change things in order to make them better (which presumes that our lives and our world can always be made better). Besides all the wonderful things that Jesus brings, he also calls for what can be a painful conversion — perhaps in different degrees for different people, but for all, some kind of turning things around. So when people hear the Good News and feel the presence of the living Spirit of Christ, it will not only delight them but frighten them. It will make demands. And the demands will usually mean that they have to give up, or turn away from, some of the practices or attitudes that they previously did not question. There will, in other words, be some form, some degree, of *replacement*.

So the Replacement Model reminds all Christians that in their meetings and conversations with other religions, there will often have to be what popularly is called "tough love." In their compassionate reaching out to others, Christians will often have to take strong stands for what Jesus is calling for. So dialogue will not always be comfortable; there will be disagreements, opposition — yes, what one of our theologians called "polemics." Though such polemics or confrontations will always be loving, respectful, humble, nonviolent — they will also be clear and firm. From the Replacement Model, all Christians can and should learn that if our dialogue with other believers is always smooth and sweet, something may be wrong. We may be diluting or forgetting the "hard" words that are also contained in Jesus' Gospel of love.

2. *The Fulfillment Model.* This model does not contradict, but does bring a needed balance to, the core concerns of the Replacement Model: the Gospel not only upsets but also *confirms*. The God whom Jesus announces is a God who is already there, already loving people, seeking to be present in their lives, calling them to peace with each other. But in connecting with, confirming, and making clear the presence of God already existing in other religious traditions, the Gospel will also *add* to it. Through an encounter with Jesus in dialogue with Christians, followers of other faiths should find that they are better off. Jesus will add something, and, though this something may not be in contradiction to what they already know and do, it will be an enhancement, a fuller revelation of what they already know. By enabling them to recognize and rejoice over the riches they already have, Jesus will add to these riches. If people are somehow

not happy about what they have heard from Christians in the dialogue, something is wrong. In some way, this model stresses, Jesus comes to complete, add to, and so fulfill other religions.

In being fulfilled, we must add, other believers will not necessarily (or usually) become Christians in the sense of joining the Christian church. But if they really meet Jesus in their dialogue with Christians, they will be different. They will, as we have heard, be "better Hindus, better Muslims, better Buddhists." According to the Fulfillment Model, if Christians are not trying to promote the betterment — the fulfillment — of others in the dialogue, they're neglecting the power and meaning of who Jesus is.

3. *The Mutuality Model.* The key reminder that this approach offers to Christians who follow the previous two models can be summarized simply: "It works both ways!" Interreligious dialogue is meant to be a truly *mutual* dialogue. Everything that Christians believe can happen to other believers in the dialogue can also happen to Christians. When Christians open themselves to others in interreligious conversations, they too must be ready to be "upset," maybe turned around, challenged to replace certain beliefs or practices that they never before questioned. Also, they should be ready to find that what they have seen and heard from a Buddhist or Muslim may confirm, and really add to, what they have already received in Jesus but never really understood. Through dialogue, Christians can come to understand Jesus in ways that never would have been possible without the dialogue. Maybe their conversations with others will even reveal truths about God and humanity that don't seem to be contained in Jesus' revelation but that fit, and so enhance, what Jesus had to say. In these different ways, mutualist Christians stress, Christians can become better Christians for having talked with and learned from Hindus or Jews or Buddhists. That means they can be *fulfilled* through such conversations.

And the reason why Christians themselves need to be open to fulfillment through dialogue, a mutuality theology of religions goes on to stress, is because the God whom Jesus has revealed to us is a Mystery and a Love that will always be more than we can ever comprehend. God's love and desire to embrace creation is *universal* and works in ways that we will never be able to pin down. Mutualist Christians remind their fellow believers that any theology of religions that wants to call itself Christian has to balance the universality of God's love with the particularity of that love's incarnation in Jesus. True, many (perhaps you would say all) of the mutualist theologians we have studied may not do a very good job of working out that balance. But the effort to achieve some such balance between the universality and particularity of God's dealing with the world has to be a pivotal part of all Christian theologies of religions.

4. *The Acceptance Model.* The gem that shines in the heart of the Acceptance Model is part of the law that all Christians find in the heart of the Gospel: the law to love, to really love, one's neighbor. Advocates of this model remind other Christians of something they too easily forget: you can't really love your neighbor unless you accept, really accept, her/his otherness. If Christians must always "let

God be God," they must also always "let their neighbor be other." Positively, this means tolerating and, as much as possible, valuing and affirming the distinct, different identity of one's neighbor. Negatively, it means not controlling, manipulating, or defining one's neighbor. To really accept and respect the otherness of one's neighbor basically means to accept and respect his/her differences.

But, we hear from the Acceptance Model, this is precisely what Christians so often fail to do, and not necessarily consciously or maliciously — but because of language. We fail to realize how much we are always looking at, judging, and reacting to the other from the perspective of our own cultural and religious language. This is one of the most valuable admonitions of this model: be aware and beware of how much our own perspectives prevent us from seeing, and therefore respecting and learning from, the otherness of the other. That means that we be conscious of how much our language can prevent us from loving our neighbor.

If we really accept the otherness of our neighbor and of the religions, if we admit that we will never be able to fully capture and understand their otherness, then we also have to accept *diversity*. There will always be "many" when it comes to "religion" — this is the radical reminder from the Acceptance Model. Or more theologically: God loves diversity. Yes, God also loves unity — but not to the point of destroying diversity. Once again, we see that any Christian theology, whether it operates from a Replacement or a Fulfillment or a Mutuality Model, will have to take on another balancing act: this time, between unity and diversity. Jesus calls us to unity, but never at the cost of diversity.

What I've just tried to do in this brief looking back at the models is somewhat dangerous. I've selected some particular gems from Christian life and belief that seem to occupy the center of concern for each model. There are other gems in each center, as I tried to show in the "insights" at the end of our review of each model. My point, and suggestion, is that each theology of religions we have pondered in this book has a number of core concerns which, though they may not be at the center for other theologies, have to be taken seriously by any Christian theology. All of which means that all the models have to check and balance — challenge and add to — each other.

All of this also implies that although you may (should?) have a "model of choice" that animates and directs your relationships with other believers, and although you may want to call this model "best for me," you should not consider it the absolute model, the only model, you make use of. Your own replacement or fulfillment or mutuality or acceptance perspective may provide you with the best means of balancing the teeter-totter we have talked about throughout this book — the balance or back-and-forth that all Christian theologies of religions have to work at between particularity and universality, diversity and unity, personal spirituality and social engagement. Yet, although your model of choice may provide you with the best balancing tools, you're really not going to be able to use them well unless you are also talking with, learning from, Christians who use other tools.

This is my first inconclusive conclusion: the need for inter-Christian dialogue about other religions. But how to do it, how to put it into workable, productive practice? We're talking about Christian ecumenism — Christians from differing denominations and historical experience trying to come closer to, and learn from, each other. We all know how difficult that can be. Which brings me to my second concluding suggestion.

The Need for Interreligious Cooperation

I really don't think an inter-Christian dialogue about a theology of religions is going to work if that's all Christians do. If we're talking only among ourselves about other religions, we're not going to get very far. So again, I'm closing the circle that represents the flow of this book: we started, in the introduction, with the need for Christians to dialogue with other religions. And that's where we're ending. The kind of inter-Christian theological conversations that I just said are *necessary for* a Christian dialogue with other religions will not be *possible without* just such a dialogue with others. In other words, what makes the inter-Christian dialogue about other religions necessary and urgent is also what makes it possible and fruitful: conversation, relationship, cooperation with persons of other religious communities.

I must admit that I am echoing the advice given by the comparative theologians in chapter 11. They urged their fellow Christians to simply dive into the encounter with others even if they don't have all their theological swimming gear in place; in fact, the comparativists claim that a theology of religions shouldn't precede dialogue, but will be born out of it. As I said earlier, I think this is the unsolvable problem of the chicken or the egg. It's not a matter of step 1 and then step 2. We need to be doing both together, moving around a circle of theology and dialogue or a circle of Christians talking among themselves and Christians talking with other believers.

So my question is: How can we best take up this dialogue with other religions? Or: Where can we plunge into the dialogue with them? More precisely: How can we encounter other believers in a way that doesn't require that we have our theological act together and that will both enrich and possibly correct our theological views of other religions? The suggestion I want to offer comes out of my own recent experience of interreligious dialogue.

Since 1996, I have been on the board of trustees of the Interreligious Peace Council. This is a group — actually a nongovernmental organization — that formed shortly after the World Parliament of Religions in 1993. The voices that called the Peace Council together came not so much from within the religions themselves as from what religious people hear all around them — the voices of the suffering earth and its suffering creatures. The members of the Council felt that religious communities spend too much time talking about problems within and between the religions and not enough about the much bigger problems that are facing and frightening us all — problems of poverty, violence, injustice, and environmental degradation. So the aim of the Peace Council is to form a group of prominent religious leaders,[1] aided by a group of trustees, who are ready to visit, by invitation, areas of the world where there is conflict and violence; the purpose of these visits is to try to offer an *interreligious* contribution to the non-violent and just resolution of the conflict. Among our places of dialogue so far are Chiapas, Mexico, Israel-Palestine, and Northern Ireland.

My own experience with the Peace Council mirrors that of other members, and it can serve, I believe, as an example of how Christians might best engage other religious believers. We come together because we all have heard the call of the suffering ones of the world and felt an ethical responsibility, as religious people, to do something. So we act together; we listen to the voices and views of all those involved in the conflict; we struggle to understand what is going on in sympathy for everyone involved but with special concern for the victims or those least able to do something about their suffering. We try to take action in meeting immediate human needs where we can (e.g., ovens for the poor of Chiapas) and also speaking compassionate truth to those in power (e.g., the military).

The first steps, therefore, in the way members of the Peace Council (councilors and trustees) relate to each other is not explicitly religious. It's ethical. We come together, first of all, not to share our beliefs but *to act out of our beliefs,* together. What motivates Christian participation in the Peace Council, for example, is not the desire to share the message of Jesus with Buddhists and Hindus but the desire to apply the message of Jesus to real people in a real situation where there is suffering and violence — and to do this *with* Buddhists and Hindus, who are there because they too want to respond to the same situation out of their experience of the Dharma. We first act together. But out of this shared action, as has become powerfully clear for all of us, there have grown deep, precious bonds of *friendship.* We have come to like each other, care about each other, respect each other. These friendships seem to be deeper — or at least, different — from the relationships that frequently result from traditional kinds of dialogue meetings. The closeness I felt with Maha Ghosananda (the leader of Cambodian Buddhists) after we both listened to and cried over the story we heard from the indigenous community of Acteal after the horrible massacre of their people in December 1997 is different from the closeness we would feel after discussing the teachings of Jesus and Buddha or meditating together. Acting, struggling, and suffering together for the cause of peace or justice make for special friendships.

But such friendships, because they were between religious people, also bear their religious, dialogical fruits. In trying to analyze the causes of violence, in

---

1. Among the peace councilors are the Dalil Boubakeur, Elise Boulding, Swami Chidananda Saraswati, Sr. Joan Chittister, Chung Hyun Kyung, Sr. Dhamananda (Chatsumarn Kabilsingh), Samdech Preah Maha Ghosananda, the Dalai Lama, Fr. Thomas Keating, Máiread Maguire, Imam W. Deen Mohammed, Chandra Muzaffar, Bishop Samuel Ruiz García, Sandhong Rinpoche, L. M. Singhvi, Bishop Desmond Tutu, and Rabbi Levi Weiman-Kelman. For more information on the Peace Council, see its website: *www.peacecouncil.org.*

seeking to determine how we should respond and what we should do, members of the Peace Council naturally have shared their religious beliefs and motivations. Usually this sharing was mutually supportive and clarifying. Sometimes, though, there were differences that produced tensions. But because we were speaking to each other as friends, because of the respect and love we felt for each other, and because our goal was not to prove who is right but to help the victims of violence as best we could, we could accept those differences, live with those tensions, and learn from them. One of the most difficult and yet richest "dialogues" I ever experienced came at the end of our meeting in Chiapas, after we had visited and listened to both the indigenous Mayan people and representatives of the Mexican government. The Christians, Jews, and Muslims wanted to issue a statement denouncing government policies; the Buddhists and Hindus warned that we must avoid all denouncing; we must, they told us, support the poor without taking sides! The compromise we worked out was one in which all sides truly listened to and learned from each other.

Because acting together as religious persons naturally leads to sharing together as religious persons — that is, sharing our own beliefs and experiences — all our Peace Council meetings end with some kind of an interreligious ritual in which not only we but the people who had invited us to share their sufferings participate. This need to carry on a more explicitly religious dialogue that arises naturally from our acting together was also the reason why the Peace Council, in September 2000, decided that we needed a more "desert" kind of meeting at the Trappist Abbey of Gethsemani where we could more easily and deeply talk together, share our Scriptures together, pray and meditate together. Religious people who act together, so it seems, stay and pray together.

So my suggestion is that this type of action-based, ethical dialogue with other religious persons be the kind of dialogue that Christians "dive into," no matter what particular theological model they are using. I trust that Christians in all the four models we have reviewed would be able to affirm that such working together with other believers for the sake of peace, justice, and the integrity of creation is a form of interreligious encounter that is permissible, pressing, and primary. After all, all Christians, no matter what their theological or denominational ilk, can agree that the Reign of God was at the heart of Jesus' message and that this Reign calls and empowers people to care about each other and about creation. Christians should have no trouble — indeed, they should feel a real obligation — to act with anyone who is also committed to caring about the human-earth community and removing its sufferings and injustices. Such a sense of urgency or obligation will only intensify when Christians also hear the mounting requests coming from political and cultural leaders that the religions make their important, if not necessary, contribution to solving the crises facing the community of nations. "There will be no peace among nations unless there is peace and cooperation among the religions!" If Christians find any truth in that statement, as many of them do, then the statement is also a call to an action-oriented dialogue.

And this kind of ethical or globally responsible dialogue will enable Christians to form new kinds of friendships with persons of other paths, friendships honed and hardened in the shared experience of truly loving and acting for the well-being of one's neighbor. Out of such friendships, as has been the experience of the Peace Council, will arise the newly acquired ability to respect the otherness of one's religious friends, to be patient with it, and perhaps to learn from and be enriched by it. Religious dialogue will grow out of ethical action. It is also likely that from this dialogue, from what Christians learn from it, they will be able to clarify, confirm, even correct the theologies that they bring to the dialogue. Dialogue will nurture theology.

This nurturing and clarifying of theology can also take place within the dialogue that Christians are having among themselves. This is what I was trying to get at when I said above that the necessary *inter-Christian* dialogue needs the help of *interreligious* dialogue. Or more clearly and personally: the friendships that Christians form with persons of other religions can nurture and animate the friendships that Christians form across their denominational borders with each other. Interreligious friends can make for better inter-Christian friends. Because we have become inter-Christian friends through our shared participation in an ethical dialogue with our interreligious friends, we Christians will be better able, I expect, to share and learn from our different theologies of religions. Our shared ethical dialogue with others will enliven and guide our shared theological dialogue with each other.

And so, both in interreligious as well as in inter-Christian relationships, dialogue and theology will form a life-giving, constantly rotating circle. Both theology (the effort to understand our own selves) and dialogue (the effort to act with and understand others) will call unto each other, enliven each other, challenge each other, transform each other. Christians need to talk to each other in order to understand other religions; but they need to engage other religions in order to be able to talk with each other. So the circle turns. But I have been suggesting that the entrance place to the circle, so to speak, is the practical, ethical, globally responsible dialogue in which Christians, among themselves and together with other religious believers, act together, work together, and talk/pray together in order to "save" the earth and its peoples/creatures from the sufferings and crises they are now facing.

Might this be consistent with what Jesus was getting at when he said, "Seek first the Reign of God and its justice and everything else will take care of itself" (Matt. 6:33)? Commit yourself first of all to acting together with your fellow Christians and your brothers and sisters in other religions in promoting the love, justice, and peace of God's Reign — and your theologies will take care of themselves. And even if this doesn't happen, even if we don't make that much theological progress, the world will still be better off.

Index